LIPSMACKIN' BACKPACKIN'

Lightweight, Trail-Tested Recipes for Backcountry Trips

Second Edition

CHRISTINE AND TIM CONNERS

FALCONGUIDES

GUILFORD, CONNECTICUT
HELENA, MONTANA
AN IMPRINT OF GLOBE PEQUOT PRESS

To buy books in quantity for corporate use
or incentives, call **(800) 962-0973**
or e-mail **premiums@GlobePequot.com**.

FalconGuides is an imprint of Globe Pequot Press.

Falcon, FalconGuides, and Outfit Your Mind are registered trademarks of Morris Book
Publishing, LLC.

All interior photos by Christine and Tim Conners unless otherwise noted.

Project Editor: David Legere

Design: Sheryl Kober

Layout Artist: Maggie Peterson

Library of Congress Cataloging-in-Publication Data is available on file.

ISBN 978-0-7627-8132-4

Printed in the United States of America

10 9 8 7 6 5 4 3 2 1

The authors and Globe Pequot Press assume no liability for accidents
happening to, or injuries sustained by, readers who engage in the
activities described in this book.

To those whose boots tread far and wide: your passion for the wild world continues to be our prime motivator as authors for explorers such as yourselves.

Be blessed by the benediction found in Psalm 18:33:

May the Lord God make your feet like those of a deer and enable you to stand upon the high places.

CONTENTS

ACKNOWLEDGMENTS

For the first edition of *Lipsmackin' Backpackin'*, we set out to produce a different kind of cookbook for the outdoor community, one more usable and with more personality than other offerings on the market. Our objective was to create a book of the highest caliber for those hitting the trail for more than just a night or two, and so we drew material mostly from those whose trail experiences exceeded ours. We didn't want our limitations to get in the way of our own book!

Our skills have naturally grown much in the fifteen years since we began work on that first edition. But we still look to the trail to learn from the experiences of others. We never cease to be surprised, and are often amazed, by the wide range of creative tips, techniques, and recipes backpackers use. We believe this kind of variety is essential for making a truly great cookbook.

With this in mind, it is to you, our backpacking friends and acquaintances—our contributors—to whom we have always been most indebted in gratitude. Our work through the first and second editions of this book would have been impossible without you. Remarkably, some folks helped with both editions, despite the many years between them. Our most sincere appreciation goes to all of you.

In one form or other, Ken Harbison has been assisting with our book projects for over ten years now. Enormously skilled as a cook, Ken is also an experienced outdoorsman, and once again he lent his talents to this latest effort, testing and reviewing recipes. Thanks to you, Ken, our go-to-guy extraordinaire!

For the first edition of this book, the paths of the High Sierra were beat relentlessly to find top-quality material worth including. The Pacific Crest Trail Association (PCTA) played a major role in getting the word out on our behalf. We remain convinced that, without the PCTA, *Lipsmackin' Backpackin'*, indeed our career as outdoor book writers, would never have left the trailhead, so to speak. To the wonderful folks at the PCTA, past and present, especially Bob Ballou and Liz Bergeron, thank you.

And to the fine folks at Globe Pequot Press and FalconGuides, especially Max Phelps and John Burbidge: We've been together for a long time now, and for good reason. In a nutshell, you're the best.

INTRODUCTION

The original edition of *Lipsmackin' Backpackin'* was our very first outdoor cookbook. We had no idea how it would be received, nor for how long the title would persist in the marketplace. It would be an understatement to say we've been pleased by the longevity of *Lipsmackin' Backpackin'* and grateful for its popularity within the backpacking world.

But, given enough time, most any book can be improved upon, and *Lipsmackin'* was certainly no exception. There were the obvious necessities we expected to address with a revision: correcting errors, improving clarity, and updating reference and resource information. But we also wanted to use the opportunity to share the additional experience we've gleaned over the years.

In the first edition of *Lipsmackin' Backpackin'*, Tim wrote of the defining moment that led to his interest in trail cooking:

> I collapsed in a stupor against the side of a fallen pine high in the Sierra Nevada Mountains of California. After weeks of grinding northward along the John Muir Trail, my bones and tendons screamed in unified agony.
>
> My will to continue would have been nonexistent had it not been for visions of the culinary wonders that awaited only a few hours ahead in the town of Mammoth Lakes, my next resupply point. It had been two weeks since I last ate food other than the revolting fare found in my backpack, and I craved something, anything, from a restaurant.
>
> I had brought along thirty pounds of rations that now occupied a very different place in my heart than when I first started the trip. As the days passed, I was eating less and less of the nutrient-laden fare that my body desperately needed simply because I couldn't tolerate the taste any longer.

The motivation for Tim's reevaluation of his trail cooking modus operandi was the miserable experience that resulted from the novice mistakes he made while preparing for three weeks on the Muir. That was twenty years ago, though. We obviously don't make such embarrassing errors any longer, right?

We wish. A truly fascinating characteristic about cooking is the nearly limitless variety of "results" that a chef can produce from just a handful of ingredients. Unfortunately, not all of those outcomes are, um, pleasant, even for the most skilled cook. One can be a student of the art of trail cooking for decades, and have several successful books on the subject under his or her belt, but the culinary world is so incredibly broad and varied that it's too much for any chef to know every rope end to end.

So, like all cooks, we've continued to learn from our own many mistakes. And, if that isn't enough, we've also paid close attention to the mistakes others have admitted to. As a result, our list of lessons has grown long over the years; and in the second edition of *Lipsmackin' Backpackin'*, we have passed along those new things we've learned.

Lipsmackin' Backpackin' began as a collection of favorite recipes and tips from some of the most experienced long-distance backpackers in the world. At the time, our formula for the book was straightforward: Keep the focus on great tasting, dependable, and simple trail recipes, and mix in some fun whenever possible. We've retained that same formula for the new edition. And through several outdoor cookbook writing ventures for Scouting over the past decade, we've learned how to better streamline recipes to make them even more reliable and easy to use. We've applied those techniques to the second edition as well. So the new *Lipsmackin' Backpackin'* has received a thorough scrubbing front to back.

We didn't want to disrupt the characteristics of the first edition that readers best appreciated, so we've retained most of the recipes while revamping each meal category with fresh titles, many of which highlight a cooking tip or technique new from the first edition. We've also preserved what many readers came to appreciate as much as we do: the crazy stories and anecdotes that some contributors provided with their recipes.

We retained the first edition's comprehensive index and links to the popular packable trail instructions. We have also greatly expanded the instructional material in the front matter, and we've added substantial resource and reference lists to the back to make the second edition more useful to readers as they plan and prepare their next expedition.

It is our desire that this thoroughly revised resource will reduce the anxieties and hassles that typically go with planning menus and packing trail food. May our book help increase your days and miles in the backcountry and, in doing so, make your time on the trail more enjoyable.

Christine and Tim Conners

Planning and Preparing Your Meals

The power of food over our physical health and well-being is obvious. However, its strong influence on the psyche is generally not as appreciated, especially by those new to backpacking. As Tim learned the hard way while on the John Muir Trail as a novice, food issues can easily make or break a long-duration backcountry outing.

Yet, despite the pitfalls of doing so, one often relegates the menu to the last step in planning for the trail, or treats it as an afterthought altogether. After all, what's the problem with stopping by an outfitter or grocer on the way to the trailhead and simply tossing a variety of food items straight into the pack? Well, nothing, as long as you are able to accurately estimate, while standing in the store aisle, all of your expected food requirements while on the trail! Some can actually pull it off, but most of us don't have that kind of acumen, even after thousands of miles of trail experience. The food equation is simply too complex.

It takes careful planning, and a lot of it, to predict how much food will be enough (many people, if not most, seriously overpack), how much spice and variety will be adequate (many trail menus end up grossly bland or monotonic), how durable the food should be for the trail conditions (ridiculously fragile items are commonly found in hikers' packs), how easy the food will be to prepare (complex, multistep recipes are a total drag before or after a long trail day), and the type of nutritional punch the meals should contain (in a nutshell, longer trips require higher quality fuel). Without much thought, it's left to chance to balance all of these variables. Ignore or misplan any one of them, and your expedition is guaranteed to become less enjoyable.

This all said, there is a somewhat obvious caveat to the above rule: For short-duration trips, spanning one or two nights on the trail, most folks, including those with little experience, can indeed throw together a menu on a whim that won't result in severe culinary misery. Even if far too much food is packed, it tastes lousy, it becomes crushed under the tent bag, it is too complicated for the trail, or it is nothing but fiber, fat, or sugar, relief by way of civilization (and restaurants) can be measured in mere hours, not days. The predicament can be laughed off in the meantime.

However, for longer trips that last several days to weeks or more, very few people are immune to the havoc wreaked by a poorly planned backpacking menu. It's no laughing matter when your food becomes repulsive or inedible and the ability to solve the problem is dozens of miles and days away by trail!

The recipes in *Lipsmackin' Backpackin'* have been selected and arranged to maximize the efficiency of the meal-planning process and steer backpackers around the usual pitfalls of trail cookery. Information is plainly presented to allow the reader to quickly judge the merits of a particular recipe while preparing for a backpacking trip; and each recipe is clearly structured for foolproof preparation once on the trail.

Ideal Attributes of Backpacking Food

The logic behind planning a great trail menu is straightforward and easy to master. In fact trail menu design becomes virtually foolproof when just a few key parameters are considered and carefully balanced.

Weight

Food obviously comprises a large fraction of total pack load, but many hikers don't realize that grub can easily exceed one-quarter of the total backpack weight on longer trips. Because of this, food weight becomes an increasingly important consideration as the length of a trip grows. For an overnight hike, for instance, canned goods, frozen meats, and fresh fruits and vegetables are all possible options, even though they tend to be heavy for their nutritional value. But on longer trips, as pack load grows, an increasing fraction of dried food must be included because of the need for lighter weight and greater nutritional density.

Food is a security blanket, and nearly every backpacker finds it necessary, when loading a pack, to fight the urge to overfill it with rations. The key to knowing how much food to carry is to pay close attention to the quantity of food one normally consumes while on the trail. Ideally this can be done by weighing the food load before the trip, then doing the same with any leftovers afterward. The difference is then used for adapting the menu prior to the next outing.

Most hikers can expect to eat between 1 to 1½ pounds of packed food per day, assuming the bulk of it is dehydrated or freeze-dried in advance. It's a common, and easy, mistake to pack more than this. Consider the implications of overpacking by about 1 pound of food per day for a weeklong trip: You'll find yourself either overeating or needlessly carrying seven extra pounds on your back (equivalent to nearly four fully filled one-quart water bottles).

As a caveat, keep in mind that the body's caloric burn grows with hiking distance and duration, with longer distance backpackers easily requiring twice the calories that a more sedentary adult needs. So either the weight of food consumed per day, or the food's caloric density, will have to increase for very long trips. Pay close attention to your body's unique requirements and plan accordingly.

Food bulk is an interesting—and frustrating—parameter, because it tends to be inversely proportional to weight. Lightweight food items, including freeze-dried meals in presealed pouches, are often less dense, and generally pack less caloric punch, than heavier foods. To compensate, more of the lightweight items are usually carried, adding to the volume of the food cache and making it all the more difficult to cram into backpacks and bear cans. Calorically dense foods make packing easier, provided that you consider the extra calories per ounce during the planning process.

Each recipe in *Lipsmackin' Backpackin',* lists the trail-ready weight per serving. This is helpful for planning and estimating proper individual serving portions and total packed food weight. Note that the weight of any water required for reconstitution is not included in the listed weight data, as drinking and cooking water is usually found along the trail.

Nutritional Value

For backpackers, the nutritional quality of packed food becomes increasingly more important in proportion to the energy expended on the trail. The harder and longer the body works, the more critical it becomes to balance one's nutritional requirements, considering total calories, quality protein, complex carbohydrates and fiber, healthy fats, electrolytes, and vitamins and minerals. The body may be able to shrug off a significant deficiency in any of these categories during an average day at home. But on the trail, the effects of an imbalanced diet are easily felt and rapidly deleterious.

Don't immediately write off a food that's heavier than others per serving without considering what it offers in nutritional value. A heavier food item may provide exceptional nutritional density, making it especially ideal for powering the body during longer days on the trail. Conversely, foods that are featherlight per serving are often lacking in caloric density, complex carbs, or protein, so you should carefully scrutinize these foods before extensively using them in your meal planning.

Adequate consumption of electrolytes is essential while on the trail. Don't shift to a low-salt diet at a time when your perspiration rate is going to skyrocket and your body will require a higher than normal level of electrolyte intake. If you are on a low-salt diet, however, don't blindly switch to higher sodium foods! Talk to your doctor first about options for safely maintaining necessary levels of electrolytes while backpacking.

The nutritional data included with each recipe in this book is designed to help you tailor your backpacking trail menus to your individual dietary requirements. Use common sense: Balance the occasional decadent recipe with one of higher nutritional quality, and you'll find yourself able to go farther and faster when on the trail.

Taste

Want to start an immediate argument with your backpacking buddies? Pronounce your favorite trail food to be the "best" and watch the sparks fly. Then narrow the argument down to the "best tasting," and the feud becomes a totally subjective free-for-all! As we all know, however, the quality of "taste" is completely personal, with no objective characteristics with which to judge its merits.

The problem is that if a food doesn't taste good, we don't want to eat it. This isn't a serious issue at home. If we don't like the food, we can select something else. However, taste, or lack thereof, can become a big problem in deep wilderness where alternate options don't exist. If you find you don't like the food you've brought along on the trail, you'll eat less, rapidly kick-starting a downward nutritional spiral.

For those new to backpacking, it may seem odd that the taste of food could even be a concern. After all, why would anyone bring along food that he or she doesn't like? Good question, but it's a remarkably common mistake, even among veteran outdoor folks. The simple reason is that recipes appropriate for backpacking are not normally eaten off the trail. Backpackers will often throw together recipes on a whim, select and use recipes for the first time from a book such as this, or grab untried freeze-dried meals off the store shelf. In the mind's eye, we're convinced the food will taste good. Think about it: We do this all the time at the grocery store or in restaurants, then find—more often than we'd like—that our choices are disappointingly different from what we imagined.

If much of the food packed for the trail ends up being an unanticipated and nasty surprise, mealtime can quickly turn into a repulsive experience, with food being choked down instead of enjoyed. Poor-tasting food really puts a damper on a long trip. And for hapless hikers who didn't give their menu more thought, it can even end an excursion prematurely.

Taste testing your selections in advance and continuously taking note of the foods that you particularly enjoy while on the trail are two ways to build and improve your backpacking menu. And when selecting options from an outdoor cookbook, look for recipes that have been carefully tested, as they have been for *Lipsmackin' Backpackin'*. Taking these steps will help you avoid unpleasant revelations in the field.

Variety

When it comes to food quality, a close cousin to taste is variety. While some folks can eat the same types of food, or even the same exact recipe, meal after meal, day after day, even week after week, most of us like to mix up the menu. Even the best-tasting recipe can quickly grow tiresome on the trail.

Variety often falls victim to poor or last-minute planning. After all, it's far easier to prepare and pack seven meals of spaghetti and sauce for a weeklong trip than it is to come up with something different for each night. But even if you're fond of Italian food, there's a good chance you'll be mighty tired of eating it after seven days. Don't underestimate this point. The mental demands on the trail can be incredibly challenging. If all you've brought are lentils and oatmeal, it won't be long before you're desperate to get off the trail and into your favorite pizza parlor.

When packing foods that are new to you, it is particularly important to diversify the menu. In the event you don't like a meal, you won't have to wait too long before you'll be dining on something different. Imagine packing nothing but a week's worth of dried hummus for snacking only to find that it doesn't rehydrate as expected nor taste as you're used to. That's a lot of hummus to have to choke down before relief comes once you're home!

Simplicity

Some folks enjoy the challenge of preparing difficult, multipot master-pieces in the wild; but most backpackers seek an easier approach to meal-time, especially before or after the end of a long day of hard hiking. The same holds true for lunch and midday snacks, when forward progress is all-important and frequent, rapid food breaks are especially valued.

Simple meals mean less cookware, less fuel to burn, and less mess to clean up. Pack weight and volume decrease with the reduction in gear and fuel. The amount of effort required to prepare and recover from mealtime is reduced as well, as is the environmental footprint left behind. And simple is most definitely better when you have to cook in the dark or in foul weather. By primarily choosing one-pot meals and easier recipes, you'll spend less time cooking and cleaning and more time resting.

Don't be fooled into thinking that simple recipes are inherently loaded with heavily processed or unhealthy ingredients. On the contrary, precooked and dried ingredients give the backpacker an endless number of tasty and healthy options that result in simple recipes ideal for the trail. In fact, all recipes in *Lipsmackin' Backpackin'* have been selected with simplicity in mind, requiring no more than a single pot to prepare.

Durability

Rounding out the list of food qualities key to enjoyable backpacking is durability. Foods that are fragile, either in terms of spoilage or crushing, have limited use on the trail and are generally only appropriate for consumption on shorter trips, not far from the trailhead. They simply wouldn't reliably survive for much longer in the challenging environment found inside a backpack.

Few are the backpacks that aren't stuffed to the hilt or whose various items don't find themselves sandwiched at some point under the heavy weight of filled water bottles. Add constant movement for hours on end, and the pack can be likened to a rock tumbler. Imagine a bag of cookies in there after a few days!

Now add heat. Even in cooler weather some areas within a pack become roasting hot in direct sunlight. Ironically the cooler regions of the pack, deep and buried, are the very places that fragile items should *not* be placed because of the weight of the gear that would rest on top of them.

You must carefully consider the warmth inside the pack if you want to bring along foods that are very perishable. Such foods *must* be eaten soon after you depart the trailhead, before they spoil. But the bulk of the food you carry on the trail for longer trips must be durable enough for the bruising environment of the pack. Well-packaged dried and dehydrated foods, tough-crust breads, hard cheeses and salami, and vegetable oils sealed in containers are all examples of durable foods that carry well and resist spoilage.

All the recipes in *Lipsmackin' Backpackin'* were selected with durability in mind. Most can be assembled at home, then safely stored for months prior to use on the trail. This quality is of particular value to the very long–distance backpacker who has a great many meals to prepare well in advance of the expedition.

Recipe Categories

This section, along with the remaining portions of this chapter, explain the general layout of *Lipsmackin' Backpackin'* and how the information presented can specifically assist with trail meal planning and preparation.

Putting recipes into categories is not as easy as it might seem. There are as many ways to organize a cookbook as there are eating styles and preferences. The approach that appears to satisfy most people, and the one used in this book, is to begin by organizing entrees according to the meal category they best belong to: breakfast, lunch, or dinner. Those recipes that could not be tagged as "main dish" were grouped into three other primary categories: breads, snacks and desserts, and drinks.

The lunch section was constructed around the premise that fast and simple meals at noontime are particularly valued. It is time-consuming to break out the stove, heat the food, and then clean the gear, so we purposely minimized these recipes. Those that are included require only very short cooking times and use foods that are easy to clean up, with clear broths and oils as opposed to sticky glop and thick sauces. It is quite common for backpackers to simply snack on a variety of foods throughout the day, with no real differentiation between lunch and any other break. A number of such options, sometimes called "walking foods," have been included as well. Adapt and apply the lunch recipes according to your hiking preferences.

Three examples of meal systems are also provided, one each for breakfast, lunch, and dinner. Meal systems provide a flexible approach for using a fixed amount of basic staples and, when used judiciously, can simplify pretrip menu planning while providing for substantial variety once on the trail.

Servings and Weights

Most of the recipes in this book require final preparation steps to be performed on the trail, with the number of servings ranging from one to four. Because of practical limitations on the size of the gear that can be packed, the average backpacking cook pot is not much larger than 2-quart capacity. Four large servings can be comfortably prepared with such cookware.

It may seem odd that many of the recipes are written to produce only a single serving. There is good reason for this, the intent being that these dishes can be replicated as required to precisely meet the needs of your particular trip. One beauty of backpacking recipes is that they tend to be readily scalable in the number of servings, either up or down. So don't hesitate to scale as required. It's easy, and single-serving recipes provide even more flexibility to do so.

Many recipes in this book, especially lunch and snack items, require preparation only at home. These recipes often produce a large number of servings that can then be portioned, divided, and packed as required for the trail.

For consistency, the estimated number of servings included with each recipe assumes the target audience to be active adults on a moderate- to high-caloric intake, consistent with the exertion level expected when backpacking on rugged or long trails. Adjust these estimates for your specific situation, keeping in mind that activity level, richness of the meal, food preferences, snacking, weather, and altitude can all influence the optimum number of servings delivered by each recipe.

For estimating the total weight of your packed food, the dried weight per serving is also included for each recipe.

Challenge Level

A three-tier system has been used to assign a challenge level to each recipe: "easy," "moderate," or "difficult." The decision was based upon the on-trail preparation and cleanup effort required, the sensitivity of the cooking technique to variation, and the attention to care necessary to avoid injury. Most of the recipes in this book have been tagged as "easy," an important quality especially for the trail setting, where simplicity is definitely welcome.

Because cooking on the trail is often challenging enough, recipes considered "moderate" and "difficult" were purposely minimized. However, give careful consideration to those that have been included. As your skills grow, you'll find these well worth the attempt.

Preparation Time

Total preparation time on the trail under pleasant weather conditions has been estimated for each recipe. This value includes time from turning on the heat through serving the dish. It is assumed that the cook will flow the preparation steps in parallel whenever possible. For instance, while water is being brought to a boil, other preparation tasks can often be accomplished simultaneously. The recipes are written to best take advantage of this.

Preparation Instructions

Instructions for each recipe include a list of ingredients along with step-by-step directions, each logically grouped and presented in numerical sequence. The use of numerical sequencing in the preparation steps is intended to help the chef stay focused and to assist in the assignment of specific tasks to any other backpackers able to lend a hand. All of the recipes require at least some preparation steps to be performed at home. These are clearly distinguished from final preparation steps required on the trail.

Remember to Pack the Instructions!

Don't make the mistake of packing your food without including instructions for what needs to be done once on the trail! Packable on-trail cooking instructions for each recipe can be found online, free of charge, at lipsmackincampin.com/packable/lbp_2ed.pdf. Download the file, print the instructions for those recipes you'll be taking with you, and place the slips of paper along with your packed food.

Options and Tips

Interesting cooking options are provided for many of the recipes. An option differs from the main instructions and produces alternate endings to the recipe. Options included with a recipe are shown separately from the main preparation steps.

Likewise, contributors occasionally offered helpful tips to assist the trail cook with purchasing ingredients or preparing the recipe in some way. As with options, tips are listed separately from the main body of the recipe. Recommendations and tips of a more generic nature, or applicable to a wider range of recipes and situations, are presented separately in the following sections.

Equipment Requirements

Essential gear in any trail cooking kit, adequate for meeting the needs of several backpackers if traveling in a group, include the following:

- Backpacking stove with windscreen and fuel for the trip
- Small maintenance kit, appropriate for the stove type
- Lightweight cook pot with stowable handle
- Cook pot lid, preferably one that can double as a frying pan
- Short wooden or plastic stirring spoon
- Short plastic spatula, if foods requiring frying are on the menu
- Liquid measuring device, such as a water bottle with measurement indicator
- Ignition device, such as a lighter, and a waterproof backup, such as a spark igniter
- Small container of hand sanitizer
- Small container of biodegradable detergent
- Small scrub pad and camp cloth
- Mesh bags for storing and airing cooking kit items

In addition, each member of a hiking group should carry his or her own own personal mess gear, which should include the following:

- Small, durable serving plate or cup
- Durable, heatproof drinking cup
- Lightweight spoon, fork, and knife (or spork, a utensil combo)
- Filled water bottles for cooking
- Mesh bag for storing personal mess kit items

If a recipe's equipment necessities go beyond the essentials noted here, those additional requirements are listed below the preparation steps to head off any mealtime surprises once on the trail.

Contributor Information

Rounding out each recipe is information about the contributors, the field experts who made the book possible. You'll learn their names, trail monikers, and place they call home. Many of our contributors included anecdotes and stories as well. Useful and often humorous, you'll find these at the top of the recipe.

All of our contributors have extensive experience in the long-trail or outdoor community. Most are accomplished long-distance backpackers. Trail marker icons next to the contributor's names highlight the National Scenic Trails, the nation's grand long trails, with which these folks have been most connected, either through long-distance trekking or major involvement in preservation and protection.

Trail Marker Icon Key

AT – Appalachian National Scenic Trail
CDT – Continental Divide National Scenic Trail
FT – Florida National Scenic Trail
NCT – North Country National Scenic Trail
PCT – Pacific Crest National Scenic Trail
PHT – Potomac Heritage National Scenic Trail
PNT – Pacific Northwest National Scenic Trail

Category System

This book uses a category system to allow the cook to rapidly assess the most appropriate recipe options when planning a menu for the trail. The key attributes for backpacking recipes were already discussed. For the attributes of weight, nutritional value, simplicity, and durability, some level of objectivity can be used to identify the characteristics of each for each recipe. Taste and variety are obviously subjective; but the recipes in this book purposely span a wide range of tastes so that most any palate should find both covered.

Regarding the objective attributes, weight is obviously straightforward, and the trail-ready measure of weight in ounces is provided for each recipe. Nutritional data is included for each recipe, allowing you to build a menu appropriate for your personal dietary requirements and the anticipated demands of the trail you'll be traveling. Data is provided on a per-serving basis for the following common parameters: calories, protein, carbohydrates, fiber, fat, sodium, and cholesterol. Naturally occurring cholesterol in food is becoming less of concern because of its weak correlation to arteriosclerosis. However, it's a useful parameter for assessing vegan food options, and so we've retained it from the first edition.

Simplicity is addressed through the challenge level assigned to each recipe—"easy," "moderate," or "difficult." For durability, all recipes in *Lipsmackin' Backpackin'* are rugged enough to withstand the rigors of long-duration trips, and so a durability characteristic doesn't require noting.

In addition to the recipe attributes noted above, the trail chef must have a firm idea of the number of servings each recipe will produce so that the recipe can be scaled, if required. Explicit serving numbers are used for this purpose. Closely associated with challenge level, the preparation time is provided and rounded to the nearest quarter hour. These data are also useful for estimating fuel requirements, as cooking time generally scales with preparation time. To help ensure that the proper gear is packed along with the food, the required cooking method necessary *on the trail*—pot, frying pan, campfire, or no cook—is indicated by the use of corresponding icons (see table on the following page).

Because of their lightweight, durable nature, dehydrated ingredients are common in backpacking foods, and the recipes in this book include them as well. Many dried ingredients can be purchased commercially, but it's easy and inexpensive to do your own drying at home using a food dehydrator. Any additional effort spent in the home kitchen drying food is usually rewarded on the trail with easier preparation, improved durability, healthier options, and less fuel used. Nevertheless, to further simplify their food preparation options at home, some prefer not to use home-dehydrated foods. To quickly call attention to recipes that require such ingredients, an icon depicting a dehydrator is used.

For backpackers looking specifically for meatless options, a **V-LO** icon identifies recipes as lacto-ovo vegetarian, meaning free of meat but containing dairy and/or egg products. For recipes free of not only meat but also dairy and egg, a **V** icon marks the selection as vegan.

To sort recipes, this book uses an approach specifically designed to assist with nearly any backpacking menu-planning scenario. Recipes are grouped at the top level by meal category, forming the main recipe chapters in the book. From there the recipes are subgrouped by cooking method, which correlates to both challenge level and preparation time. Recipes are then subgrouped by weight per serving. Number of servings, weight data, preparation time, and challenge level are summarized in a prominent box in the sidebar of each recipe.

Recipe Icons Category System
Required Equipment and Preparation Method

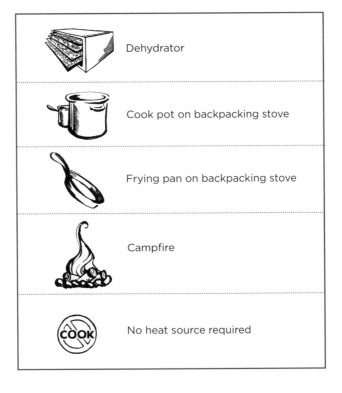

Dehydrator

Cook pot on backpacking stove

Frying pan on backpacking stove

Campfire

No heat source required

Supplemental Information for the Trail Cook

Additional information is included in the front and back sections of this book to assist the backpacking chef with the challenge of cooking on the trail. An important chapter on safety highlights the most common risks associated with trail cooking and what can be done to help reduce the probability of an accident while far from a hospital. Please err on the side of caution and review this material, especially if you are new to trail cooking.

Hand in hand with safety comes skill. Expert trail chefs are far less likely to inflict injury or illness to either themselves or their fellow backpackers. A chapter on basic skills reviews the competencies that outdoor chefs should seek to understand and master, with an emphasis from the vantage of cooking on the trail. Tips and techniques for home dehydrating are covered in a chapter devoted to saving weight and improving durability through the use of dried foods.

The appendices cover a wide variety of helpful reference information, including measurement conversions, sources of trail-cooking equipment and ingredients, a bibliography of additional books and information on outdoor cooking, and techniques for reducing the environmental impact of cooking while on the trail. And if you're looking for even more reasons to hit the nation's long-distance trails, check out the information provided on the National Trails System.

Healthy Pairings

Wise choices and moderation are the two keys to maintaining a healthy diet while on the trail. If care is taken not to overpack, moderation will be guaranteed, since there will only be so much food to be found in your pack!

But regarding wise choices, these begin and end with the planning process. When choosing recipes that lean toward higher fats and sugars, balance your meals with healthier options the remainder of the day. This is especially critical on treks of longer duration, when high-quality fuel is what your body needs and craves. Sure, bring along a couple of king-size candy bars, but retain them as a reward for making it up and over grueling mountain passes!

Drinks containing electrolytes can be appropriate when the weather is warm and the level of exertion very high. But, otherwise, make the bulk of your liquid intake pure, cool filtered water from wild streams and springs, a rare treat that few people in this day have the opportunity to experience.

Trail Cooking Safety

The process of cooking presents some of the more significant hazards that backpackers will face during their stay outdoors. Most people have learned to successfully manage dangers in the home kitchen through caution and experience. But outdoor cooking presents many new and unique hazards that, if not appreciated and controlled, can cause severe injury or illness. The following information on trail cooking safety highlights the most common risks and what can be done to help reduce the probability of an accident.

While the goal should always be zero accidents, minor injuries, including cuts and burns, are common while cooking outdoors. Keep the first-aid kit handy for these. Never acceptable, however, are more serious injuries or food-borne illness. Extreme care and caution should always be used to prevent accidents that could send you to the hospital. This point is even more important while on the trail, where the time to get to help can be measured in days.

Always be careful! A razor-sharp pocketknife can go deep into your body before your brain has time to register what is happening. Fuel leaking from a pack stove can explode into a fireball, burning your face. Harmful bacteria, left alive due to improper cooking, can leave you so ill that you can't even walk.

Learn to respect every step of the cooking process, from preparation at home to clean up on the trail. Always think about what you are about to do and ask yourself, "Is this safe?" If it isn't, or even if you are uncomfortable for reasons you don't understand, trust your instinct. Stop and determine how to do the job better, either by using more appropriate techniques and equipment or by asking others for assistance or advice. Move slowly and methodically. No matter how hungry you might be, no meal is worth compromising your health and well-being.

With care and attention, any cooking risk can be managed to an acceptable level. The following list of guidelines for safety will help you do just that.

Setup and Assistance

- When cooking on the trail, schedule pressure often occurs while you're trying to break camp in the morning, when foul weather

16

is moving in quickly, or when nightfall is fast approaching. If you find yourself trailing, don't rush to catch up. The chances of an accident and injury will only increase. And don't be a martyr if you're cooking for more than one, silently suffering under the burden. You'll only fatigue yourself all the more quickly. Instead, immediately enlist help from others to get the meal preparation back on track.

- If traveling in a group, establish your cooking zone in an area away from the main traffic in your trail camp. Especially at the end of a long day, with the natural desire for camaraderie, it's tempting to cook in the middle of where the action is. But pack stoves sit naturally low to the ground and are prone to being inadvertently kicked asunder in areas with a lot of activity.

Food Poisoning

- To decrease the probability of illness from parasites, bacteria, or viruses, all water taken from natural sources must be properly purified while on the trail. Do not assume that the heat from the cooking process will be adequate to sanitize your water. It often is not! There are many reliable devices on the market designed for water purification while backpacking. The best choice for your situation will depend on the water quality in the area you'll be visiting as well as your personal preference on the method of purification.

- The inside of a backpack can become toasty over the course of a long day, especially when the weather is warm. However, the surface of a backpack becomes downright hot when exposed to direct sunlight. Store foods away from the surfaces of the backpack. Instead, place them deeper in the center of the pack to reduce the temperature that the food is exposed to and extend its shelf life.

- Do not bring raw meat or eggs on the trail unless they are to be cooked and consumed soon after leaving the trailhead. This is especially true in warm weather. Raw meats that are brought along should first be frozen hard, then thoroughly sealed, then buried deep in a well-insulated region of the backpack. Do not allow the meat to completely thaw and become warm before using. If the meat discolors, or if meat or eggs develop an off odor, do not use.

- Cold and wet weather significantly affect cooking time. High altitude will as well, because it lowers the boiling temperature of water. Consider these factors and plan to cook your food longer to be certain is it thoroughly heated throughout.

- All food should be packaged tightly and securely to reduce the risk of spoilage. Loose seals on containers or ziplock bags give entry to moisture and contaminants, both of which decrease the shelf life of food. This is especially important if packing for a trip lasting more than a day or two. Now is not the time to cut corners: Always use high-quality ziplock bags and containers. Heavy-duty ziplock bags are recommended for foods with a rough, jagged nature that might otherwise puncture thin walls of less expensive bags.

- Certain elements of backpacking, especially when answering nature's call, require fastidious attention to the cleanliness of one's hands. Bring a small container of hand sanitizer, enough to last the trip, for thoroughly cleansing hands before handling food at mealtime. This is particularly needed in areas where water for cleaning is in short supply.

- Carefully clean all cookware and utensils following each use. If they are greasy or smell strongly of the meal just prepared, then keep washing. Not only will you avoid unwanted animal interest by reducing odors, but you will reduce the chances of any food remnants becoming spoiled and then creating a hazard the next time you cook. And don't make the common mistake of overlooking your pocketknife if you've used it to slice cheese or meats. The blade slots, grooves, and joints of a knife collect food bits that must be cleaned carefully after such use. Wipe your cookware and utensils dry following cleaning to help remove any remaining protozoa, cysts, or other nasties that may have survived washing.

- A final line of protection: If any food smells or looks odd, or if you see signs of mold or patches of discoloration, discard it! Do not take the risk. Even the mildest case of food poisoning can be a miserable experience when you're deep in the wilderness.

Physical Dehydration

- Heavy exertion can dehydrate the body very rapidly, placing it at increased risk of cramping, injury, and ailment. To stay properly hydrated, you will easily require more than 1 gallon of water on hot days when trekking with a heavy backpack. When urine becomes a deeper shade of yellow, that's a sign to up your water intake pronto. Don't rely on your sense of thirst, which often only develops after your body has become dehydrated. Keep a water bottle or hydration pack filled and handy at all times, and get in the habit of taking frequent sips while on the trail.

- Electrolytes, such as sodium and potassium, are essential to the proper metabolic functioning of the body. When you drink large quantities of water on warm days, more electrolytes are flushed from the body through perspiration, and they require replacement. A typical diet will normally provide enough sodium, but supplementation is often required to maintain adequate reserves of other electrolytes, either through energy bars, sport drink mixes, or mineral tablets. Have these types of items available on the trail and use them, especially if you feel your energy reserves diminishing or begin to cramp.

Cuts and Burns

- With many backpacking recipes, much of the cutting and chopping occurs at home and not on the trail. But an occasional recipe does require knife work at mealtime. A kitchen knife is too large for the pack. Heavy folding knives are also inappropriate and unnecessary. A standard pocketknife should be adequate for accomplishing any food-preparation job on the trail.

- Cutting utensils are inherently dangerous, and it goes without saying that they should be handled with care. Dull knife blades unintentionally slip much more easily when you're slicing or chopping, and they can quickly end up in the side of your finger instead of in the food you're cutting. Maintain the sharpness of knife blades to help ensure they do what you expect them to. When slicing and chopping, always keep your hands and fingers away from the underside of the cutting edge and from in front of the blade tip.

- Backpacking stoves are small and lightweight for good reason, but that small size makes them somewhat unstable, especially when used with larger cook pots or skillets. Improve the stability by setting the stove on a solid, level surface such as the top of a flat rock. Before leaving for the trail, check to be sure that your cookware is not too large for the stove. If the stove or cookware may tip easily, look for a smaller pot or skillet. Use care while cooking by bracing the pot or skillet handle with one hand while stirring with the other. If your cookware is not properly stabilized, it—and the hot food inside—could end up tipping onto the ground or your unprotected skin.

- Handles are easy to inadvertently snag, and so they become a frustratingly simple way to accidentally tip a pot or skillet. Use cookware that has retractable or removable handles so that they don't get in the way while the pot or skillet is on the stove.

- Stoves become red hot during use. Fortunately, because of their small size, they take only a few minutes to cool off. But their small size also makes them easy to grab and move without giving it much thought. And that is where the danger lies. Inadvertently grabbing a searing-hot stove from the top will leave a spectacular pattern of burns on your fingers and palm. This is sure to impress your friends, but it won't be very fun while you wait for them to heal.

- Be extra cautious with plastic food bags containing hot water, as the bags can potentially tip or rupture, covering your skin in scalding liquid. Brace the bag, such as by placing it in an empty cook pot, before pouring hot water into the bag, then minimize handling of the bag until it cools to a safe temperature.

Fire Safety

- It is imperative that any applicable fire regulations be strictly adhered to. These are often posted at trailheads. But a surer way to gather this information is to contact the appropriate authorities for the area you plan to visit. It is not uncommon for campfires to be banned while the use of backpacking stoves is permissible. In very dry conditions, any type of open fire may be banned, including stoves. Ignorance is no excuse. Make no assumptions regarding the law. The potential legal, financial, and environmental consequences are enormous should you ignore the law or lose control of your fire.

- All cooking must be performed in a fire-safe area, clear of natural combustibles like dry leaves, grass, and trees. Instead of creating a human-made fire-safe zone about your cooking area, and potentially leaving behind the ugly evidence, take your cooking to a durable area naturally free of combustibles, such as the surface of a large flat rock or an area of bare soil or sand. Imagine the size of the fireball that might occur should your stove leak fuel and burst into flames, then place the stove at least that far from the nearest combustibles, including overhanging trees.

- Cooking fuel is an obvious hazard, both to you and to the environment. Care should always be taken when lighting a stove, no matter what its design. A stove that is leaking liquid or propane fuel under pressure can produce an impressive fireball that, if you're fortunate, won't do anything more than burn the hair off your forearms. But you shouldn't let the situation get that far. Before striking a match—and with the stove assembled, pressurized, and the valve off—listen and sniff for fuel leaks. If you note a problem, repair the stove, using a maintenance kit if necessary, before proceeding. If you are unable to repair the stove, do not use it! Better to eat a cold dinner than to burn either yourself or the forest. Finally, always use care when starting a normally functioning stove. A stove will often flash while lighting, so keep your face well away when doing so. Understand how to properly operate your stove before using it for the first time, and especially before using it on the trail.

- Many stoves come with a metal windscreen, and some also come with a base plate to go underneath. Both the windscreen and base plate are designed to help keep heat where you want it: on the pot. But both also serve an important safety function. A base plate can help prevent bits of duff from igniting under the stove while it is in use, while a windscreen can prevent windblown sparks from reaching nearby combustibles. Use a base plate, if your stove comes with one, and always use a windscreen if the weather is gusty.

- Keep loose and combustible items, such as jackets, sleeves, towels, plastic bags, and hair, away from the stove when it is in operation or cooling down following cooking. Alcohol stoves burn with a colorless flame that is almost impossible to see in sunlight. Without the visual cue, these stoves are notorious for burning clothing (and skin), and extra care is required for their use.

- Avoid building campfires for the sole reason of cooking while on the trail. Bring a backpacking stove for this purpose. Used properly, a stove will not leave behind evidence of its use; and, compared to a campfire, a properly maintained stove poses less chance of creating a wildfire.

- Have filled water bottles at the ready to extinguish any flames that might otherwise threaten to escape your fire-safe zone.

- Never attempt to cook in a sleeping tent! The fully enclosed walls can concentrate deadly gases and cause asphyxiation. Or the tent walls or floor could rapidly catch fire, trapping the occupants. A flat tarp—set at an angle above head height to safely vent noxious fumes and positioned well out of range of the flames of the stove—can serve to protect the stove during rainy or snowy weather.

Allergies and Special Diets

When planning a menu for a group outing, ask your fellow hikers if they have food allergies or health issues that might require special dietary restrictions. Once on the trail and far from medical assistance, a severe allergic reaction could be life-threatening. At the least a dietary reaction can make the trip very uncomfortable for the poor soul struck with such a malady. Do not assume, just because they haven't told you, that none of your trail companions have such issues. Selecting foods that meet everyone's tastes and requirements might seem impossible in these circumstances, but many recipes can be modified for special dietary needs while satisfying everyone else in the group. This approach can be far easier on the cook than attempting to adhere to a parallel special-requirements menu.

Wild Animals

- Critters searching for food can pose a danger to backpackers either through aggression or disease. Food bags; odorous items such as toiletries; dirty cookware and utensils left unattended; and leftover food waste improperly disposed of all will eventually attract unwanted animal attention and can create a major problem when in bear country. Wildlife that gains access to such goodies will surely come back for more, placing these animals at risk of harm along with the people who must interact with or remove them. A camp that is neat and clean, with food and garbage properly stored and secured, is far less attractive to the local fauna. Practice low-impact principles and adhere to any food storage regulations unique to your area, such as a requirement for bear bagging.

- In areas with the potential for bear activity, cook and eat far downwind from your sleeping area to reduce the chance of it becoming of nocturnal interest to bruins looking to satisfy their incessant hunger. Better yet, pause for an early dinner while still on the trail, then walk the final mile or two to your stopping point for the day. By doing so you'll leave the enticing aromas well behind.

No list can cover every danger lurking in every situation, and the above is surely no exception. But by learning to cook with a mind fixated on safety, few circumstances will catch you ill prepared or by surprise.

Basic Skills and Equipment for the Trail Chef

Cooking a great meal out of a backpack might seem magical, perhaps impossible. It's neither, of course. And a strong foundation in the fundamentals of outdoor cooking in general, and trail cooking in particular, will make it all the more likely you'll be successful. With this in mind, the following section covers the essential skills for cooking when one's kitchen is in a backpack.

Planning for the Obvious . . . and the Unexpected

- If you are new to trail cooking, keep your backpacking menu simple, especially for longer trips. Raise the challenge level only after you've become more skilled and confident in your abilities. Taking on more than one can manage is a common mistake, and the botched meal that results is sure to disappoint your famished stomach.

- Foul weather adds a powerful variable to the outdoor cooking equation. And bugs and wild animals further distract by keeping the cook on the defensive. Prior to any outing, weather and critters should be considered and appropriately planned for. Be realistic about what you can handle under the circumstances you're likely to encounter. The more trying the conditions, the simpler the menu should be.

- When traveling in a group, enlist help and divide cooking and cleanup duties among everyone in the group. The recipes in this book use numerical sequencing for the instructions. Use this feature to best assign tasks to helpers.

- Make sure you can manage the additional workload when assigning tasks to new chefs. If cooking in inclement weather or under an extreme time crunch, there will come a better time to engage the assistance of inexperienced cooks.

- Groceries account for a large fraction of cost on most outings, and it's natural to attempt to keep these expenses reasonable. However, cost cutting can be taken to an extreme, with ingredients of such low quality that it's painfully obvious, meal after meal. Be prudent about cost-cutting measures. Spend the extra money when it makes sense. Once on the trail the difference will be appreciated.

- Any dish can end its short life tragically dumped in the dirt by fate or accident. Many miles from the nearest road, Plan B's are hard to come by in the wilderness. If mealtime goes awry, you'll have no choice but to replan the menu for the remainder of the trip to offset the lost food. One such event shouldn't cause undue hardship to you and any folks traveling with you.

- Now, if a bear happens to abscond with the entire food stash, or the meal bag is inadvertently dropped over a cliff into a raging river, that's another story. Quickly take stock of your remaining inventory. If reserves are low, carefully plan how to stretch the remaining food and be prepared to head straight back to civilization, recognizing that a couple of days without grub never hurt anyone. As your stomach grumbles, don't forget to stay properly hydrated. Your

24

body needs the water more than the food, and it can help lessen the hunger pains until that wondrous moment when you finally make it off the trail and into the nearest restaurant.

Menu Selection and Preparation at Home

- The typical adult or older teen will eat no more than about 1½ pounds of packed food per day, assuming that most, if not all, of the food has been dried. This weight value easily doubles or even triples when you're carrying fresh foods or canned goods. For a long trek spanning a week, about 10 pounds of mostly dried food will be adequate for most hikers. (In contrast, if canned goods comprised most of the food items, the weight would increase to nearly 30 pounds!) Total pack weight should not exceed one-quarter of your body weight to avoid overstressing joints and muscles, and food should not exceed one-quarter to one third of pack weight to leave adequate room for other critical gear. For a 40-pound pack, then, foods other than dried generally become too heavy once the trip length exceeds a few days.

- One-pot meals are the backbone of most trail menus, because less equipment, fuel, and effort are required for preparation compared to multicourse meals. But don't think that one-pot recipes make meals boring. There are many very good one-pot recipes, including those in this book, that stand perfectly well on their own.

- It's easier to prepare for a backpacking trip by multiplying good recipes for use on more than one day instead of preparing a unique recipe for every meal. But even a great recipe can become tiring if eaten too often, so balance convenience with variety when planning your menu.

- Most backpacking recipes are easy to prepare on the trail; but even many of the easiest require fairly accurate measurements of water or oils for final preparation. For these in particular, it is important that the on-trail directions be included with the recipe. Don't forget them! See www.lipsmackincampin.com/packable/lbp_2ed.pdf to print packable on-trail directions for all recipes in this book.

- For overnight trips, special food preparation is usually unnecessary. With plenty of room in the backpack, canned goods, fresh fruits and vegetables, and larger and heavier cooking gear can be managed. If you do bring canned goods on short trips, don't forget the can opener! Many are the stories of frustrated backpackers who've had to resort to opening their cans with blows from rocks.

- For longer trips spanning more than a few days, it becomes difficult to justify the substantial weight penalty associated with foods that have not been dried. A larger portion of your meals should consist of dried foods on treks like these. For trips spanning four days or more, almost all foods should be dried, for reasons of weight and durability.

- Water accounts for most of the weight of fresh fruits and vegetables, about 80 percent of which can be eliminated through drying. For canned goods, the fraction saved may be even higher as the can itself accounts for as much as one-quarter of the weight. By eliminating the can, draining the liquid, drying the contents in a dehydrator, and repackaging the food in a plastic food bag, as much as 90 percent of the initial weight can be eliminated.

- When bringing along dried foods originally prepackaged in boxes, such as rice mixes, repackage the contents in ziplock bags for the trail. By removing the packaging, trail trash is reduced and some weight is saved in the process. In addition, ziplock bags pack more efficiently than boxes, because the bags are free to conform to the confines of the pack. Be sure to clip any relevant directions from the box and place them along with the food in the ziplock bag.

- Package dry foods and ingredients in high-quality ziplock bags just large enough to do the job. Standard ziplock bags are usually appropriate, but for more aromatic or jagged foods—or for challenging duty, such as when used with water in rehydrating foods on the trail—heavy-duty freezer-type bags are a better choice. Less expensive or generic-brand bags tend to have thinner walls or less robust seals, so use these with caution.

- Once filled, squeeze as much air as possible from storage bags, then seal tightly. Recheck the seal to be sure it is securely shut, then store the bag in the refrigerator or freezer until ready to head to the trail. When it's time to load the backpack, ingredients packaged individually for a given recipe can be gathered together into a larger size bag to create a self-contained meal.

- Always label ziplock bags with the recipe name, number of servings, and date packaged. Other useful information to note could include simple instructions, such as the amount of water required.

- Lightweight and durable, condiment packets are an excellent way to liven up foods on the trail. Ketchup, taco sauce, soy sauce, barbecue sauce, hot sauce, relish, mayonnaise, mustard, honey, syrups, jellies, lemon juice, grated Parmesan cheese, and dried red pepper are some of the choices available. Save any extras from restaurants that you frequent or purchase them online in bulk from wholesale suppliers.

- Fresh butter is suitable for short treks but lacks durability for longer trips. Dried butter substitutes, such as Butter Buds, are an easy, good-tasting, and durable alternative for many recipes.

- Soy milk powder can often be exchanged in like amounts for dairy milk powder; and olive oil can typically be exchanged for butter, ounce for ounce.

- Use an accurate kitchen scale when preparing foods for the trail. Be sure the final weight is close to that specified by the recipe. If it isn't, this is a telltale sign that something is amiss, either with the recipe or the preparation; troubleshoot the problem before you hit the trail. A bath scale is valuable for determining the combined weight of the packed gear, to help with keeping the total weight of the pack below target, and for equally distributing the gear and food load between other backpackers who may be traveling with you.

- When packing equipment for the trail, use a checklist. By doing so you are less likely to forget a critical piece of gear. Review the list after each trip and modify it as required as you gain experience. Checklists tend to be very personal, and you'll soon discover that no two ever seem to be the same.

- To decrease the risk of their failure in a situation when you can least afford it, test recipes at home or on short trips before relying on them during longer or more challenging expeditions.

- Don't neglect nutrition on the trail. It's important to balance fats, carbohydrates, and proteins while backpacking. Carbohydrates provide a more rapidly available source of energy than do fats, and by combining the two, short- and long-term energy levels are more likely to be sustained. Proteins are valuable for extending the utilization of carbohydrates. Fats at suppertime are particularly useful in cold weather, as they help the body sleep more warmly throughout the night. Constipation is a common problem on the trail, but a fiber-rich diet, along with plenty of water, will help maintain regularity. Choose healthier fats, such as olive oil, when cooking, and avoid filling up on empty calories from simple sugars.

- If a bear-proof food canister is not required for the area you'll be visiting, gather all meals together into a large sturdy food sack for the backpack. Avoid placing your food at the bottom of the backpack, where it will be subjected to weight from heavy items above it. Instead, position the bag in the center of the pack, close to the forward (strap-side) wall of the backpack. This positions the food in a less compressed and cooler area of the pack while keeping the center of gravity farther forward, a more comfortable location for the backpacker.

Preparation on the Trail

- Review and understand your recipes before commencing preparation in the field. You are less likely to make a critical mistake if you do so. And be sure to have everything needed before starting to cook by first gathering together all ingredients and utensils.

- A lot of purified water is an obvious requirement during the high exertion of walking the trail. But a surprisingly large amount is also required in camp for cooking, cleaning, and replenishing the body's reserves. To minimize wilderness impact, a trail camp should never be established next to a water source unless a dedicated area has been created for the purpose. Of course, one drawback to camping away from water is the need to haul it from the source back to camp. For this reason, a collapsible plastic water carrier or dromedary bag, with a capacity of a gallon or more, is an ideal way of keeping a supply of water close at hand. The carrier can be quickly filled with raw water at the source then purified as needed at camp.

- An extension of the previous point is to avoid the vicinity of water altogether when stopping for the night, and instead, look for out-of-the-way areas with incredible vistas . . . and fewer bugs. Often called "dry camping," the idea is to purposely tank up on water at the source, with reserves adequate for the night and following morning, then continue along the trail to a campsite with a grand view or other redeeming quality. This is a liberating technique that moves campsite wear-and-tear away from the more heavily used water sources, while opening up a vastly larger world of camping opportunities along the trail.

• Nonfat dry milk powders are notorious for clumping during reconstitution, more so when using water that is cold. Of course warm water, and therefore warm milk, does not make for a good bowl of cold cereal in the morning. A method for avoiding clumping is to first add a very small amount of water, warm or cold, to the powder in a drinking cup, stirring until it becomes a thick, smooth paste. The remainder of the water, even if cold, can then be added and blended with no resulting clumping.

• Whole-fat milk powders generally reconstitute with less clumping compared to nonfat varieties. Many people find the taste more pleasing as well. Whole milk powder, such as Nestlé's Nido, can be found in the Hispanic food section at the grocery store. It is also widely available online.

• Carry a selection of favorite herbs and spices on the trail to satisfy individual preferences. Small containers specifically for this purpose are available from backpacking suppliers.

• Etch water bottles, containers, or mugs in measures of a cup and fractions of a cup for determining required amounts of water when cooking on the trail. Many transparent or translucent water containers come premarked with measuring lines specifically for this purpose. Learn to estimate one teaspoon and one tablespoon as measured using your backpacking spoon.

• Although possibly necessary when carrying fresh vegetables, chopping and slicing isn't required for most trail recipes using dried ingredients. However, when knife work is called for, the clean inside bottom of a bare-metal cook pot or lid makes an adequate substitute for a cutting board.

- With the type of cooking equipment and methods now available, it can be hard to imagine how much effort went into camp cooking in the not-too-distant past. Roasting pits and trenches, roaring fires, wooden tripods, and cooking boards all had a reason and a place at one time but left behind a scar in the wilderness that was slow to heal. With modern gear these damaging methods and techniques are no longer necessary on the trail. Use appropriate tools and equipment to minimize your impact to the trail environment and to truly leave no trace.

Managing the Heat

- Become familiar with your cooking stove and how much fuel is required to prepare a meal. Don't forget fuel required for heating water for coffee, tea, and other hot drinks. Bring extra for contingency, especially if the weather is to be wet or cold. Monitor fuel consumption while on the trail and adjust your use accordingly if burning too much too quickly. Test your cooking equipment before leaving home, looking for clogging or leaks. Be sure your gear is in good working order, and carry a repair kit for contingency. Maintenance kits are very lightweight and take little room in the pack.

- Use a windscreen and, if your stove comes with one, a base plate to improve fuel efficiency. Both reflect heat back onto the pot or skillet and should be employed to save fuel even if the weather isn't windy. Likewise, place the lid on your pot when cooking to help retain heat.

- Pack ovens are wonderful devices that open up a world of baked food options on the trail. If baking with a pack oven that uses water, never allow the oven to boil dry. Otherwise the plastic oven bag is likely to melt and create a truly nasty mess in your cook pot.

- For some recipes, ziplock food storage bags make attractive cooking containers, because they can simplify food preparation and reduce the hassle of cleanup. However, some plastics used in food storage bags may begin to soften at temperatures close to the boiling point of water. There is growing debate over the safety implications of such. However, dehydrating foods in storage bags using hot water, as opposed to boiling the bag directly, is generally considered safe, because the temperature of boiled water very quickly drops once the water is removed from the heat source and introduced to the bag. If rehydrating foods in storage bags using hot water is a concern for you, stick with your cook pot instead.

- An alternative to rehydrating foods in plastic storage bags with hot water is to use roasting bags instead. These are specifically designed for use at temperatures much higher than the boiling point of water and are correspondingly more expensive. While these bags can't be sealed in ziplock fashion, the open necks can be twisted and tied, with the top of the bag positioned so as not to collect steam or water.

- The boiling point of water decreases with altitude, dropping, for example, by nearly 20°F at 12,000 feet elevation compared to sea level. Because the water temperature is lower, foods will take longer to cook, requiring more time on the stove and more fuel. Bring extra fuel for contingency at high altitude and be prepared to stir often and to sample your food more frequently to be sure it's ready to serve.

Dealing with the Weather

- Perhaps the most challenging of all outdoor cooking situations involves rain. In a heavy downpour, the only options may be to cease and desist and wait it out, serve no-cook foods, or move the stove under a fire-safe tarp if you're fortunate to have one. Never cook in a sleeping tent.

- In light rain the pot itself, along with a windscreen, is usually adequate for shielding the burner, allowing cooking to commence and continue. This is also the moment when you'll be glad to have brought along a box of waterproof matches!

- Snow presents its own unique challenges to cooking; usually the most difficult is locating a decent place to set the stove. In mountainous areas, the tops of large rocks or boulders can often be found free of snow, as can the ground along the downwind side of the same. In areas with rapidly changing topography, it usually is just a matter of time before a snow-free area can be found along the trail. If snow stretches as far as the eye can see, but isn't deep, a suitable spot can be cleared by hand and foot. Place the stove on a pot lid set into packed snow if it's deep.

Keeping It Clean While Cooking on the Trail

- Maintain a close eye on your food while cooking so that it doesn't burn. Charred grub is difficult to remove from cookware and requires much more time, water, and detergent during cleanup.

- Use dishwashing detergent sparingly during cleanup, just enough for the job. Only detergents that are biodegradable should be used outdoors. Bring a small piece of scrub pad for tackling stuck-on foods. Clean coarse sand or small scree, along with a little water, are also very effective for cleaning the insides of pots and pans, provided the cookware isn't coated in nonstick material, which would otherwise be damaged by the bits of rock.

- Grease and stuck-on food are cut more easily, and with less detergent, when you use warm water. If you can spare the fuel, throw a little water in the soiled pot or skillet, warm the water briefly, splash it around, then let the cookware sit for a few minutes before scrubbing.

- Dispose of wash and rinse water, also called "gray water," in a manner acceptable for your particular area. Never dump gray water directly into a stream or lake. If the rinse water contains large bits of food, strain these out and dispose of them with your pack trash. If the area you are visiting is particularly sensitive ecologically or contains wild animals that may be especially interested in your food, then gray water should be disposed of like fecal matter—in a cat hole covered with several inches of soil and located at least 200 feet from the nearest water source. Always follow any local regulations regarding waste disposal.

- Dirty cookware left to lie will eventually attract bugs and wild animals. To avoid such interest, ensure that all utensils have been washed and rinsed before leaving base camp during the day or when retiring for the evening.

- Minimize the use of aluminum foil, which tends to shred into small pieces that are easy to miss during cleanup and remain unsightly for years. Likewise, keep a close eye on smaller trash bits, such as empty condiment packs, bouillon cube wrappers, and the like. A good practice is to immediately place small trash items in a larger bag before they are dropped and possibly forgotten.

- Reclaimed ziplock bags, used to carry food for your trip but now empty following the meal, make excellent trash receptacles. Squeezed to remove air then sealed tightly, they can be placed bag in bag to isolate aromatic and rotting waste. If carrying your dried food in ziplocks, you are unlikely to find yourself short on trash containers.

- Bear-proof food canisters are the best option when visiting areas with high bruin activity. They are neither inexpensive nor lightweight, but the piece of mind and convenience they bring over conventional bear bagging can't be overstated. In fact in some areas and parks, their use is required by law.

- When bear bagging, use a large sack to pack all foods along with any aromatics that could attract animal attention, including trash and toiletries. All items should be in waterproof storage bags, such as ziplocks, to keep them dry in case of rain. Be sure to use a stout sack to hold your stash, beefy enough to suspend it all off the ground without rupturing like a piñata in the middle of the night. You also need a long, strong hanging rope, at least 40 feet in length, to hoist it all. As any experienced backpacker knows, the perfect bear-bagging tree is a cruel myth. But try to find it anyway, one with a thick tree limb 15 or more feet from, and parallel to, the ground. Toss the rope over the limb and hoist the food bag. The bag should hang at least 6 feet off the trunk of the tree so that a climbing bear can't reach out and grab it. Likewise, the bag should rest several feet under the branch from which it hangs. Securely tie off the loose end of the rope to a neighboring tree.

- In some areas the bears are smart enough to defeat the bagging techniques described, and the more-involved process of counterbalancing may be required. Even that may not stop Yogi. However, if the bears in the area are this intelligent, local regulations most likely require the use of a bear-proof container anyway.

Key Equipment for Trail and Home

- All backpackers seem to have a strong personal preference regarding stoves, and there are persuasive pros and cons for each design. There are four major classes of the most common trail stoves: gasoline, alcohol, propane canister, and solid fuel. Gasoline stoves, some of which also burn kerosene, diesel, or even jet fuel, operate under pressure, generate tremendous heat, and work well at all altitudes. Because of their stability, gasoline stoves are arguably the best option for frying, especially when using larger pans. Alcohol stoves operate unpressurized and are very compact and lightweight. They are most useful for preparing single servings in a small metal cup or pot and are not well suited for cooking for groups. Propane stoves are also very lightweight and compact, with good heat output and excellent simmering capability for more delicate foods, but they are generally less stable than gasoline stoves, and their fuel canisters are bulky for the amount of energy they pack. The fuel remaining in a canister can also be difficult to judge, making it more challenging to manage fuel reserves. Solid fuel stoves use combustible tablets and are perhaps the lightest and simplest system to use. But, like alcohol stoves, they work best for heating water in small quantities and not for cooking for long periods of time. Some fuel tablets have a strong, somewhat off odor requiring layers of packaging to prevent transfer to other gear.

- Your cookware should be well matched to your stove and the types of recipes you'd like to prepare. For a lightweight alcohol stove, for instance, a single-serving metal cup is all that would be required for cookware. However, for recipes that make more than one serving, a true pot and sturdy stove may be necessary. And if frying is on the menu, you'll also need a lid that can also serve as a skillet.

- The selection of backpacking cookware is large and somewhat bewildering, but if you plan to cook for more than yourself, and would like to occasionally do some frying, all you'll need is a simple pot and multifunction lid. For packability and safety, select gear that has retractable or removable handles. Pots of about 2½-quart capacity are very good for handling six-serving recipes or less. Pack a small pot or simply a large metal cup when cooking for only yourself or a couple of people at most. Larger pots are too massive and unstable for most stoves, unnecessarily large for most backpack recipes, and more difficult to pack.

- Cookware comes in an assortment of metals and coatings, and some is sold in sets specifically designed to work with certain stoves. Standard aluminum is the least expensive material, but it's also the least durable. Anodized aluminum is a tougher variant with modest nonstick quality, but it is more expensive. Stainless steel is rugged but tends to be heavier than other metals. Titanium alloys are extremely light and tough, but they are also significantly more expensive than the other options. Nonstick surfaces definitely make cleanup easier in the wilderness, but some coatings are prone to damage and can eventually begin to flake off. The final choice regarding materials and coatings comes down to personal preference and budget.

- A pack *oven,* as opposed to a pack *stove,* isn't required, but can definitely broaden your repertoire, as it offers many new baking options on the trail. A lightweight and inexpensive insert, the pack oven is an ingenious modification of the simple trivet. It turns a cook pot into a double-boiler oven in water-based units, like the BakePacker. Breads, pancakes, and desserts are baked in high-temperature plastic roasting bags. The results are wonderful, and cleanup is easy. A few of the recipes in this book call for a pack oven. If you haven't used one before, consider trying it. Pack ovens can require a significant amount of time for baking, but if you have the fuel to spare, and don't mind the extra few ounces in weight, they are simple to use and a lot of fun.

- Don't forget cooking and serving utensils for the trail. A short wooden spoon is ideal for stirring. A small plastic spatula is a must for frying pancakes and other foods that require flipping. Pack all cooking gear into a mesh bag of appropriate size to allow the equipment to breathe and dry when it is in your backpack.

- At home, a blender is essential for pureeing chunky foods so they can produce smooth fruit and sauce leathers. A food processor is handy for slicing or chopping foods to a uniform consistency prior to drying. And a food scale is invaluable for weighing ingredients and evenly subdividing a recipe into smaller serving sets.

- A food dehydrator is indispensable for vastly expanding the range of trail cooking options, adapting your favorite home recipes for the trail, and maximizing and customizing the nutrition content of your trail foods. It is a surprisingly easy appliance to use. For more information, see the next section, where dried foods and dehydration are given exclusive treatment.

Reducing Weight and Improving Durability with Dried Foods

Whether performed at a factory for common food items found at the grocery store, or done at home for use on the trail, the reason for drying foods is the same: Water makes up most of the weight of many food items and is an essential prerequisite for spoilage. So by removing the water through the process of drying, the food becomes much lighter and lasts longer. Dried foods are also more resistant to rough handling than those with a high water content. For all of these reasons, the process of drying food provides benefits that are ideal for backpackers.

Freeze-drying and dehydrating are the two primary techniques used to dry foods for the trail. Reconstitution is the process of rehydrating dried food back to its original state. On the trail this is usually done with hot water, although cold water often works, given enough time.

Freeze-drying is performed commercially using industrial equipment to remove moisture through a rapid deep-freezing process. Most prepackaged meal options available at outfitters have been freeze-dried. Just like entrees found in the freezer at the grocery store, freeze-dried meals are a convenient option for the backpacker who is short on time or prefers to minimize the cooking effort. However, freeze-dried meals have some disadvantages: They are expensive per serving, the packages are often bulky for the quantity of food provided, and the serving sizes can be awkward for the actual group size. While many freeze-dried meals are quite tasty, many aren't; and costly surprises can await the backpacker on the trail, unless each menu selection is sampled previously. These disadvantages make freeze-dried meals less desirable, especially when packing for longer trips or preparing food for a group of backpackers.

On the other hand, *dehydrating* is the process of using low heat over a period of hours or days to slowly and gently remove moisture from food. It is a simple and inexpensive process, and it can be performed easily at home using an appliance called a food dehydrator. A new, high-quality home food dehydrator can be purchased for about the same cost as a good quality blender. Dehydrators come in two primary designs. One design uses stackable round trays with a blower at either the top or bottom of the unit, the other uses a rectangular cabinet and slide-out trays over which warm air is blown. Each design has its advantages, depending on the task, but either performs well in drying foods for the trail. All models provide some method for adjusting temperature; and fine-mesh screens are usually included to permit drying of small-size food items, such as rice, that would otherwise fall through the trays. Additional accessories can make the drying process more convenient, but they aren't required for the recipes in this book.

Dehydrating foods and ingredients at home allows you to customize an endless variety of your favorite recipes for the trail. Serving sizes and amounts can be tailored to your needs. And to top it off, the ingredients shrink dramatically in size once dry, taking up less volume in your pack. For all of these reasons, combined with the cost-effective nature of home drying, dehydrated foods are a great option for backpacking trips.

Entire books have been written about the art of food dehydrating, but that doesn't mean you have to read one to successfully dry foods. The finer points of drying food are certainly worth learning, but they often relate to preparing foods for very long storage times or to those foods that are less common on the trail. You should understand the nuances of your own dehydrator, of course, to help ensure safe use and predictable results, but by becoming familiar with the following list of drying tips and recommendations, you'll be ready to tackle most any backpacking menu.

Steps for Maximizing Shelf Life and Improving Food Quality

- To minimize the chance of contaminating your food, thoroughly clean and dry your hands, preparation surfaces, cooking utensils, and dehydrating trays before commencing.

- Properly dried and sealed meats have a shelf life measured in weeks, whereas fruits, vegetables, and grains can last a year or more. Remember: The more moisture or oils remaining in a dried food, the shorter its shelf life. Refrigeration greatly extends the life of foods once they've been dried, freezing even more so. Sealing dried foods tightly in high-quality food storage bags is necessary to maximize the longevity and preserve the taste.

- In very humid kitchen environments, dry the foods as usual, place in airtight containers for a few days to give any remaining moisture time to redistribute, then return the food to the drying trays for another round. This is an effective way to reduce the probability of spoilage due to mold.

- To dry cooked ground beef, begin by using lean meat, then allow the fried beef to drain in a colander. Finally, rinse the meat in hot water or pat it with a paper towel. Removing as much fat and oil as possible helps extend the shelf life of any meat. See *Ground Beef Gravel,* a recipe in this book, for one popular approach to drying hamburger meat.

- Always closely inspect your dried foods before packing them for the trip and cooking on the trail. Any patches of discoloration or molding, or an odd aroma, is an indication that the food has begun to spoil and should be discarded.

Planning for Drying

- Many food items can be dried overnight, but some foods may need as much as a full day or more to dehydrate, especially thick purees or leathers. If a lot of drying will be required for an upcoming trip, consider the capacity of your dehydrator and be sure to set aside enough time to do the entire job. It can take more than a week to dry the food required for a very long excursion.

- Dried foods tend to pack a lot of nutrients per ounce, and this is especially true of fruit leathers. Some fruits make better tasting leathers than others; and some combinations, apple-and-berry combos, for instance, are truly wonderful. Certain fruits, like blueberries, produce a better texture when blended with other fruits before drying.

- The kitchen oven is naturally attractive for drying because of its large capacity, provided that the door can be held open slightly to allow moisture to escape. But the lowest achievable temperature on many ovens is much higher than that recommended for drying non-meat items. Some ovens reach down to the range recommended for drying meats, but the unit may not be able to accurately hold the temperatures there. Before relying on your oven to dry large batches of meat, be sure it works properly in the required temperature range.

- Foods that contain a large fraction of high-fructose corn syrup, such as some canned fruits or pie fillings, can be impossible to dry, forever remaining very sticky to the touch. If attempting to dehydrate these types of foods, the results may be disappointing.

Preparing Foods for Drying

- The more finely chopped the ingredients and the more consistent the sizes of the pieces, the more uniformly they will dehydrate and the better they will reconstitute on the trail. Also ensure that pieces are spaced evenly on the drying trays for better air circulation.

- Don't mix different types of highly aromatic foods in the same drying batch to avoid intermingling flavors. The same holds true when mixing odorous foods with less aromatic types. As an example, it would be unadvisable to dry garlic and onions with a batch of fruit leathers.

- When drying sauce for spaghetti or soup on the trail, use a blender to puree chunky blends into a smooth consistency before drying. Texture can be introduced back to the sauces and soups at camp by adding dried vegetables and the like at the time of cooking.

- Thick liquids, such as spaghetti sauces and purees, can be dried in shallow pools on parchment paper, cut to the proper shape for your trays, or on reusable liners specifically designed for this purpose. Depending on the design of your dehydrator, very runny liquids are sometimes best dried in solid plastic trays specially made for your unit.

- Darkening of fruit and vegetables during and following drying naturally occurs due to oxidation. This doesn't affect the taste of the food, but it can be surprising to the uninitiated. There are several ways to reduce or eliminate the occurrence of oxidation when drying, but a reasonably effective and easy method is to soak sliced fruits and vegetables for 5 minutes in a bath of ¼ cup lemon juice to 1 quart water prior to drying.

- Blanching is the process of lightly steaming or boiling, but not thoroughly cooking, fruits or vegetables prior to dehydrating. Blanching is helpful in that it can extend a food's shelf life and improve its appearance once dried. It can also help speed the rehydration process for some foods. But, while beneficial, blanching is not a requirement, especially if the trip you're preparing for will occur within the next couple of months. Blanching produces no benefit to onions, tomatoes, and mushrooms, which have naturally long shelf lives and stable appearance when dried.

- Precooking, or parboiling, pasta and rice then drying in the dehydrator will greatly reduce cooking and reconstitution time on the trail. When parboiling, it even becomes possible to have excellent cold pasta and rice salads on the trail, because many parboiled foods can fully reconstitute using cold water.

- Corn, legumes (peas and beans, for example), and root crops (carrots, in particular) should always be thoroughly cooked before drying. They will not dry or reconstitute satisfactorily otherwise.

- Jerkies generally begin with raw meat and are preserved through both the drying and heavy salting processes. Regular unsalted meats can also be dried, but they should be thoroughly cooked before doing so. Slice or chop thinly after cooking, rinse under hot water to remove oils, then pat dry before dehydrating.

Maintaining the Proper Drying Environment

- Typical drying temperatures range from the upper 90s to low 100s°F for drying fragile leafy vegetables, through 125°F for most chopped or sliced vegetables, to 135°F for fruits and purees, to 155°F and higher for meat jerkies. Follow the specific guidelines and settings that come with your dehydrator.

- It may be tempting to crank the temperature beyond recommended to hasten the drying process, but there's a very good reason for keeping to the specified range. When setting the temperature too high with fruits and vegetables, not only are healthful enzymes potentially destroyed, but the outer surface of the food pieces can rapidly dry and harden, trapping moisture in the interior and leading to rapid spoilage. By drying at lower temperatures, the dehydration process progresses more uniformly from inside to out. But don't take the temperature below the recommended range: The dehydration process can take so long that your food items can actually begin to spoil before drying is complete.

- When drying foods that tend to clump, such as rice, break up the clusters after half a day or so of dehydrating, then redistribute. This will hasten the remaining process and help ensure more uniform drying. If your dehydrator is new to you, check the progress of the drying every few hours to learn the subtleties. Rotate or restack trays to keep the drying uniform.

- Some foods retain a leathery and pliable texture once fully dried, whereas other types of foods become very crisp. With a little experience you'll find that you rarely underdry food. The instruction manual that comes with your dehydrator can help you identify the drying characteristics of a large variety of foods to help you get it right the first time.

Packaging Dried Foods

- Once removed from the dehydrator, allow dried foods to cool to room temperature, then immediately transfer them to tightly sealed storage bags or containers.

- Quality ziplock bags with a sturdy seal are excellent for storing dehydrated foods. Pack a few extra bags for the trail just in case a seal breaks or a seam ruptures on a bag holding your dried foods.

- Remove fruit leather while it is still warm and pliable but not sticky. If overdried or allowed to cool, the leather may become brittle and more difficult to roll, though certainly still edible. Fruit leathers can be individually rolled on sheets of wax paper to prevent sticking.

- Vacuum sealing has little value for extending the life of some packaged trail foods, because the jagged edges of dried foods can puncture the tightly compressed walls of the vacuum bag, defeating the original objective of an airtight seal and permitting the entry of moisture from the air.

Bringing Your Dried Food Back to Life on the Trail

- Some dehydrated foods can be slower to rehydrate than others while cooking. And dehydrated foods tend to rehydrate more slowly than their freeze-dried counterparts. Don't expect all dehydrated foods to return to the same predried state once rehydrated. Many do not, being slightly smaller or chewier in texture. This is inconsequential to most recipes, since the goal is soft and tasty, not pretty.

- The best method for reconstituting dried food depends on the specific item and how it was dried. An extended simmer is usually required for foods that were not thoroughly cooked prior to drying, such as fresh vegetables. Foods that were precooked prior to drying are usually restored simply by pouring hot water over the dried food in a cup or pot, then setting it aside for an appropriate amount of time, covering it to help trap heat and moisture. Some precooked foods restore well using cold water, although the time for reconstitution takes longer than when using hot water. The recipes in this book specify the method most appropriate for the foods being rehydrated.

- Not all trail recipes require dehydrating foods at home, but many require dried foods of some sort, whether purchased at the grocery store or online. There are several web-based retailers of dried ingredients, and the types of foods now available is truly incredible. Check out the list of suppliers in Appendix B and challenge your creativity.

Breakfast

BOULDER LAKE BREAKFAST BARS

V-LO

Total Servings: 16 (1 bar per serving)
As Packaged for the Trail: Individual servings as required
Weight per Serving: About 2 ounces
Preparation Time on the Trail: None
Challenge Level: Easy

"In my search for a good homemade granola bar recipe that could also serve as a no-cook breakfast, I came across this one combining two of my favorite foods: chocolate and peanut butter! The bars are very dense and filling. A little goes a long way. Great for those mornings when you need to make a quick departure."

2 cups quick oats

2 cups Health Valley Date-Almond granola

1 cup raisins

⅓ cup brown sugar

¼ cup all-purpose flour

1 cup semisweet chocolate chips

½ cup (1 standard stick) butter

½ cup maple syrup

½ cup chunky peanut butter

Required Equipment on the Trail:
None

Nutrition Information per Serving:
Calories: 340
Protein: 6 g
Fat: 12 g
Carbohydrates: 56 g
Fiber: 4 g
Sodium: 140 mg
Cholesterol: 15 mg

Preparation at Home:

1. Preheat oven to 350°F.
2. In a large bowl combine oats, granola, raisins, brown sugar, flour, and chocolate chips. Break apart any clumps in the raisins and granola.
3. Melt butter in a saucepan over low heat, then stir in maple syrup and peanut butter until well blended.
4. Drizzle butter mixture over oat blend and toss, thoroughly coating all.
5. Turn oat mixture into a greased 9x13-inch baking pan, pressing firmly and evenly into place with greased fingers.
6. Bake bars for 20 minutes.
7. Remove pan from oven, thoroughly cool, then cut into approximately 16 bars.
8. Pack bars in small ziplock bags for the trail.

Preparation on the Trail:
Eat a breakfast bar for a quick, no-cook breakfast.

Option: Try substituting your favorite granola for the date-almond flavor specified in the recipe.

Ann Marshall
Port Orchard, Washington

"I eat a breakfast bar or snack first thing in the morning so that I can get on the trail early. Beating the hot sun is a priority for me."

Steve "Switchback" Fuquay, Las Vegas, Nevada

Photo by Ted Ayers

BLACK AND BLUE GRANOLA

Total Servings: 12
As Packaged for the Trail: 1 serving
Weight per Serving: About 3 ounces
Preparation Time on the Trail: None
Challenge Level: Easy

¼ cup sunflower oil

1 (18-ounce) jar Smucker's black raspberry jelly

2 cups lightly salted cashews, finely chopped

1 (16-ounce) package Bob's Red Mill 5-Grain rolled hot cereal

1 cup sweetened shredded coconut

3 ounces dried blueberries

Optional: instant dry milk and water, added on the trail

Required Equipment on the Trail:
None

Nutrition Information per Serving:
Calories: 420
Protein: 9 g
Fat: 27 g
Carbohydrates: 62 g
Fiber: 6 g
Sodium: 80 mg
Cholesterol: 0 mg

Preparation at Home:

1. Warm oil and jelly in a saucepan over low heat until thin.

2. Add cashews to saucepan along with cereal and coconut. Stir until jelly liquid thoroughly covers cereal mixture.

3. Evenly spread cereal mix in a nonstick jelly roll pan.

4. Bake granola at 225°F for 2 hours. Stir periodically to prevent uneven heating.

5. Set granola aside to cool, add dried blueberries, and stir.

6. Divide cereal mixture evenly among 12 (1-pint) ziplock bags.

7. Pack optional dry milk separately for the trail.

Preparation on the Trail:

A single ziplock bag provides 1 serving. Eat as is or serve with optional instant dry milk and water, hot or cold.

Christine and Tim Conners
Statesboro, Georgia

LOST VALLEY GRANOLA

V-LO

Total Servings: 26
As Packaged for the Trail: 1 serving
Weight per Serving: About 3 ounces
Preparation Time on the Trail: None
Challenge Level: Easy

Preparation at Home:
1. Preheat oven to 250°F.
2. In a very large bowl, combine and toss all ingredients except for oil, vanilla extract, and raisins.
3. Combine oil and vanilla extract in a small bowl and stir well before drizzling over the oat mixture in the large bowl.
4. Toss oat mixture to distribute oil throughout.
5. Divide oat mixture evenly among 4 large baking pans.
6. Bake granola in oven until coconut becomes a golden brown, about 2 hours.
7. Remove granola from oven, return it to the large bowl, and toss with raisins.
8. Allow granola to cool, then package in 26 (1-pint) ziplock bags, adding about 1 cup granola mix to each bag.
9. Pack optional instant dry milk separately for the trail.

Preparation on the Trail:
A single ziplock bag provides 1 serving. Eat as is or serve with optional instant dry milk and water, hot or cold.

Ann Marshall
Port Orchard, Washington

10 cups regular oats

4 cups sweetened flaked coconut

1 cup buttermilk

3 cups All-Bran cereal

1 cup brown sugar

1 cup wheat germ

1 cup sesame seeds

2 cups sunflower seed kernels

1 cup almonds

1 1/2 cups sunflower oil

1 teaspoon vanilla extract

3 cups raisins

Optional: instant dry milk and water, added on the trail

Required Equipment on the Trail:
None

Nutrition Information per Serving:
Calories: 550
Protein: 13 g
Fat: 31 g
Carbohydrates: 62 g
Fiber: 9 g
Sodium: 80 mg
Cholesterol: 3 mg

GOOSE'S MULTIGRAIN GRANOLA

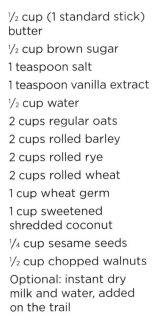

V-LO

Total Servings: 10
As Packaged for the Trail: 1 serving
Weight per Serving: About 4 ounces
Preparation Time on the Trail: None
Challenge Level: Easy

"Can be eaten as is, with cold milk, or as a hot breakfast with boiling water."

½ cup (1 standard stick) butter

½ cup brown sugar

1 teaspoon salt

1 teaspoon vanilla extract

½ cup water

2 cups regular oats

2 cups rolled barley

2 cups rolled rye

2 cups rolled wheat

1 cup wheat germ

1 cup sweetened shredded coconut

¼ cup sesame seeds

½ cup chopped walnuts

Optional: instant dry milk and water, added on the trail

Required Equipment on the Trail:
None

Nutrition Information per Serving:
Calories: 510
Protein: 15 g
Fat: 21 g
Carbohydrates: 73 g
Fiber: 12 g
Sodium: 340 mg
Cholesterol: 24 mg

Preparation at Home:
1. Melt butter in a large cook pot over low heat, then add brown sugar, salt, vanilla extract, and water. Stir until dissolved.
2. Add remaining ingredients. Stir and toss until granola is thoroughly moistened by the butter mixture.
3. Spread granola over two ungreased cookie sheets.
4. Bake for 2 hours at 250°F, stirring occasionally with a fork.
5. Remove from oven, cool, then package about 1 cup granola in each of 10 (1-pint) ziplock bags.
6. Pack optional instant dry milk separately for the trail.

Preparation on the Trail:
A single ziplock bag provides 1 serving. Eat as is or serve with optional instant dry milk and water, hot or cold.

Option: 8 cups uncooked Quaker Multigrain hot cereal can be substituted for the oats, barley, rye, and wheat.

*Kathleen "The Old Gray Goose" Cutshall
Conneaut, Ohio*

BACKPACKING CEREAL

Total Servings: 5
As Packaged for the Trail: 1 serving
Weight per Serving: About 5 ounces
Preparation Time on the Trail: None
Challenge Level: Easy

"I've had this cereal most mornings for breakfast, on the trail and at home, for the past 25 years. It's a very filling recipe, packed with healthy fats. Plan for a smaller amount each day initially until your system adjusts to it."

Preparation at Home:
1. Combine oats, wheat germ, flour, brown sugar, and walnuts in a bowl.
2. Drizzle oil over the mixture and toss well.
3. Package about 1 cup cereal in each of 5 (1-pint) ziplock bags.
4. Pack optional instant dry milk separately for the trail.

Preparation on the Trail:
A single ziplock bag provides 1 serving. Eat as is or serve with optional instant dry milk and water, hot or cold.

Option: To make granola with this recipe, bake in the oven at 275°F for 1 to 2 hours on pans, stirring occasionally to prevent burning.

Ann Marshall
Port Orchard, Washington

2 cups quick oats

1 cup wheat germ

1 cup whole wheat flour

¼ cup loose-packed brown sugar

1 cup finely chopped walnuts

¾ cup sunflower oil

Optional: instant dry milk and water, added on the trail

Required Equipment on the Trail:
None

Nutrition Information per Serving:
Calories: 760
Protein: 17 g
Fat: 52 g
Carbohydrates: 64 g
Fiber: 10 g
Sodium: 1 mg
Cholesterol: 0 mg

BIG RIVER APRICOT GRANOLA

Total Servings: 7
As Packaged for the Trail: 1 serving
Weight per Serving: About 5 ounces
Preparation Time on the Trail: None
Challenge Level: Easy

"This recipe makes for a very hearty and nutritious breakfast."

¼ cup vegetable oil

¼ cup honey

¼ cup maple syrup

1½ teaspoons vanilla extract

1 tablespoon nutritional yeast

½ cup wheat germ

2½ cups regular oats

1 cup rolled wheat

1 cup rolled rye

½ cup unsweetened shredded coconut

1 cup dried cranberries

1 cup chopped dried apricots

½ cup chopped dates

⅓ cup chopped almonds

½ cup unsalted sunflower seed kernels

Optional: instant dry milk and water, added on the trail

Required Equipment on the Trail:
None

Nutrition Information per Serving:
Calories: 680
Protein: 16 g
Fat: 19 g
Carbohydrates: 107 g
Fiber: 12 g
Sodium: 30 mg
Cholesterol: 0 mg

Preparation at Home:

1. In a medium-size cook pot over low heat, combine and stir oil, honey, and syrup until thin.

2. Add vanilla extract, yeast, wheat germ, oats, rolled wheat, and rye, stirring well following each addition.

3. Remove mixture from heat and spread evenly and loosely over a cookie sheet.

4. Bake at 250°F for 1½ to 2 hours, stirring mixture periodically.

5. Remove mixture from oven, cool, then pour into a large bowl.

6. Add fruits, nuts, and seeds to the bowl and stir well.

7. Package for the trail, adding about 1 cup granola mix to each of 7 (1-pint) ziplock bags.

8. Pack optional instant dry milk separately for the trail.

Preparation on the Trail:
A single ziplock bag provides 1 serving. Eat as is or serve with optional instant dry milk and water, hot or cold.

Brian Guldberg
Bozeman, Montana

KOOGER'S WOLF CREEK GRANOLA

Total Servings: 8
As Packaged for the Trail: 1 serving
Weight per Serving: About 5 ounces
Preparation Time on the Trail: None
Challenge Level: Easy

V

Preparation at Home:

1. In a saucepan, heat oil, maple syrup, and honey until boiling, then reduce heat to a simmer.
2. Add vanilla extract, cinnamon, and orange peel to the syrup. Continue to simmer for 15 minutes.
3. While syrup simmers, preheat oven to 275°F.
4. Remove syrup from heat and stir in lemon juice concentrate.
5. In a large bowl, combine oatmeal, wheat germ, coconut, pecans, sunflower seed kernels, almonds, and cranberries.
6. Pour syrup over mixture in the bowl and toss contents to thoroughly coat.
7. Spread mixture evenly over two greased cookie sheets and bake for 30 minutes, stirring every 10 minutes or so, checking occasionally to ensure granola doesn't burn.
8. Remove granola from oven and cool, then divide equally among 8 (1-pint) ziplock bags, adding about 1 cup granola mixture to each.
9. Pack optional instant dry milk separately for the trail.

Preparation on the Trail:

A single ziplock bag provides 1 serving. Eat as is or serve with optional instant dry milk and water, hot or cold.

Option: For crunchier granola, use a little less honey or maple syrup and bake at 335°F.

*Emmett "Ol Kooger" Autrey
Amarillo, Texas*

¼ cup sunflower oil

1 cup maple syrup

¼ cup honey

½ teaspoon vanilla extract

1 tablespoon ground cinnamon

3 tablespoons fresh grated orange peel

2 tablespoons lemon juice concentrate

2 cups regular oatmeal

1 cup wheat germ

½ cup sweetened flaked coconut

½ cup chopped pecans

½ cup sunflower seed kernels

½ cup slivered almonds

½ cup dried cranberries

Optional: instant dry milk and water, added on the trail

Required Equipment on the Trail:
None

Nutrition Information per Serving:
Calories: 550
Protein: 12 g
Fat: 20 g
Carbohydrates: 75 g
Fiber: 7 g
Sodium: 20 mg
Cholesterol: 0 mg

GRAVEL ROAD GRANOLA

V

Total Servings: 13
As Packaged for the Trail: 1 serving
Weight per Serving: About 5 ounces
Preparation Time on the Trail: None
Challenge Level: Easy

½ cup brown sugar

½ cup sunflower oil

½ cup honey

½ teaspoon vanilla extract

5½ cups regular oats

1½ cups unsalted peanuts, chopped

1½ cups sweetened shredded coconut

1½ cups sunflower seed kernels

1 cup dried soybeans

2 cups chopped dried pears

Optional: instant dry milk and water, added on the trail

Required Equipment on the Trail:
None

Nutrition Information per Serving:
Calories: 610
Protein: 18 g
Fat: 34 g
Carbohydrates: 51 g
Fiber: 13 g
Sodium: 50 mg
Cholesterol: 0 mg

Preparation at Home:

1. Preheat oven to 325°F.
2. Combine brown sugar, oil, honey, and vanilla extract in a small bowl. Stir.
3. In a large bowl, combine all remaining ingredients except for pears. Toss well.
4. Drizzle brown sugar mixture over oat mix, tossing again. Use a hand mixer on a low setting to thoroughly combine all ingredients.
5. Evenly spread oat mixture on two nonstick or greased cookie sheets.
6. Bake granola for 15 minutes until golden brown, stirring and turning mixture every 3 to 5 minutes to prevent burning.
7. Remove granola from oven and stir in chopped pears.
8. Allow granola to cool before dividing evenly among 13 (1-pint) ziplock bags, adding about 1 cup granola to each bag.
9. Pack optional instant dry milk separately for the trail.

Preparation on the Trail:
A single ziplock bag provides 1 serving. Eat as is or serve with optional instant dry milk and water, hot or cold.

*Deborah Brill and Scott "Marty" Place
Berkeley, California*

CONGAREE CHEESE GRITS

V-LO

Total Servings: 2
As Packaged for the Trail: 2 servings
Weight per Serving: About 3 ounces
Preparation Time on the Trail: 15 minutes
Challenge Level: Easy

Preparation at Home:
Combine all dry ingredients, including optional bacon bits, in a pint-size ziplock bag.

Preparation on the Trail:
1. To prepare both servings, bring 2 cups water to a boil in cook pot.
2. Add grit mix to water and cook for about 5 minutes or until grits become soft.

Scott Simerly
Apex, North Carolina

½ cup quick grits

¼ teaspoon salt

⅓ cup grated Parmesan cheese

1 tablespoon Butter Buds

Optional: bacon bits

2 cups water, added on the trail

Required Equipment on the Trail:
Cook pot

Nutrition Information per Serving:
Calories: 220
Protein: 10 g
Fat: 6 g
Carbohydrates: 33 g
Fiber: 2 g
Sodium: 640 mg
Cholesterol: 15 mg

CATOCTIN MOUNTAIN POTATO OMELET

Total Servings: 2
As Packaged for the Trail: 2 servings
Weight per Serving: About 3 ounces
Preparation Time on the Trail: 30 minutes
Challenge Level: Easy

"This recipe was created for a warm-up backpacking trip along the Chesapeake and Ohio Canal. My older scouts were practicing their cooking techniques for an upcoming high-adventure week in West Virginia."

½ cup whole egg powder

1 (4.2-ounce) package Hungry Jack dried hash browns

¼ cup cheese powder

2 tablespoons dried minced onion

¼ cup bacon bits

2 tablespoons dried bell pepper flakes

Optional: black pepper to taste

3 cups water plus additional for pack oven, added on the trail

Required Equipment on the Trail:
Pack oven and small oven bag

Cook pot with lid

Nutrition Information per Serving:
Calories: 490
Protein: 27 g
Fat: 25 g
Carbohydrates: 48 g
Fiber: 5 g
Sodium: 1420 mg

Cholesterol: 434 mg

Preparation at Home:
1. Combine egg powder, hash browns, cheese powder, dried onion, bacon bits, and dried bell pepper flakes in a quart-size ziplock bag.
2. Pack optional black pepper separately.

Preparation on the Trail:
1. To prepare both servings, place pack oven in cook pot. Add water to top of pack oven grid.
2. Pour dried ingredients along with 3 cups water into oven bag and mix thoroughly by kneading.
3. Spread bag over pack oven grid and fold top loosely. Cover pot with a lid.
4. Bring water to a boil for about 20 minutes.
5. Carefully serve omelet from bag.

Linda Nosalik
Upper Marlboro, Maryland

CHERRY-WALNUT COUSCOUS PORRIDGE

Total Servings: 2
As Packaged for the Trail: 2 Servings
Weight per Serving: About 4 ounces
Preparation Time on the Trail: 15 minutes
Challenge Level: Easy

V-LO

"My wonderful sister-in-law discovered and prepared this recipe for my trek along the Pacific Crest Trail in 1997. I found it to be easy, nourishing, and very tasty."

Preparation at Home:
Combine all dry ingredients in a pint-size ziplock bag.

Preparation on the Trail:
1. To prepare both servings, bring 1¼ cups water to a boil in a cook pot.
2. Add couscous mix to the boiling water and stir.
3. Remove pot from heat, cover, and allow to rest for 10 minutes.
4. Stir and serve.

Cathy Czachorowski
Torrington, Connecticut

½ cup instant couscous

½ cup instant dry nonfat milk

¼ cup dried cherries

¼ cup finely chopped walnuts

3 tablespoons light brown sugar

½ teaspoon ground cinnamon

1 dash salt

1¼ cups water, added on the trail

Required Equipment on the Trail:
Cook pot with lid

Nutrition Information per Serving:
Calories: 460
Protein: 17 g
Fat: 9 g
Carbohydrates: 80 g
Fiber: 9 g
Sodium: 240 mg
Cholesterol: 3 mg

BACKCOUNTRY CINNAMON ROLLS

Total Servings: 4
As Packaged for the Trail: 4 Servings
Weight per Serving: About 3 ounces
Preparation Time on the Trail: 45 minutes
Challenge Level: Moderate

V-LO

½ cup powdered sugar

2 tablespoons ground cinnamon

3 tablespoons chopped pecans

1½ cups Bisquick pancake mix

2 tablespoons instant dry buttermilk

3 tablespoons sunflower oil

⅓ cup water plus additional for pack oven, added on the trail

Required Equipment on the Trail:
Pack oven and small oven bag

Cook pot with lid

Nutrition Information per Serving:
Calories: 330
Protein: 5 g
Fat: 14 g
Carbohydrates: 46 g
Fiber: 2 g
Sodium: 420 mg
Cholesterol: 3 mg

Preparation at Home:
1. Combine powdered sugar, cinnamon, and pecans in a pint-size ziplock bag.
2. Add Bisquick and instant dry buttermilk to a quart-size ziplock bag.
3. Pack oil separately for the trail.

Preparation on the Trail:
1. To prepare all 4 servings, place pack oven in cook pot. Add water to top of pack oven grid.
2. Add 3 tablespoons sunflower oil to the pecan mixture, reseal bag, and mush contents together.
3. Add ⅓ cup water to the Bisquick mixture, reseal bag, and knead contents well.
4. Remove dough ball from the bag and place on a clean, flat surface, such as the bottom of a pot lid.
5. Work dough into a rough square about 10 inches on a side and about ¼ inch thick (thinner is better if you have the surface area to work with).
6. Evenly spread sugary nut paste over the dough.
7. Roll dough into a log and slice into disks, each about 1 inch thick.
8. Place rolls side-by-side in oven bag, fold top of bag over, then place on pack oven grid. Place lid on pot.
9. Bake, boiling over low heat, until buns rise and become firm, about 20 to 30 minutes.
10. Do not allow water to fully evaporate from pot.
11. Remove rolls from oven and allow to cool before serving.

Recipes for pack ovens usually require longer cooking times than more traditional backpacking recipes. Be sure to carry extra fuel when bringing along the oven.

A sturdy cylindrical water bottle serves nicely as a rolling pin for this recipe.

Jeffrey Hare
Citrus Heights, California

"I love my pack oven! I use it to cook most of my meals, because, with it, I never have to wash dishes and I never burn food."

Will "The Green Ghost" O'Daix,
Indianapolis, Indiana

Photo by Ted Ayers

CORNMEAL MUSH

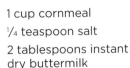

Total Servings: 2
As Packaged for the Trail: 1 serving
Weight per Serving: About 4 ounces
Preparation Time on the Trail: 15 minutes
Challenge Level: Easy

V-LO

"Don't let the name of this recipe fool you. It's delicious!"

1 cup cornmeal

¼ teaspoon salt

2 tablespoons instant dry buttermilk

2 tablespoons brown sugar

¼ teaspoon ground cinnamon

1 tablespoon sunflower oil per serving

¾ cup water per serving, added on the trail

Required Equipment on the Trail:
Cook pot with lid

Nutrition Information per Serving:
Calories: 400
Protein: 7 g
Fat: 16 g
Carbohydrates: 59 g
Fiber: 5 g
Sodium: 350 mg
Cholesterol: 4 mg

Preparation at Home:
1. Combine all dry ingredients in a small bowl, then evenly divide between 2 pint-size ziplock bags.
2. Pack oil separately for the trail.

Preparation on the Trail:
1. To prepare 1 serving, bring ¾ cup water to a boil in a cook pot and add 1 tablespoon sunflower oil.
2. Slowly add contents of 1 bag cornmeal mix to the boiling water. Stir while heating for about 1 minute.
3. Remove pot from heat, cover with lid, and allow to rest for about 5 minutes.
4. Stir then serve.

Wrapping the covered pot in a towel or other heat-resistant insulator immediately after removing from the stove allows the cornmeal to reconstitute more rapidly.

Irwin Reeves
Beaumont, California

PCT

"Grits provide good energy, cook up just fine, and taste good. By the final months of my Pacific Crest Trail thru-hike, I had given up on other foods because they didn't pack the energy punch that rice and grits do."

Charlie Thorpe, Huntsville, Alabama

CAMEL RIDER OMELET

Total Servings: 1
As Packaged for the Trail: 1 serving
Weight per Serving: About 5 ounces
Preparation Time on the Trail: 15 minutes
Challenge Level: Easy

"Camel Rider is a common name for a pita-based breakfast sandwich in the South. Most any mom-and-pop sandwich shop has one on the menu."

Preparation at Home:
1. Combine all dry ingredients, except for the pita, in a pint-size ziplock bag.
2. Pack pita bread separately for the trail.

Preparation on the Trail:
1. To prepare a single serving, bring ⅔ cup water to a boil in a cook pot. Reduce heat to a simmer.
2. Add egg mixture and stir until water is fully absorbed, about 10 minutes. Remove pot from stove.
3. Slice pita in half and divide the cooked egg between the pockets of the pita halves.

Jason Cagle
Jacksonville, Florida

2 tablespoons whole egg powder

¼ cup bacon bits

¼ cup grated Parmesan cheese

2 tablespoons dried onion flakes

1 dash ground black pepper

1 tablespoon McCormick Perfect Pinch Salt-Free Garlic and Herb Seasoning

Optional: 2 tablespoons dried bell pepper flakes

1 whole wheat pita bread

⅔ cup water, added on the trail

Required Equipment on the Trail:
Cook pot

Nutrition Information per Serving:
Calories: 430
Protein: 32 g
Fat: 17 g
Carbohydrates: 36 g
Fiber: 4 g
Sodium: 1590 mg
Cholesterol: 241 mg

OUTBACK OATMEAL

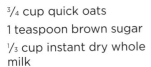

V-LO

Total Servings: 1
As Packaged for the Trail: 1 serving
Weight per Serving: About 5 ounces
Preparation Time on the Trail: 15 minutes
Challenge Level: Easy

³/₄ cup quick oats

1 teaspoon brown sugar

¹/₃ cup instant dry whole milk

¹/₄ cup dried fruit (your choice)

1 dash salt

3 tablespoons chopped cashews

1¹/₂ cups water, added on the trail

Required Equipment on the Trail:
Cook pot

Nutrition Information per Serving:
Calories: 620
Protein: 20 g
Fat: 25 g
Carbohydrates: 80 g
Fiber: 10 g
Sodium: 310 mg
Cholesterol: 30 mg

Preparation at Home:
1. Combine all dry ingredients, except for the nuts, in a pint-size ziplock bag.
2. Carry cashew pieces in a snack-size ziplock bag.

Preparation on the Trail:
1. To prepare a single serving, bring 1¹/₂ cups water to a boil in a cook pot.
2. Add oat mixture to the boiling water. Stir, then remove pot from heat.
3. Allow pot to rest for about 5 minutes. Stir in cashews and serve.

Options: Dehydrated strawberries are especially good with this recipe. Dry at home after slicing to about ¹/₈ inch thick. Other dried fruit options: Craisins, cherries, raisins, and mango.

Ken Harbison
Rochester, New York

KITCHEN CREEK BREAKFAST RICE

V

Total Servings: 2
As Packaged for the Trail: 2 Servings
Weight per Serving: About 5 ounces
Preparation Time on the Trail: 15 minutes
Challenge Level: Easy

Preparation at Home:
Combine all dry ingredients in a pint-size ziplock freezer bag.

Preparation on the Trail:
1. To prepare both servings, bring 1¼ cups water to a boil in a cook pot.
2. Add contents of rice bag to the boiling water. Reduce heat to low.
3. Stir, then cover, simmering for 10 minutes or until rice is tender. Be sure to maintain low heat to keep rice from burning, stirring as required.

Options: Substitute any chopped dried fruit in equal quantity for the raisins.

Instant dry milk, spices, or just about anything you can scrape off the bottom of your pack can also be added to this recipe!

Ursula Brower
South Lake Tahoe, California

1 cup instant brown rice
¼ cup raisins
¼ cup chopped pecans
2 tablespoons brown sugar
1 teaspoon ground cinnamon
¼ teaspoon salt
1¼ cups water, added on the trail

Required Equipment on the Trail:
Cook pot with lid

Nutrition Information per Serving:
Calories: 400
Protein: 6 g
Fat: 9 g
Carbohydrates: 74 g
Fiber: 3 g
Sodium: 310 mg
Cholesterol: 0 mg

MOUNTAIN CORN CAKES

Total Servings: 4
As Packaged for the Trail: 4 Servings
Weight per Serving: About 2 ounces
Preparation Time on the Trail: 30 minutes
Challenge Level: Moderate

"I've prepared this as a side dish in the morning and carried the leftovers wrapped in tissue paper in a side pouch to eat as I walk or to have later for lunch."

1 (8.5-ounce package) Jiffy Corn Muffin mix

1 tablespoon whole egg powder

2 tablespoons instant dry nonfat milk

¼ cup sunflower oil

½ cup water, added on the trail

Required Equipment on the Trail:
Frying pan

Spatula

Nutrition Information per Serving:
Calories: 290
Protein: 6 g
Fat: 11 g
Carbohydrates: 45 g
Fiber: 1 g
Sodium: 580 mg
Cholesterol: 30 mg

Preparation at Home:
1. Remove corn muffin mix from package and combine with remaining dry ingredients in a quart-size ziplock bag.
2. Pack oil separately for the trail.

Preparation on the Trail:
1. To prepare all 4 servings, add ½ cup water to the corn cake mixture in the bag. Reseal bag and knead the contents well.
2. Grease frying pan with 1 tablespoon sunflower oil, then warm the oil over a low flame.
3. Carefully drop heaping spoonfuls of batter into the frying pan. The batter will spread slightly, so leave adequate room between each cake.
4. Once bubbles appear over the surface of the batter, carefully flip cake onto its uncooked side.
5. Fry for an additional 30 to 40 seconds or until the cake sounds hollow when lightly tapped.
6. Repeat steps 2 through 5 for remaining oil and batter.

> The batter should be spoonable, so add water gradually and be prepared to use less or more to avoid overly runny or thick batter.

Craig "Smitty" Smith
Springfield, Missouri

62

SCRAMBLING-UP-THE-SIERRA EGGS

Total Servings: 2
As Packaged for the Trail: 2 Servings
Weight per Serving: About 3 ounces
Preparation Time on the Trail: 15 minutes
Challenge Level: Moderate

V-LO

Preparation at Home:
1. Combine all dry ingredients in a quart-size ziplock bag.
2. Pack olive oil separately for the trail.

Preparation on the Trail:
1. To prepare both servings, add 1½ cups water to the egg mixture in the bag.
2. Reseal bag and knead contents until lumps disappear. Set bag aside to rest for 5 to 10 minutes.
3. While eggs rest, grease frying pan with 1 tablespoon olive oil then warm oil over low flame.
4. Pour mixture into hot pan and scramble until thoroughly cooked, being careful not to burn the eggs.

Christine and Tim Conners
Statesboro, Georgia

1½ cups whole egg powder

¼ teaspoon ground black pepper

2 tablespoons dried bell pepper flakes

1 tablespoon dried onion

4 teaspoons instant dry buttermilk

1 teaspoon garlic powder

1 tablespoon olive oil

1½ cups water, added on the trail

Required Equipment on the Trail:
Frying pan
Spatula

Nutrition Information per Serving:
Calories: 330
Protein: 41 g
Fat: 7 g
Carbohydrates: 16 g
Fiber: 0 g
Sodium: 710 mg
Cholesterol: 960 mg

CAMERON CANYON CARAMEL ROLLS

Total Servings: 4
As Packaged for the Trail: 4 Servings
Weight per Serving: About 3 ounces
Preparation Time on the Trail: 30 minutes
Challenge Level: Moderate

V-LO

1 (8-ounce) package Jiffy Buttermilk Biscuit mix

1/4 cup chopped pecans

1/4 cup brown sugar

2 tablespoons sunflower oil

1/2 cup water, added on the trail

Optional: Butter Buds to taste

Required Equipment on the Trail:
Nonstick frying pan and cover

Spatula

Nutrition Information per Serving:
Calories: 390
Protein: 5 g
Fat: 16 g
Carbohydrates: 59 g
Fiber: 1 g
Sodium: 540 mg
Cholesterol: 4 mg

Preparation at Home:

1. Transfer biscuit mix to a quart-size ziplock bag.

2. Combine pecans with brown sugar and seal in a pint-size ziplock bag.

3. Pack oil separately for the trail.

Preparation on the Trail:

1. To prepare all 4 servings, add 1/2 cup water to bag of biscuit mix.

2. Seal bag, squeezing out the air, then knead contents until reasonably smooth. A few lumps won't cause a problem.

3. Grease frying pan with 2 tablespoons sunflower oil and warm over low heat.

4. Add pecan and brown sugar mixture to the hot oil in the pan and stir to coat. Sprinkle with optional Butter Buds.

5. Cut a corner from the bottom of the bag containing the biscuit batter.

6. Squeeze batter thinly over as much of the pecan and brown sugar mixture as possible.

7. Cover pan loosely while dough mixture bakes. Maintain low heat level, checking frequently to ensure the sugar mixture doesn't char.

8. Remove rolls from heat once dough becomes biscuit-like in texture, about 20 minutes.

9. Allow rolls to cool before serving.

*Christine and Tim Conners
Statesboro, Georgia*

APPALACHIAN APPLE BANNOCK

Total Servings: 5
As Packaged for the Trail: 1 serving
Weight per Serving: About 3 ounces
Preparation Time on the Trail: 30 minutes
Challenge Level: Moderate

V

Preparation at Home:
1. In a medium-size bowl, combine Bisquick mix and dried apple pieces. Stir well.
2. Dividing evenly, place a little less than ½ cup Bisquick-apple mix into each of 5 (1-pint) ziplock bags.
3. Pack oil and optional jam, jelly, or honey separately for the trail.

Preparation on the Trail:
1. To prepare 1 serving, add 3 tablespoons (a little more than 1 ounce) water to contents of a single bag of bannock mix. Seal bag and knead contents thoroughly.
2. Grease frying pan with 1 tablespoon sunflower oil, then warm over low heat.
3. Drop biscuit-size blobs of bannock batter into the hot pan and flatten slightly with a spatula.
4. Continue to cook over low heat for a few minutes, then flip, finishing with a brief period of frying on the opposite side. Do not allow dough to burn.
5. Repeat steps 3 and 4 with any remaining batter.
6. Serve with optional jam, jelly, or honey.

2 cups Bisquick Heart Smart pancake mix

¼ cup chopped dried apples

1 tablespoon sunflower oil per serving

Optional: jam, jelly, or honey

3 tablespoons water per serving, added on the trail

Required Equipment on the Trail:
Frying pan

Spatula

Nutrition Information per Serving:
Calories: 200
Protein: 4 g
Fat: 6 g
Carbohydrates: 35 g
Fiber: 2 g
Sodium: 410 mg
Cholesterol: 0 mg

Option: Try substituting freeze-dried banana pieces for the dried apple.

Walt and Jane Daniels
Mohegan Lake, New York

WHOLE WHEAT PALISADES PANCAKES WITH SYRUP

V-LO

Total Servings: 5
As Packaged for the Trail: 1 serving
Weight per Serving: About 4 ounces
Preparation Time on the Trail: 15 minutes
Challenge Level: Moderate

Pancake Mix:
2 tablespoons whole egg powder

1½ cups instant dry buttermilk

¼ teaspoon salt

½ cup cornmeal

1 cup whole wheat flour

½ teaspoon baking soda

2 teaspoons baking powder

Syrup:
10 tablespoons brown sugar

1 tablespoon sunflower oil per serving

About ½ cup water per serving, added on the trail

Preparation at Home:
1. Stir together all pancake mix ingredients in a large bowl.
2. Place about ½ cup dry mixture into each of 5 (1-pint) ziplock bags.
3. For syrup mixture, place 2 tablespoons brown sugar into each of 5 snack-size ziplock bags. Place 1 sealed bag brown sugar into each of the 5 bags of pancake mix.
4. Pack oil separately for the trail.

Preparation on the Trail:
1. To prepare 1 serving, remove ziplock bag containing brown sugar from a single bag of pancake mix.
2. Add slightly less than ½ cup water to pancake mixture. Reseal the bag, squeezing out the air, then knead the contents. Don't overwork the batter.
3. Cut a small corner from bottom of the ziplock bag.
4. Grease frying pan with 1 tablespoon sunflower oil. Warm the oil over low heat.
5. Squeeze some of the batter into the hot greased pan, forming a single pancake.
6. Maintain heat at a low setting. If flame temperature remains too high, hold the pan slightly above the stove to prevent burning while the pancake cooks.
7. Flip immediately after bubbles begin to form in the batter and continue to cook for a few more moments.
8. Repeat steps 5 through 7 for the remainder of the batter.

9. Add 1 tablespoon water to brown sugar in its bag and knead until lumps disappear. Pour syrup over cooked pancakes before serving.

Option: Lightly sprinkle pancakes with Butter Buds when serving.

Christine and Tim Conners
Statesboro, Georgia

Required Equipment on the Trail:
Frying pan

Spatula

Nutrition Information per Serving:
Calories: 450
Protein: 18 g
Fat: 14 g
Carbohydrates: 70 g
Fiber: 3 g
Sodium: 440 mg
Cholesterol: 24 mg

PACIFIC CREST PANCAKES

Total Servings: 11
As Packaged for the Trail: 1 serving
Weight per Serving: About 4 ounces
Preparation Time on the Trail: 15 minutes
Challenge Level: Moderate

V-LO

"My plan for hiking the Pacific Crest Trail was to have an occasional pancake breakfast for variety. Making pancakes takes more effort than other options, and I wasn't always able to spare the time in the mornings before breaking camp. So I ended up occasionally preparing this recipe in the evening as 'bread' to go along with dinner."

4 cups all-purpose flour

3/4 cup instant dry buttermilk

1/2 cup Backpacker's Pantry scrambled egg mix

1 tablespoon baking soda

1 tablespoon vegetable shortening per serving

1/2 cup water per serving, added on the trail

Required Equipment on the Trail:
Frying pan

Spatula

Nutrition Information per Serving:
Calories: 290
Protein: 6 g
Fat: 15 g
Carbohydrates: 33 g
Fiber: 1 g
Sodium: 380 mg
Cholesterol: 33 mg

Preparation at Home:
1. Mix all dry ingredients together in a large bowl, mashing out lumps.
2. Place about 1/2 cup dry mixture into each of 11 (1-pint) ziplock bags.
3. Securely pack shortening for the trail. Double sealing in a snack-size ziplock bag is one method for doing so.

Preparation on the Trail:
1. To prepare a single serving, add 1/2 cup water to 1 bag of pancake mix.
2. Seal the bag, squeezing out the air, then knead the contents. Don't overwork the mixture, which can prevent the pancakes from rising properly while cooking.
3. Cut a small corner from the bottom of the ziplock bag.
4. Melt 1 tablespoon shortening in the frying pan over low heat. Spread the melted shortening around the pan.
5. Squeeze about half the batter into the hot greased pan, forming a single pancake.
6. Maintain heat at a low setting. If flame temperature remains too high, hold the pan slightly above the stove to prevent burning while the pancake cooks.
7. Immediately flip the pancake after bubbles begin to form in the batter, and continue to cook for a few more moments.
8. Repeat steps 5 through 7 for the remainder of the batter.

It takes much less time to fry the flip side of
a pancake than the initial side.

Ann Marshall
Port Orchard, Washington

BLUE RIDGE BLUEBERRY PANCAKES

Total Servings: 4
As Packaged for the Trail: 1 serving
Weight per Serving: About 4 ounces
Preparation Time on the Trail: 30 minutes
Challenge Level: Moderate

V-LO

1 cup whole-wheat flour

1/2 cup yellow cornmeal

3 tablespoons instant dry buttermilk

2 tablespoons egg white powder

1 1/2 tablespoons granulated sugar

1 1/2 teaspoons baking powder

3/4 teaspoon baking soda

1/2 teaspoon ground cinnamon

1/2 teaspoon salt

1/2 cup dried blueberries

1/3 cup finely chopped almonds

1 1/4 teaspoons sunflower oil per serving

Optional: pancake syrup to taste

1/4 cup water per serving, added on the trail

Required Equipment on the Trail:
Frying pan

Spatula

Nutrition Information per Serving:
Calories: 320
Protein: 11 g
Fat: 11 g
Carbohydrates: 49 g
Fiber: 8 g
Sodium: 610 mg
Cholesterol: 4 mg

Preparation at Home:
1. Combine all dry ingredients in a medium-size bowl.
2. Divide ingredients equally among 4 (1-pint) ziplock bags, adding slightly more than 1/2 cup mixture per bag.
3. Pack oil and optional syrup separately for the trail.

Preparation on the Trail:
1. To prepare 1 serving, add 1/4 cup water and about 1/4 teaspoon sunflower oil to a single bag of pancake mix.
2. Reseal the bag, squeezing out the air, then knead the contents. Don't overwork the batter.
3. Let batter rest for about 15 minutes, giving it time to rise.
4. Grease frying pan with about 1 teaspoon sunflower oil, then warm over low heat.
5. Cut a corner from the bottom of the ziplock bag.
6. Squeeze about half the batter into the pan to form a single pancake.
7. Maintain heat at a low setting. If flame temperature remains too high, hold the pan slightly above the stove to prevent burning while the pancake cooks.
8. Flip pancake immediately once bubbles begin to form in the batter, then quickly finish on the opposite side.
9. Repeat steps 6 through 8 for remaining batter.
10. Serve with optional pancake syrup.

Cathy Czachorowski
Torrington, Connecticut

Lunch

CALIFORNIA BEEF JERKY

Total Servings: 10
As Packaged for the Trail: Individual servings as required
Weight per Serving: About 1 ounce
Preparation Time on the Trail: None
Challenge Level: Easy

1½ pounds flank steak

½ cup soy sauce

2 tablespoons garlic salt

2 tablespoons lemon pepper

Required Equipment on the Trail:
None

Nutrition Information per Serving:
Calories: 110
Protein: 14 g
Fat: 5 g
Carbohydrates: 1 g
Fiber: 0 g
Sodium: 1,000 mg
Cholesterol: 33 mg

Preparation at Home:
1. Trim fat from steak and cut lengthwise along the grain in slices about ½ inch thick.
2. Lay beef strips in a large bowl and cover thoroughly with soy sauce.
3. Place meat strips in a single layer on a cooling rack set on a baking sheet.
4. Sprinkle half of the garlic salt and lemon pepper over meat, coating thoroughly.
5. Place a second rack over the beef and flip the two racks over.
6. Remove the top rack to expose the unseasoned side and sprinkle the beef again with the remainder of the seasoning.
7. Dry beef strips in oven, with door closed, for about 10 to 12 hours at 155°F to 175°F.
8. Remove jerky from the oven and blot up beads of fat on the surface of the meat with paper towels.
9. Allow jerky to cool completely before packaging in ziplock bags for the trail.
10. Keep jerky refrigerated until time to leave for the trailhead.

Preparation on the Trail:
Eat a couple of pieces of jerky as a side at lunch. To reduce risk of spoilage, use all jerky within a week or so of removing it from the refrigerator at home.

> Cut across the grain of the meat for a more tender jerky texture or with the grain for a chewier texture.

Peg Spry
Agua Dulce, California

WILD TURKEY JERKY

Total Servings: 12
As Packaged for the Trail: Individual servings as required
Weight per Serving: About 1 ounce
Preparation Time on the Trail: None
Challenge Level: Easy

Preparation at Home:
1. To facilitate slicing, partially freeze the turkey meat, then cut it into very thin slices, no more than 1/8 inch thick.
2. Combine all marinade ingredients in a small bowl. Stir well.
3. Layer meat slices in a plastic container with a tight-fitting lid and pour the marinade over the turkey, being sure to wet all surfaces.
4. Seal container with lid and place in the refrigerator for about 12 hours. Occasionally invert the container to keep all surfaces of the meat saturated in marinade.
5. Place meat slices in a single layer on cooling racks set on a baking sheet.
6. Dry the meat in the oven, with door closed, for about 4 hours at 155°F, or at your oven's lowest temperature setting if higher than that.
7. Reduce oven temperature to 130°F, or its lowest setting if higher than that, and continue heating until thoroughly dry. When ready, jerky should be tough but not brittle.
8. Remove jerky from the oven and blot up any beads of fat on the surface of the meat with paper towels.
9. Allow jerky to cool completely before packaging in ziplock bags for the trail.
10. Keep jerky refrigerated until time to leave for the trailhead.

Preparation on the Trail:
Eat a few pieces of jerky as a side at lunch. To reduce risk of spoilage, use all jerky within a week or so of removing it from the refrigerator at home.

Bob Ballou
Minden, Nevada

2 pounds cooked lean turkey breast

Marinade:
1 teaspoon salt
1 teaspoon ground black pepper
1 tablespoon brown sugar
1/4 cup Worcestershire sauce
1/4 cup soy sauce
1 teaspoon liquid smoke

Required Equipment on the Trail:
None

Nutrition Information per Serving:
Calories: 100
Protein: 18 g
Fat: 1 g
Carbohydrates: 2 g
Fiber: 0 g
Sodium: 1,000 mg
Cholesterol: 23 mg

APPALACHIAN TRAIL JERKY

Total Servings: 12
As Packaged for the Trail: Individual servings as required
Weight per Serving: About 1 ounce
Preparation Time on the Trail: None
Challenge Level: Easy

"While on a trek in the 100 Mile Wilderness, we enjoyed Appalachian Trail Jerky both as a staple food and as a bite on the go."

2 pounds flank steak

Marinade:
1/3 cup teriyaki sauce

2 tablespoons liquid smoke

1/4 cup low-sodium soy sauce

2 tablespoons Worcestershire sauce

1 tablespoon garlic powder

1/2 teaspoon onion powder

2 teaspoons ground black pepper

2 teaspoons crushed red pepper

2 tablespoons brown sugar

Required Equipment on the Trail:
None

Nutrition Information per Serving:
Calories: 160
Protein: 20 g
Fat: 8 g
Carbohydrates: 4 g
Fiber: 0 g
Sodium: 500 mg
Cholesterol: 45 mg

Preparation at Home:
1. Trim fat from steak and cut lengthwise along the grain in slices about 1/4 inch thick by 1 1/2 inches wide.
2. Combine marinade ingredients in a large bowl. Stir well.
3. Add beef strips to the bowl and stir, thoroughly coating all pieces.
4. Cover bowl with lid or plastic wrap and marinate for about 12 hours.
5. Place meat strips in a single layer on two large cookie sheets.
6. Dry in the oven, with door closed, for about 10 to 12 hours at 155°F, or at your oven's lowest temperature setting if higher than that.
7. Remove jerky from oven and blot up beads of fat on the surface of the meat with paper towels.
8. Allow jerky to cool completely before packaging in ziplock bags for the trail.
9. Keep jerky refrigerated until time to leave for the trailhead.

Preparation on the Trail:
Eat a couple of pieces of jerky as a side at lunch. To reduce risk of spoilage, use all jerky within a week or so of removing it from the refrigerator at home.

Option: Chuck tender roast can be substituted for the flank steak.

Mark "Doc" and Jen "Thumper" Watson
Mechanic Falls, Maine

OAK CREEK CHEESE COOKIES

V-LO

Total Servings: 9 (4 cookies per serving)
As Packaged for the Trail: Individual servings as required
Weight per Serving: About 2 ounces
Preparation Time on the Trail: None
Challenge Level: Easy

"The Pacific Crest Trail cuts above the Oak Creek Canyon south of the town of Tehachapi, California, our former home. It's a beautiful area, an oasis surrounded by desert, where wild horses still run the canyon floor."

Preparation at Home:
1. Preheat oven to 350°F.
2. In a medium-size bowl, knead flour and butter together.
3. Add remaining ingredients to the bowl and thoroughly mix.
4. Roll batter into 36 balls, flattening each on a large cookie sheet.
5. Bake for 8 to 10 minutes.
6. Allow cookies to cool, then package for the trail.

Preparation on the Trail:
Eat about 4 cookies for a quick, no-cook lunch.

Christine and Tim Conners
Statesboro, Georgia

1 cup whole-wheat flour
½ cup (1 standard stick) butter, softened
1 cup grated cheddar cheese
½ cup cream cheese, softened
¼ cup chopped pecans
¼ cup flaxseed
1 dash ground cayenne pepper

Required Equipment on the Trail:
None

Nutrition Information per Serving:
Calories: 280
Protein: 8 g
Fat: 24 g
Carbohydrates: 20 g
Fiber: 1 g
Sodium: 200 mg
Cholesterol: 56 mg

CONGAREE COLESLAW

Total Servings: 2
As Packaged for the Trail: 2 servings
Weight per Serving: About 2 ounces
Preparation Time on the Trail: 5 minutes (plus about 1 hour to rehydrate)
Challenge Level: Easy

V-LO

"Congaree National Park, located in South Carolina, is the spectacular home to the largest tract of intact bottomland forest in the United States. It holds the world's largest known examples of at least fifteen kinds of hardwood trees."

½ cup white vinegar

¼ cup granulated sugar

1 teaspoon prepared mustard

3 cups pre-cut coleslaw vegetable mix

1 (2.5-ounce) container Lay's Smooth Ranch dip

¼ cup water, added on the trail

Required Equipment on the Trail:
None

Nutrition Information per Serving:
Calories: 200
Protein: 2 g
Fat: 6 g
Carbohydrates: 44 g
Fiber: 3 g
Sodium: 290 mg
Cholesterol: 3 mg

Preparation at Home:

1. Heat vinegar, sugar, and mustard in a saucepan to boiling, then immediately remove from stove.

2. Pour vinegar blend over slaw mix in a medium-size heatproof bowl.

3. Toss slaw, cover, and set aside for about 1 hour, occasionally stirring to recoat slaw.

4. Drain slaw and transfer to lined dehydrator trays.

5. Dry the slaw mix, occasionally breaking apart any clumps.

6. Transfer dried coleslaw to a quart-size ziplock freezer bag.

7. Pack ranch dip separately in its original container for the trail.

Preparation on the Trail:

1. To prepare both servings, add ¼ cup water and the ranch dip to the slaw mix about an hour before lunch.

2. Carefully reseal the bag, gently knead the contents, then place bag in the top of your backpack before continuing to hike.

3. At lunchtime, once slaw is rehydrated, serve straight from the bag.

Ken Harbison
Rochester, New York

HUDSON BAY BREAD

V-LO

Total Servings: 16 (2 bars per serving)
As Packaged for the Trail: Individual servings as required
Weight per Serving: About 3 ounces
Preparation Time on the Trail: None
Challenge Level: Easy

"My favorite food on the Pacific Crest Trail was Hudson Bay Bread. It was always the first thing I ate when I'd pick up my food drop at each post office resupply."

Preparation at Home:
1. Preheat oven to 350°F.
2. Melt butter in a large saucepan. Add sugar and stir. Remove from heat.
3. Stir 3 cups oats into the butter-sugar mixture.
4. Pour honey into a microwave-safe bowl and heat in a microwave oven for about 30 seconds, until it becomes runny.
5. Add honey, along with raisins, peanuts, and remaining oats, to saucepan. Stir well.
6. Allow oat mixture to cool until safe to touch, then thoroughly blend by hand.
7. Turn oat batter onto a large ungreased baking pan.
8. Bake for 25 to 30 minutes, until golden brown.
9. Remove from oven and cool for about 10 minutes before cutting into 32 bars.
10. After cutting, let bread cool for another 10 minutes before flipping out of pan.
11. Allow bread to completely cool before packaging for the trail.

Preparation on the Trail:
Eat a couple of bars for a quick, no-cook lunch.

1 cup (2 standard sticks) butter
1 1/2 cups granulated sugar
6 cups regular oats
2/3 cup honey
1/2 cup raisins
1/2 cup dry-roasted peanuts

Required Equipment on the Trail:
None

Nutrition Information per Serving:
Calories: 380
Protein: 6 g
Fat: 16 g
Carbohydrates: 44 g
Fiber: 4 g
Sodium: 128 mg
Cholesterol: 32 mg

> Though more like a sweet snack than a bread, this recipe has a history of use as a staple which is why it's included in the Lunch section.

Alan Young
Scottsdale, Arizona

BACKPACKER'S SNACK ATTACK BARS

V-LO

Total Servings: 18 (2 bars per serving)
As Packaged for the Trail: Individual servings as required
Weight per Serving: About 2 ounces
Preparation Time on the Trail: None
Challenge Level: Easy

"The recipe was adapted, with permission, from an article about backpacking published in the Schenectady Gazette *over thirty years ago. It has become a classic."*

6 ounces frozen orange juice concentrate, thawed
1/2 cup quick oats
1/2 cup chopped pitted prunes
1/2 cup chopped dried apricots
1/2 cup raisins
1/2 cup chopped unsalted peanuts
1/4 cup chopped dates
1/4 cup wheat germ
1/4 cup sesame seeds

1 tablespoon vegetable shortening
1/2 cup granulated sugar
1/2 cup unsulphured molasses
1 egg
2 cups all-purpose flour
1/4 teaspoon salt
1 teaspoon baking soda
1 teaspoon ground ginger
1 teaspoon ground cinnamon

Preparation at Home:

1. Preheat oven to 325°F.
2. In a large bowl, mix orange juice concentrate, oats, prunes, apricots, raisins, peanuts, dates, wheat germ, and sesame seeds.
3. In a second large bowl, blend shortening and sugar using a hand mixer.
4. To the second bowl, add molasses and the egg, then mix well once again.
5. In a third bowl, combine the remaining ingredients.
6. Add contents of third bowl to that of the second bowl, then stir together.
7. To the second bowl, add contents of first bowl and thoroughly blend.
8. Turn batter into a greased 13 x 9 x 2-inch baking pan and spread to an even depth.
9. Bake for 35 minutes.
10. Remove baking pan from oven, cool, then cut into 36 3 x 1-inch bars.
11. Package bars for the trail.

Preparation on the Trail:

Eat a couple of bars for a quick, no-cook lunch.

David and Sandra Geisinger
Schenectady, New York

Required Equipment on the Trail:
None

Nutrition Information per Serving:
Calories: 220
Protein: 6 g
Fat: 8 g
Carbohydrates: 38 g
Fiber: 2 g
Sodium: 120 mg
Cholesterol: 8 mg

This recipe's long list of wholesome ingredients makes it excellent as a lunch staple; but it's also great for a snack, as the name implies.

To save even more weight, Snack Attack Bars can be dried.

SKY LAKES GORP

Total Servings: 14
As Packaged for the Trail: 1 serving
Weight per Serving: About 3 ounces
Preparation Time on the Trail: None
Challenge Level: Easy

½ cup sunflower oil

¼ cup Worcestershire sauce

2 teaspoons garlic salt

2 tablespoons barbecue sauce

½ cup wheat germ

1 (24-ounce) package Mini Wheats cereal

2 cups mini pretzels

2 cups Cheese Nips crackers

2 cups honey-roasted peanuts

2 cups Cheerios cereal

Required Equipment on the Trail:
None

Nutrition Information per Serving:
Calories: 380
Protein: 11 g
Fat: 13 g
Carbohydrates: 50 g
Fiber: 6 g
Sodium: 450 mg
Cholesterol: 1 mg

Preparation at Home:
1. Preheat oven to 350°F.
2. In a large bowl, combine oil, Worcestershire sauce, garlic salt, barbecue sauce, and wheat germ. Mix well.
3. Add Mini Wheats to the bowl. Toss to thoroughly coat the cereal.
4. Evenly spread gorp mix on a cookie sheet.
5. Bake for 15 minutes or until lightly browned.
6. Return gorp mix to the bowl and add pretzels, Cheese Nips, peanuts, and Cheerios. Toss and set aside to cool.
7. Using about 1 cup in each, divide gorp among 14 (1-pint) ziplock bags.

Preparation on the Trail:
A single ziplock bag provides 1 serving. Enjoy as a side at lunch or as a snack while walking.

Option: Enjoy with peanut butter on a pita or tortilla for lunch.

All gorp recipes have been placed in the Lunch section of the book because many backpackers eat nothing but gorp during their midday break; and many folks view it more as a staple than a treat.

Alyssa Pinkerton and Jean Capellari
Allen Park, Michigan

MATT FOOD

V-LO

Total Servings: 8
As Packaged for the Trail: Individual servings
    as required
Weight per Serving: About 4 ounces
Preparation Time on the Trail: None
Challenge Level: Easy

Preparation at Home:
1. Combine all ingredients in a medium-size bowl and thoroughly mix together.
2. Pack for the trail using any of several methods: in a container; in ziplock freezer bags; or rolled into logs, then wrapped in plastic.

Preparation on the Trail:
    For lunch, eat a couple of thick slices, if rolled into a log, or several large spoonfuls, if packed in a container or ziplock bag.

Option: Matt Food is great with crackers, bread, oatmeal, and chocolate!

Deborah Brill and Scott "Marty" Place
Berkeley, California

2 cups creamy peanut butter

2 cups instant dry nonfat milk

$\frac{1}{2}$ cup honey

1 cup regular oats

Optional: nuts, shredded coconut, dried fruit, ground cinnamon, vanilla extract, wheat germ

Required Equipment on the Trail:
None

Nutrition Information per Serving:
Calories: 560
Protein: 24 g
Fat: 28 g
Carbohydrates: 40 g
Fiber: 4 g
Sodium: 360 mg
Cholesterol: 8 mg

SIERRA SZECHWAN CHICKEN SALAD

Total Servings: 6
As Packaged for the Trail: 1 serving
Weight per Serving: About 3 ounces
Preparation Time on the Trail: 5 minutes (plus 3 hours to rehydrate)
Challenge Level: Easy

"While we trudge along the trail in the morning, each yummy morsel is reabsorbing the water removed days prior. By lunchtime, a succulent salad is ready!"

½ cup low-sodium soy sauce

1 teaspoon Szechwan chili oil

1 teaspoon Dijon mustard

1 pound somen (Japanese) noodles

1 (10-ounce) can water-packed chunk chicken, drained

6 green onions, thinly sliced

1 red bell pepper, chopped

1 green bell pepper, chopped

2 cups matchstick carrots

1 (8-ounce) can sliced bamboo shoots, drained and chopped

1 (15-ounce) can baby corn on the cob (unpickled), drained and chopped

8 ounces frozen petite peas, thawed

1 tablespoon dried cilantro

2 tablespoons sesame seeds, lightly toasted

Optional: 2 tablespoons sesame oil

¾ cup water per serving, added on the trail

Preparation at Home:

1. In a large bowl, combine soy sauce, chili oil, and Dijon mustard. Stir.

2. Cook somen noodles in boiling water until al dente. Drain.

3. Add noodles to bowl with soy sauce mixture and toss, coating noodles thoroughly.

4. Spread noodles in a thin layer on drying trays and dehydrate.

5. Break chicken into pieces and dehydrate along with onions, red and green bell peppers, carrots, bamboo shoots, baby corn, and peas.

6. Once somen noodles have dried, break them into smaller pieces, about 1 inch long, and combine in a large bowl with all other dehydrated ingredients. Add cilantro and sesame seeds. Toss well.

7. Evenly divide mixture into 6 (3-ounce) portions, packaging each portion in its own quart-size ziplock freezer bag.

8. Pack optional sesame oil in a small bottle.

Preparation on the Trail:
1. Several hours before lunch, add ¾ cup water to a single-serving bag dried salad mix. Carefully reseal the bag.
2. Place salad bag in a safe location at the top of your pack.
3. Enjoy salad for lunch, adding optional 2 tablespoons sesame oil.

Option: This salad can also be served after chilling for a few minutes in a cold stream or warming briefly over a stove.

Pam Coz-Hill
Visalia, California

Required Equipment on the Trail:
None

Nutrition Information per Serving:
Calories: 380
Protein: 19 g
Fat: 6 g
Carbohydrates: 62 g
Fiber: 5 g
Sodium: about 1,100 mg
Cholesterol: 29 mg

PEANUT BUTTER AND RAISIN ROLL-UPS

V

Total Servings: 2 (1 roll per serving)
As Packaged for the Trail: 2 servings
Weight per Serving: About 4 ounces
Preparation Time on the Trail: Less than 5 minutes
Challenge Level: Easy

"Simple, no cooking , no cleanup, and very tasty!"

2 heaping tablespoons peanut butter

2 heaping tablespoons raisins

2 medium-size flour tortillas

Required Equipment on the Trail:
None

Nutrition Information per Serving:
Calories: 380
Protein: 18 g
Fat: 16 g
Carbohydrates: 50 g
Fiber: 4 g
Sodium: 410 mg
Cholesterol: 0 mg

Preparation at Home:
Pack each ingredient separately for the trail.

Preparation on the Trail:
1. To prepare both servings, spread half of the peanut butter over each tortilla.
2. Divide raisins evenly between each tortilla.
3. Roll like a burrito or *taquito*, then serve.

Option: *Try substituting honey or jam for the raisins.*

Kevin Corcoran
Palmdale, California

"We switched from pita bread to tortillas as our bread source. The tortillas hold up better on the trail, weigh less, and make great cheese, tuna, or peanut butter and jelly roll-up sandwiches."

—Joe "Mongoose" and Claire "Buttercup" Hageman, Trenton, North Carolina

GREEN MOUNTAIN FRUIT GORP

Total Servings: 7
As Packaged for the Trail: 1 serving
Weight per Serving: About 5 ounces
Preparation Time on the Trail: None
Challenge Level: Easy

Preparation at Home:
1. Mix all ingredients together in a large bowl.
2. Using about 1 cup in each, divide gorp evenly among 7 single-serving (1-pint) ziplock bags.

Preparation on the Trail:
A single ziplock bag provides 1 serving. Enjoy as a side at lunch or as a snack while walking.

Most gorp recipes are healthy and filling, with 1 cup going a long way. Open a serving at lunch, and there should be plenty left over to snack on throughout the afternoon while hoofing it down the trail. That a small amount of gorp can do double duty is an important point to take note of when planning an afternoon snack menu.

Allmuth "Curly" Perzel
Tolland, Connecticut

1 cup hazelnuts

1 cup walnuts

1 cup pumpkin seeds, roasted and salted

1 cup dried papaya, chopped

1 cup dried pineapple, chopped

1 cup dried figs, chopped

1 cup dried prunes

Required Equipment on the Trail:
None

Nutrition Information per Serving:
Calories: 470
Protein: 13 g
Fat: 28 g
Carbohydrates: 44 g
Fiber: 7 g
Sodium: 10 mg
Cholesterol: 0 mg

CREAMY CILANTRO TUNA SALAD

Total Servings: 4
As Packaged for the Trail: 1 serving
Weight per Serving: About 4 ounces
Preparation Time on the Trail: 5 minutes (plus 3 hours to rehydrate)
Challenge Level: Easy

Salad:
1 (12-ounce) bag rotini pasta

1½ cups finely shredded green cabbage

1 cup chopped celery

½ cup chopped cucumber

½ cup sliced and chopped radishes

½ cup packed minced fresh cilantro

½ cup chopped green onion

1 (5-ounce) can water-packed tuna, drained

¾ cup chopped walnuts

Dressing:
¼ cup safflower oil

¼ cup rice vinegar

1 teaspoon garlic powder

4 teaspoons Dijon mustard

2 teaspoons brown sugar

½ teaspoon salt

1 condiment packet mayonnaise per serving, added on the trail

¾ cup water per serving, added on the trail

Preparation at Home:
1. Cook pasta according to package directions, rinse, then drain.

2. In a large bowl, toss pasta with remaining salad ingredients.

3. Evenly spread about 2¼ cups pasta mixture onto 4 separate drying trays, then dehydrate. Each tray will produce a single serving.

4. While pasta mixture dries, combine all dressing ingredients in a small bowl. Mix well. Before the spices settle, immediately package for the trail in a leakproof bottle.

5. Once the pasta mix is thoroughly dry, pack the contents from each tray into a separate quart-size ziplock freezer bag.

6. Pack mayonnaise packets separately for the trail.

Preparation on the Trail:

1. Several hours before lunch, add ¾ cup water to a single-serving bag of dried salad mix. Carefully reseal the bag.
2. Place salad bag in a safe location at the top of your pack.
3. At lunchtime, pour a single-serving's worth of dressing over salad along with contents of a mayonnaise packet. Mix dressing with salad and allow to marinate for a few minutes.
4. Enjoy straight from the ziplock bag.

Pam Coz-Hill
Visalia, California

Required Equipment on the Trail:
None

Nutrition Information per Serving:
Calories: 770
Protein: 25 g
Fat: 45 g
Carbohydrates: 71 g
Fiber: 6 g
Sodium: 680 mg
Cholesterol: 21 mg

COZ-HILL CHICKEN CURRY SALAD

Total Servings: 6
As Packaged for the Trail: 1 serving
Weight per Serving: About 4 ounces
Preparation Time on the Trail: 5 minutes (plus 3 hours to rehydrate)
Challenge Level: Easy

Salad:
5 cups cooked brown rice

1/2 cup rice vinegar

4 (5-ounce) cans chicken breast, drained

1 cup diced celery

1 cup diced carrots

1 cup diced apples

1/2 cup minced parsley

1/2 cup minced bell pepper

2 tablespoons minced dried onion

1/2 cup sunflower seed kernels

Dressing:
1/4 cup olive oil

1/4 cup safflower oil

2 teaspoons brown sugar

1/2 teaspoon salt

1 teaspoon garlic powder

2 teaspoons curry powder

1 teaspoon cumin powder

3/4 cup water per serving, added on the trail

Preparation at Home:

1. In a large bowl, toss cooked brown rice and vinegar. Set aside to marinate for 30 minutes.

2. Break chicken into small pieces and add to rice along with remainder of the salad ingredients. Toss well.

3. On 6 drying trays, evenly spread about 1 3/4 cups rice mixture, then dehydrate. Each tray will produce a single serving.

4. While rice mixture dries, combine dressing ingredients in a small bowl. Mix well. Immediately package for the trail in a leak-proof bottle.

5. Once the rice mix is thoroughly dry, pack the contents from each tray into a separate quart-size ziplock freezer bag.

Preparation on the Trail:

1. Several hours before lunch, add 3/4 cup water to a single-serving bag of dried salad mix. Carefully reseal the bag.

2. Place salad bag in a safe location at the top of your pack.

3. At lunchtime, pour a single-serving's worth of dressing over the salad. Mix dressing with salad and allow to marinate for a few minutes.

4. Enjoy straight from the ziplock bag.

Note that the recipe calls for 5 cups *cooked* brown rice, not 5 cups dry rice that are then cooked. If the latter is mistakenly performed, you'll be swimming in starch!

Pam Coz-Hill
Visalia, California

Required Equipment on the Trail:
None

Nutrition Information per Serving:
Calories: 610
Protein: 30 g
Fat: 29 g
Carbohydrates: 54 g
Fiber: 6 g
Sodium: 600 mg
Cholesterol: 59 mg

Photo by Ken Harbison

BOMBACI'S TASTY TRAIL GORP

Total Servings: 8
As Packaged for the Trail: 1 serving
Weight per Serving: About 5 ounces
Preparation Time on the Trail: None
Challenge Level: Easy

V-LO

"Ever wonder where the name gorp comes from? It's an acronym for 'good old raisins and peanuts.' As you can see, this recipe, and others in this section, take the definition a little further!"

1 cup unsalted cashews

1 cup unsalted sunflower seed kernels

1 cup sweetened shredded coconut

1 cup dried banana chips

1 cup raisins

1 cup regular M&Ms

1 cup unsalted dry-roasted peanuts

1 cup dates

Required Equipment on the Trail:
None

Nutrition Information per Serving:
Calories: 660
Protein: 14 g
Fat: 36 g
Carbohydrates: 96 g
Fiber: 8 g
Sodium: 70 mg
Cholesterol: 4 mg

Preparation at Home:
1. Combine all ingredients in a large bowl and mix well.
2. Using about 1 cup in each, divide gorp evenly among 8 single-serving (1-pint) ziplock bags.

Preparation on the Trail:
A single ziplock bag provides 1 serving. Enjoy as a side at lunch or as a snack while walking.

Rick Bombaci
Enterprise, Oregon

GOOSE'S GORP

V-LO

Total Servings: 12
As Packaged for the Trail: 1 serving
Weight per Serving: About 5 ounces
Preparation Time on the Trail: None
Challenge Level: Easy

Preparation at Home:
1. Mix all ingredients together in a large bowl.
2. Using about 1 cup in each, divide gorp evenly among 12 single-serving (1-pint) ziplock bags.

Preparation on the Trail:
A single ziplock bag provides 1 serving. Enjoy as a side at lunch or as a snack while walking.

Option: Use your favorite dried fruit blend in place of the Sun Maid mixed fruit.

*Kathleen "The Old Gray Goose" Cutshall
Conneaut, Ohio*

2 cups gumdrops candy

2 cups regular M&Ms

1/2 cup pepitas, roasted and salted

1/2 cup dry-roasted and salted peanuts

2 (7-ounce) packages Sun Maid dried mixed fruit

1/2 cup roasted and salted sunflower seed kernels

4 cups Honey Nut Cheerios cereal

1/2 cup raisins

Optional: shredded coconut to taste

Required Equipment on the Trail:
None

Nutrition Information per Serving:
Calories: 450
Protein: 7 g
Fat: 13 g
Carbohydrates: 87 g
Fiber: 7 g
Sodium: 240 mg
Cholesterol: 4 mg

SMITTY'S LUNCH AT LOST LAKE

Total Servings: 2 (6 crackers per serving)
As Packaged for the Trail: 2 Servings
Weight per Serving: About 5 ounces (including sardine can)
Preparation Time on the Trail: Less than 5 minutes
Challenge Level: Easy

"I really like simple lunches. My brother and I first had this one at Lost Lake, about 4 miles from the trailhead in the Beartooth Mountains. The lake is quite small and faced on the south by impressive rock buttresses. The winds that day were pushing 50 miles per hour!"

12 Triscuit Hint of Salt crackers

3 prewrapped slices American cheese

1 (3 ³/₄-ounce) can sardines, added on the trail

Required Equipment on the Trail:
None

Nutrition Information per Serving:
Calories: 320
Protein: 11 g
Fat: 18 g
Carbohydrates: 22 g
Fiber: 3 g
Sodium: 630 mg
Cholesterol: 57 mg

Preparation at Home:
Pack crackers, cheese slices, and sardines separately for the trail. Keep sardines and cheese slices in their original packaging.

Preparation on the Trail:
1. To prepare both servings, fold each piece of cheese in half twice to create 12 squares.
2. On each cracker, place a piece of cheese, then a bit of sardine.
3. After lunch, rinse the sardine can well and wrap it tightly with your trash to seal the aroma.

Option: Substitute your favorite crackers for the Triscuits, but be sure to select types that will hold up to the rigor of your backpack's interior.

Craig "Smitty" Smith
Springfield, Missouri

HAWK MOUNTAIN ROLLS-UPS

Total Servings: 1
As Packaged for the Trail: 1 serving
Weight per Serving: About 5 ounces
Preparation Time on the Trail: 5 minutes (plus 1 hour to rehydrate)
Challenge Level: Easy

V-LO

Preparation at Home:
1. Combine bean mix, chili powder, and cumin in a pint-size ziplock freezer bag.
2. Pack cheese and tortilla separately for the trail.

Preparation on the Trail:
1. To prepare a single serving, about 1 hour before lunch, add ½ cup water to the bean mix.
2. Carefully reseal the bag and knead the contents well.
3. Place bag in the top of your pack or other safe location and continue hiking.
4. Once it's time for lunch, spread beans on the tortilla, top with pieces of cheese, and roll like a burrito or *taquito*.

½ cup (about ⅓ of 7-ounce package) Fantastic Foods refried bean mix

¼ teaspoon chili powder

1 dash cumin

1 slice jalapeno jack cheese

1 medium-size whole wheat tortilla

½ cup water, added on the trail

Required Equipment on the Trail:
None

Walt and Jane Daniels
Mohegan Lake, New York

Nutrition Information per Serving:
Calories: 470
Protein: 23 g
Fat: 14 g
Carbohydrates: 64 g
Fiber: 15 g
Sodium: 1,160 mg
Cholesterol: 25 mg

Authors' Note:
Thanks to Ken Harbison for reworking the original recipe from the first edition to accommodate changes in available ingredients.

TREKKER'S TABOULI ON PITA

V-LO

Total Servings: 4 (1 pita per serving)
As Packaged for the Trail: 1 serving
Weight per Serving: About 5 ounces
Preparation Time on the Trail: 5 minutes (plus about 2 hours to rehydrate)
Challenge Level: Easy

1 small zucchini, diced

1 bell pepper, diced

1 (6-ounce) package Fantastic Foods tabouli salad mix

2 tablespoons minced dried onion

1 tablespoon dried oregano

1 tablespoon dried basil

2 bay leaves, crumbled

1 teaspoon dried sage

1 teaspoon dried parsley

1 tablespoon nutritional yeast

4 whole wheat pitas

¼ cup olive oil

4 slices Swiss cheese

⅓ cup water per serving, added on the trail

Required Equipment on the Trail:
None

Nutrition Information per Serving:
Calories: 540
Protein: 21 g
Fat: 26 g
Carbohydrates: 65 g
Fiber: 8 g
Sodium: 1,250 mg
Cholesterol: 25 mg

Preparation at Home:
1. Dry zucchini and bell pepper in a dehydrator.
2. In a medium-size bowl, thoroughly combine dried zucchini and pepper, tabouli mix, minced onion, oregano, basil, bay leaves, sage, parsley, and nutritional yeast.
3. Evenly divide tabouli blend among 4 (1-pint) ziplock freezer bags.
4. Pack pitas, oil, and cheese separately for the trail.

Preparation on the Trail:
1. A couple of hours before lunch, prepare 1 serving by adding ⅓ cup water and 1 tablespoon olive oil to a bag of tabouli blend.
2. Seal bag and knead contents, then set aside in your pack for the remainder of the morning while you continue to hike.
3. At lunchtime, place a slice of cheese in a pita pocket.
4. Snip a corner from the bottom of the bag of tabouli blend and squirt contents into the pita and serve.

> For those who'd prefer to not dehydrate their own ingredients, see Appendix B for online sources of dehydrated fruits, vegetables, and other food items.

Sandy Lee Burns
Prospect, Oregon

TROPICAL TRAIL SALAD

V

Total Servings: 4
As Packaged for the Trail: 1 serving
Weight per Serving: About 5 ounces
Preparation Time on the Trail: 5 minutes (plus 3 hours to rehydrate)
Challenge Level: Easy

Preparation at Home:
1. Cook brown rice according to package directions.
2. Toss rice in a large bowl with lemon juice and coconut milk. Set aside for 30 minutes to marinate.
3. Add remaining ingredients, excluding water, then mix well.
4. On 4 separate drying trays, evenly spread about 2¼ cups of rice mixture, then dehydrate. Each tray will produce a single serving.
5. Once the rice mix is thoroughly dry, package the contents from each tray into a separate quart-size ziplock freezer bag.

Preparation on the Trail:
1. Several hours before lunch, add 1 cup water to a single-serving bag of dried salad mix. Carefully reseal the bag.
2. Place salad bag in a safe location at the top of your backpack.
3. When it's time to stop for lunch, enjoy your salad straight from the ziplock bag.

Option: Substitute your favorite dried fruits for the apricots and dates.

Pam Coz-Hill
Visalia, California

PCT

2½ cups Minute Brown Rice
½ cup lemon juice
½ cup coconut milk
1 carrot, peeled and grated
1 apple, peeled, cored, and grated
2 stalks celery, thinly sliced
1 cup shredded cabbage
1 cup chopped dried apricot
½ cup chopped dates
¼ cup almonds, toasted
1 tablespoon dried parsley flakes
1 teaspoon salt
¼ cup honey
1 cup water per serving, added on the trail

Required Equipment on the Trail:
None

Nutrition Information per Serving:
Calories: 580
Protein: 11 g
Fat: 17 g
Carbohydrates: 108 g
Fiber: 8 g
Sodium: 640 mg
Cholesterol: 0 mg

BMCS

Total Servings: 2 (1 bagel per serving)
As Packaged for the Trail: 2 servings
Weight per Serving: About 6 ounces
Preparation Time on the Trail: Less than 5 minutes
Challenge Level: Easy

"I first made bagel, meat, and cheese sandwiches (BMCS) at a small lake in the Wind River Range. The lake provided the most incredible trout fishing I'd ever experienced. 'Which lake?' you ask. I'm not telling."

2 bagels

2 ounces summer sausage

2 slices sharp cheddar cheese

Optional: condiment packets, such as hot mustard

Required Equipment on the Trail:
None

Nutrition Information per Serving:
Calories: 440
Protein: 20 g
Fat: 18 g
Carbohydrates: 58 g
Fiber: 2 g
Sodium: 1,270 mg
Cholesterol: 45 mg

Preparation at Home:
Package ingredients, including optional condiments, individually for the trail.

Preparation on the Trail:
1. To prepare 1 serving, split a bagel, then layer half of the meat and cheese on the bread as you would a sandwich.
2. Add optional condiments.
3. Repeat steps 1 and 2 for the second serving.

Options: Try different types of bagels; dried chipped beef or pepperoni instead of the summer sausage; or another hard cheese, such as pepper jack, instead of cheddar.

Craig "Smitty" Smith
Springfield, Missouri

TUNA-SPINACH COUSCOUS

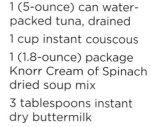

Total Servings: 2
As Packaged for the Trail: 1 serving
Weight per Serving: About 6 ounces
Preparation Time on the Trail: 5 minutes (plus 1 hour to rehydrate)
Challenge Level: Easy

Preparation at Home:
1. Dry tuna in a dehydrator.
2. In a medium-size bowl, thoroughly combine dried tuna with couscous, soup mix, and dry buttermilk.
3. Evenly divide tuna-couscous mixture between 2 (1-quart) ziplock freezer bags.

Preparation on the Trail:
1. To prepare 1 serving, add 1 cup water to a bag of couscous mix about an hour before lunch.
2. Reseal bag, mush contents, place in a safe place at the top of your backpack.
3. At lunchtime, serve straight from the bag.

Option: If the extra weight isn't a concern, the home dehydrating process can be bypassed for this recipe, with the tuna carried in easy-open foil pouch packaging, then combined with the couscous mix on the trail. Be sure to use a little less water for reconstituting with this method.

Diane King
Somers, Connecticut

1 (5-ounce) can water-packed tuna, drained

1 cup instant couscous

1 (1.8-ounce) package Knorr Cream of Spinach dried soup mix

3 tablespoons instant dry buttermilk

1 cup water per serving, added on the trail

Required Equipment on the Trail:
None

Nutrition Information per Serving:
Calories: 600
Protein: 35 g
Fat: 12 g
Carbohydrates: 89 g
Fiber: 4 g
Sodium: 1,440 mg
Cholesterol: 39 mg

"Learn the joys of couscous! It's high in protein, needs no rinsing, and takes less time to cook than pasta; but it can be used in all the same ways."

Dan and Sara Rufner, San Diego, California

EGG SOUP

Total Servings: 1
As Packaged for the Trail: 1 serving
Weight per Serving: About 1 ounce
Preparation Time on the Trail: 15 minutes
Challenge Level: Easy

"I like this recipe because it tastes great, is loaded with protein for its weight, and has a way of getting the motor running."

1 regular-size cube low-sodium chicken bouillon

2 tablespoons whole egg powder

1 tablespoon dried chives

1 1/2 cups water, added on the trail

Required Equipment on the Trail:
Cook pot

Nutrition Information per Serving:
Calories: 80
Protein: 6 g
Fat: 5 g
Carbohydrates: 2 g
Fiber: 0 g
Sodium: 620 mg
Cholesterol: 205 mg

Preparation at Home:
Combine bouillon cube, egg powder, and chives in a snack-size ziplock bag.

Preparation on the Trail:
1. To prepare a single serving, combine egg mixture and 1 1/2 cups water in a cook pot. Stir well.
2. Bring soup to a boil while breaking up clumps.
3. After a few minutes of boiling, the egg will have congealed at the top. Once it does, remove from heat and serve.

Thomas Leggemann
Greensboro, North Carolina

WANDERING WONTON SOUP

Total Servings: 2
As Packaged for the Trail: 2 servings
Weight per Serving: About 2 ounces
Preparation Time on the Trail: 15 minutes
Challenge Level: Easy

Preparation at Home:
1. Chop wontons into small pieces.
2. Dry wonton pieces on a lined dehydrator tray.
3. Place dried wontons in a pint-size ziplock bag along with soup packet and chives.

Preparation on the Trail:
1. To prepare both servings, add wontons, chives, and contents of soup packet to 3 cups water in a cook pot. Stir well.
2. Bring soup to a boil and continue to cook for a few minutes until wontons fully rehydrate.

Ken Spiegel
Farmingville, New York

4 ounces frozen precooked wontons (your favorite), thawed

1 (0.28-ounce) packet Dynasty wonton soup base mix

2 tablespoons dried chives

3 cups water, added on trail

Required Equipment on the Trail:
Cook pot

Nutrition Information per Serving:
Calories: 150
Protein: 4 g
Fat: 2 g
Carbohydrates: 20 g
Fiber: 1 g
Sodium: 1,110 mg
Cholesterol: 19 mg

PINE NUT SOUP

Total Servings: 2
As Packaged for the Trail: 2 servings
Weight per Serving: About 3 ounces
Preparation Time on the Trail: 15 minutes
Challenge Level: Easy

"On a Boy Scout outing once, I prepared this dish on the fly using what I could find in my backpack."

1 (1.4-ounce) package Knorr vegetable recipe mix

1/4 cup pine nuts

1/4 cup chopped walnuts

1 (1.5-ounce) box raisins

1 tablespoon honey

3 cups water, added on the trail

Required Equipment on the Trail:
Cook pot

Nutrition Information per Serving:
Calories: 370
Protein: 7 g
Fat: 21 g
Carbohydrates: 40 g
Fiber: 4 g
Sodium: 1,400 mg
Cholesterol: 0 mg

Preparation at Home:
1. Combine vegetable recipe mix, pine nuts, and walnuts in a pint-size ziplock bag.
2. Carry raisins in the box and pack honey separately.

Preparation on the Trail:
1. To prepare both servings, add vegetable recipe mixture, raisins from the box, and 1 tablespoon honey to 3 cups water in a cook pot. Stir well.
2. Bring soup to a boil, then remove from stove and allow to rest for 5 minutes before serving.

Ken Spiegel
Farmingville, New York

SIMMERING POT FRUIT SOUP

Total Servings: 4
As Packaged for the Trail: 4 servings
Weight per Serving: About 5 ounces
Preparation Time on the Trail: 15 minutes
Challenge Level: Easy

V

Preparation at Home:
1. If not in small pieces already, chop dried fruit, then package it for the trail.
2. Pack pudding mix separately in a pint-size ziplock bag.

Preparation on the Trail:
1. To prepare all 4 servings, bring 3 cups water to a boil, then add dried fruit.
2. Lower heat to a simmer for about 10 minutes, stirring occasionally while the fruit rehydrates.
3. Add 1 cup cold water to the pudding mix in a ziplock bag. Seal bag and knead mixture until dissolved.
4. Pour pudding mix into fruit soup, stir until well blended, and serve.

1 pound dried fruit (your favorite)

1 (3.4-ounce) package instant lemon pudding mix

4 cups water, added on the trail

Required Equipment on the Trail:
Cook pot

Nutrition Information per Serving:
Calories: 390
Protein: 4 g
Fat: 0 g
Carbohydrates: 104 g
Fiber: 8 g
Sodium: 400 mg
Cholesterol: 0 mg

It used to be hard to find a wide selection of dried fruit at the typical grocery store, but not anymore. Look for pears, apples, pineapple rings, papaya, peaches, apricots, and, of course, prunes and dates. Or dry your favorites yourself at home!

Sandy Lee Burns
Prospect, Oregon

WAGON MOUND TORTILLA CHIPS

V

Total Servings: 2
As Packaged for the Trail: 2 servings
Weight per Serving: About 4 ounces
Preparation Time on the Trail: 15 minutes
Challenge Level: Easy

⅓ cup peanut oil

2 medium-size flour tortillas

¼ teaspoon salt

Required Equipment on the Trail:
Frying pan

Spatula

Nutrition Information per Serving:
Calories: 530
Protein: 5 g
Fat: 43 g
Carbohydrates: 36 g
Fiber: 2 g
Sodium: 640 mg
Cholesterol: 0 mg

Preparation at Home:
Pack all ingredients separately for the trail.

Preparation on the Trail:
1. To prepare both servings, warm ⅓ cup peanut oil in a frying pan over medium heat.
2. Slice each tortilla into six or so wedges.
3. Carefully fry tortilla wedges in small batches until light brown and crispy on the bottom, then flip and repeat on the other side.
4. Remove tortillas from the oil, salting lightly before serving.
5. Fry remaining tortillas following steps 3 and 4.

Option: Salsa is extremely easy to dry and rehydrate and makes an excellent addition to this recipe. Try this on the trail, and you are guaranteed to be the envy of your group!

> Do not overcrowd the pan with tortillas while frying, as it becomes difficult to flip and move the chips to avoid burning.

*Christine and Tim Conners
Statesboro, Georgia*

WHITE MOUNTAINS HUMMUS BURRITOS

V-LO

Total Servings: 4
As Packaged for the Trail: 4 servings
Weight per Serving: About 5 ounces
Preparation Time on the Trail: 15 minutes
Challenge Level: Easy

Preparation at Home:
Pack all ingredients separately for the trail.

Preparation on the Trail:
1. To prepare all 4 servings, add 1½ cups water to dry hummus mix, knead the bag, and set aside for a few minutes to reconstitute.
2. Meanwhile, grease frying pan with 1 tablespoon peanut oil and warm over low heat.
3. Spread a quarter of the reconstituted hummus mix evenly over the top of 1 tortilla and place 1 slice cheese over the hummus.
4. Set tortilla in frying pan. Cover pan and warm tortilla until cheese has melted.
5. Repeat steps 2 through 4 for the remaining tortillas and hummus.

Option: Try grated Parmesan instead of provolone or sprouts instead of cheese.

Walt and Jane Daniels
Mohegan Lake, New York

1 (6-ounce) package Fantastic Foods Original Hummus mix

1½ cups water, added on the trail

¼ cup peanut oil

4 medium-size reduced-fat whole wheat tortillas

4 slices provolone cheese

Required Equipment on the Trail:
Frying pan and cover

Spatula

Nutrition Information per Serving:
Calories: 450
Protein: 20 g
Fat: 28 g
Carbohydrates: 41 g
Fiber: 9 g
Sodium: 1,020 mg
Cholesterol: 19 mg

DOMELAND NACHOS

Total Servings: 2
As Packaged for the Trail: 2 servings
Weight per Serving: About 6 ounces
Preparation Time on the Trail: 15 minutes
Challenge Level: Easy

V-LO

"I came down with the backpacking bug when I was twenty-seven years old while on a day hike with friends in the incredible Domeland Wilderness of the Southern Sierra. Before the trip, I was a reluctant participant. Afterward, I couldn't wait to return. The following month, I did just that. Inexperienced and improperly equipped for November mountain weather, I headed into the wilderness. Several days later, I limped back out, injured and exhausted, but with a love of the mountains that hasn't faded."

—TIM

¼ cup peanut oil

2 medium-size flour tortillas

3-ounce block sharp cheddar cheese, cut from a larger block

Required Equipment on the Trail:
Frying pan

Spatula

Nutrition Information per Serving:
Calories: 700
Protein: 16 g
Fat: 57 g
Carbohydrates: 37 g
Fiber: 2 g
Sodium: 610 mg
Cholesterol: 45 mg

Preparation at Home:
Pack all ingredients separately for the trail.

Preparation on the Trail:
1. To prepare the first of 2 servings, grease a frying pan with 2 tablespoons peanut oil and warm over low heat.
2. Slice a tortilla into six or so wedges.
3. Cut half of the cheese block into thin slices, 1 slice for each wedge of tortilla.
4. Fry tortilla pieces in oil for a couple of minutes, then flip.
5. Add a piece of sliced cheese to each of the tortilla wedges and cover pan.
6. Once the cheese melts, serve, then repeat steps 1 through 5 with the remaining ingredients.

Christine and Tim Conners
Statesboro, Georgia

Dinner

TEHACHAPI TRAIL SPROUTS

Total Servings: 2
As Packaged for the Trail: 2 servings
Weight per Serving: Less than 1 ounce
Preparation Time on the Trail: 5 minutes
   (plus 3 to 6 days for soaking and sprouting)
Challenge Level: Moderate

"Growing sprouts on a long trek is a great way to enjoy fresh, healthy greens at a time when your body is craving them and when they would otherwise be impossible to come by. Corrine Edwards's recipe, Trail-Grown Sprouts, in the first edition of this book was the inspiration for the version here."

2 tablespoons sprout seeds: alfalfa, red clover, chia, mung, green pea, fenugreek, mustard, radish, bean mix, lentil, garbanzo, rye, hard or soft wheat, red pea, or barley

Required Equipment on the Trail:
Sprout bag and dry sack

Nutrition Information per Serving:
Varies by type, but sprouts are generally a good source of protein, vitamins A and C, and calcium.

Preparation at Home:
   Pack sprout seeds in a snack-size ziplock bag for the trail.

Preparation on the Trail:
1. Soak seeds in a little water inside the ziplock bag for 8 to 10 hours.
2. Place seeds in sprout bag and soak the bag in water for several minutes.
3. Close sprout bag and place it in a second bag, one reasonably waterproof, such as a dry sack, then hang the assembly from your pack. Don't seal the bag tightly shut, because the seeds need fresh air.
4. At least twice each day, such as when stopping to fill your water bottles, remove the seed bag from the waterproof bag, and pour some filtered water over the seed bag to keep it fresh and moist. Massage the seeds very gently through the wall of the seed bag to help keep the air circulating before returning the seed bag to the waterproof bag.
5. Following this process most varieties of grains and beans will be fully sprouted and ready to eat in 3 to 6 days, producing plenty of sprouts for 2 people.

A variety of bag materials can be used to grow sprouts, including cheesecloth, muslin, hosiery socks, ringless aquarium filter bags, gauze, and even mosquito netting.

Keep sprouts moist continuously.

Extreme outdoor temperatures, hot or cold, will adversely affect sprouting performance.

To add deeper green to your sprouts, expose them periodically to indirect sunlight.

Christine and Tim Conners
Statesboro, Georgia

SANDY'S WEED SALAD

V

Total Servings: 1
As Packaged for the Trail: 1 serving
Weight per Serving: About 1 ounce (dressing only)
Preparation Time on the Trail: 15 minutes
Challenge Level: Difficult

"Dandelion, plantain, chicory, chickweed, yellow dock, lamb's quarters, sheep sorrel, and miner's lettuce are abundant in many areas of the Western mountains of the United States during the summer months. Fresh greens are a great source of calcium and a refreshing treat for the long-distance hiker."

Dressing:
2 tablespoons (1 ounce) fresh-squeezed lemon

Salt, black pepper, dried oregano, or other seasonings to taste

Olive oil, to taste

Herbs and Weeds from the Trail:
Dandelion, plantain, chicory, chickweed, yellow dock, lamb's quarters, sheep sorrel, miner's lettuce, red clover, wild and prickly lettuce

Required Equipment on the Trail:
2 quart-size ziplock bags

Nutrition Information per Serving:
Varies by the kinds of greens collected and the type of dressing used.

Preparation at Home:
Mix dressing ingredients and store in a small container for the trail.

Preparation on the Trail:
1. Collect greens while traveling along the trail.
2. Immediately splash picked greens with filtered water.
3. Store greens in an unsealed quart-size ziplock bag. Save this ziplock as your greens collection bag for future use.
4. When ready for your salad, wash greens in filtered water, shake dry, and chop into bite-size pieces.
5. Add greens to a second, clean quart-size ziplock bag, then toss with 2 tablespoons dressing to produce a single serving.
6. Rinse the second bag once finished and save this ziplock as the greens serving bag for future use.

Caution!
You must be able to positively identify plants safe for consumption before using this recipe. This is where the recipe's challenge lies. If you're unsure, or if the leaves don't appear green and fresh, don't pick!

> To avoid spoilage, don't place the collection bag in a warm location of your pack or wait more than a few hours to use the greens.

> In support of leave-no-trace, if greens are scarce in the area you're traveling through, leave them for the local fauna. And when picking greens, select plants well off the trail, where any evidence of foraging will go unnoticed by other hikers.

Sandy Lee Burns
Prospect, Oregon

Authors' Note:
We hope that Sandy's Weed Salad recipe will inspire backpackers to look beyond the grocery store for valuable food sources while on long-distance treks, when fresh greens are otherwise few and far between.

"It's not impossible to have a fresh salad on the trail. I combine leaf lettuce, string beans, snow peas, and chopped herbs. I find that leaf lettuce will keep two or three days when rolled in paper towels and stored in a plastic bag. For dressing, I use leftover juice from sweet pickles."

—Jack Konner
Beaverton, Oregon

KIRK'S NO-COOK PIZZA

V-LO

Total Servings: 1
As Packaged for the Trail: 1 serving
Weight per Serving: About 6 ounces
Preparation Time on the Trail: 15 minutes
Challenge Level: Easy

1 (5-ounce) packet
Boboli pizza sauce

2 tablespoons grated
Parmesan cheese

2 whole wheat pitas

⅓ cup water, added on
the trail

**Required Equipment on
the Trail:**
None

**Nutrition Information
per Serving:**
Calories: 460
Protein: 20 g
Fat: 9 g
Carbohydrates: 76 g
Fiber: 6 g
Sodium: 1,350 mg
Cholesterol: 15 mg

Preparation at Home:
1. Dry Boboli sauce on lined trays in a dehydrator until the consistency of tough leather.
2. Tear dried sauce into small pieces.
3. Seal dried sauce along with Parmesan cheese in a pint-size ziplock bag.
4. Pack pitas separately for the trail.

Preparation on the Trail:
1. To prepare a single serving, add ⅓ cup water to the dried sauce mix in the bag.
2. Seal bag and carefully knead for a few minutes to speed rehydration of the pizza sauce.
3. With the sauce rehydrated, cut a corner from the bottom of the sauce bag and squirt about half over the top of each pita.

Option: If weight isn't a concern, the Boboli sauce can be carried in its original packaging, avoiding the dehydration step.

*Kirk Ikens
Rogers City, Michigan*

PCT

JOE'S EXCITING SANDWICHES

Total Servings: 1 (2 sandwiches per serving)
As Packaged for the Trail: 1 serving
Weight per Serving: About 7 ounces
Preparation Time on the Trail: Less than 5 minutes
Challenge Level: Easy

"My advice is to leave the stove at home! I hiked the entire Pacific Crest Trail without cooking, and I never missed it. During foul weather, it was especially nice to simply climb into the tent and eat a couple of sandwiches. No fuel or dirty dishes and no water needed for cleaning up. Give it a try!"

Preparation at Home:
Pack all items separately for the trail.

Preparation on the Trail:
1. To prepare a single serving, use 1 slice cheese and 2 slices ham on each of the 2 hamburger buns.
2. Add optional condiments.

2 small hamburger buns

2 slices Tillamook cheddar cheese

4 slices Hillshire Farm Deli Select ham

Optional: favorite condiments in single-serving packets

Required Equipment on the Trail:
None

Caution!

Prudence must be exercised when carrying nondried meats. The salt and preservatives added to deli ham help prevent spoilage, but the meat must also be kept cool and sealed to prevent bacteria from growing. This may not be possible in some trail environments or during warmer months. If in doubt, don't risk making yourself ill!

Nutrition Information per Serving:
Calories: 500
Protein: 29 g
Fat: 24 g
Carbohydrates: 45 g
Fiber: 2 g
Sodium: 1,230 mg
Cholesterol: 67 mg

Joe Sobinovsky
Citrus Heights, California

Authors' Note:
Joe's recipe is included in Lipsmackin' Backpackin' *because it's so simple that it's otherwise easy to overlook as a real option. Most backpackers are unlikely to hike an entire long trail without cooking, because hot food is such an important part of their outdoor experience. But Joe's approach is definitely worth considering, especially for long, dry sections of trail where water for cleanup is scarce, when time is of the essence, or during periods of inclement weather.*

ALASKAN CHIPPED BEEF

Total Servings: 2
As Packaged for the Trail: 2 servings
Weight per Serving: About 1 ounce
Preparation Time on the Trail: 15 minutes
Challenge Level: Easy

"This was one of our favorite meals when we visited the Harding Ice Flow on the Kenai Peninsula in Alaska."

1 (2.25-ounce) jar Armour sliced dried beef

⅓ cup instant dry nonfat milk

1 tablespoon Coffee-mate nondairy creamer

1 tablespoon all-purpose flour

2 tablespoons sunflower oil

1 cup water, added on the trail

Required Equipment on the Trail:
Cook pot

Nutrition Information per Serving:
Calories: 250
Protein: 13 g
Fat: 16 g
Carbohydrates: 13 g
Fiber: 0 g
Sodium: 1,430 mg
Cholesterol: 27 mg

Preparation at Home:
1. Dry beef even further using a dehydrator, then break beef into pieces.
2. Combine dried beef, instant dry milk, creamer, and flour together in pint-size ziplock bag.
3. Pack oil separately for the trail.

Preparation on the Trail:
1. To prepare both servings, combine 2 tablespoons sunflower oil and contents from ziplock bag in a cook pot. Stir well.
2. Add 1 cup water, stir, then place pot over low flame.
3. Simmer, stirring often, until thick, then serve.

Option: Pour sauce over toast, instant rice, or mashed potatoes to make a quick, delicious, and hearty meal.

Jeff and Chris Wall
Lancaster, California

PASCAGOULA BAY SHRIMP AND GRITS

Total Servings: 1
As Packaged for the Trail: 1 serving
Weight per Serving: About 3 ounces
Preparation Time on the Trail: 15 minutes
Challenge Level: Easy

Preparation at Home:
Combine all dry ingredients in a pint-size ziplock bag.

Preparation on the Trail:
1. To prepare a single serving, add 1¼ cups water to a cook pot along with the grit mixture. Stir.
2. Allow pot to rest for a few minutes while shrimp begins to rehydrate.
3. Place pot on stove and bring to a boil, cooking for 5 to 7 minutes or until grits soften.

Option: Shrimp can be purchased predried, but it's easy to dry it yourself. Start with precooked, frozen medium-size shrimp. Thaw, pinch off the tail, then rinse. Slice each shrimp crosswise into 4 or 5 pieces, arrange in a single layer on a dehydrator tray, and dry at about 155°F until firm. There should be no moisture remaining when a piece is sliced. Refrigerate or freeze until ready to use.

Dried powdered cheeses are available from online sources. See Appendix B.

Marc Robinson
Canton, Michigan

¼ cup quick grits

¼ cup dried shrimp

1 tablespoon McCormick Perfect Pinch salt-free garlic and herb seasoning

1 tablespoon dried minced onion

1 tablespoon instant dry whole milk

2 tablespoons cheese powder

1¼ cups water, added on the trail

Required Equipment on the Trail:
Cook pot

Nutrition Information per Serving:
Calories: 370
Protein: 29 g
Fat: 16 g
Carbohydrates: 36 g
Fiber: 4 g
Sodium: 1,450 mg
Cholesterol: 252 mg

NCT   CDT
PHT   PNT

ROMAN HILLS RAMEN

Total Servings: 1
As Packaged for the Trail: 1 serving
Weight per Serving: About 4 ounces
Preparation Time on the Trail: 15 minutes
Challenge Level: Easy

"Ramen is designed to be rapidly rehydrated, so it's great for making a quick spaghetti dish that saves backpackers fuel, water, and time."

1 (5-ounce) packet Boboli pizza sauce

1 (3-ounce) package ramen noodles, seasoning packet removed

Optional: toppings to taste, such as garlic powder, dried basil, dried oregano, onion powder, red pepper flakes, and grated Parmesan cheese

1½ cups water, added on the trail

Required Equipment on the Trail:
Cook pot

Nutrition Information per Serving:
Calories: 480
Protein: 14 g
Fat: 14 g
Carbohydrates: 72 g
Fiber: 4 g
Sodium: 970 mg
Cholesterol: 0 mg

Preparation at Home:
1. Dry Boboli sauce on lined trays in a dehydrator until it's the consistency of tough leather.
2. Tear dried sauce into small pieces.
3. Pack dried sauce in a pint-size ziplock bag.
4. Pack ramen noodles in a separate pint-size ziplock bag. Do not include the ramen seasoning packet; it isn't required for this recipe.
5. Carry optional toppings in a snack-size ziplock bag or spice kit.

Preparation on the Trail:
1. Bring 1½ cups water to a boil, then add ramen noodles and pizza sauce. Continue to cook until noodles are tender and sauce begins to rehydrate, just a few minutes.
2. Remove pot from heat, stirring in any optional spices or cheese, then serve.

Option: If weight isn't a concern, the Boboli sauce can be carried in its original packaging, avoiding the dehydration step.

Curt "The Titanium Chef" White Forks, Washington

FORESTER PASS MASHED POTATOES

Total Servings: 2
As Packaged for the Trail: 2 servings
Weight per Serving: About 4 ounces
Preparation Time on the Trail: 15 minutes (plus 1 hour to rehydrate)
Challenge Level: Easy

Preparation at Home:
1. Combine vegetables and textured vegetable protein (TVP) together in a gallon-size ziplock freezer bag.
2. Pack potato flakes in a separate pint-size ziplock bag.
3. Carry gravy mix in its original package.

Preparation on the Trail:
1. To prepare both servings, about an hour before dinner add 3 1/2 cups water to bag containing the vegetable-TVP mixture.
2. Reseal the bag and place in a safe place until dinner.
3. When time to eat, pour rehydrated contents of vegetable-TVP bag into cook pot and bring to a boil.
4. Add contents of gravy packet to the pot and stir.
5. Add potato flakes to pot and continue to stir. If all the liquid is absorbed by the rehydrating mixture, add water, a little at a time, as necessary.

1 cup freeze-dried Just Veggies mixed vegetables

1/4 cup Bob's Red Mill TVP

1 cup instant potato flakes

1 (1.2-ounce) package Knorr instant gravy

3 1/2 cups water, added on the trail

Required Equipment on the Trail:
Cook pot

Nutrition Information per Serving:
Calories: 340
Protein: 21 g
Fat: 5 g
Carbohydrates: 63 g
Fiber: 9 g
Sodium: 1,250 mg
Cholesterol: 10 mg

Option: One pound of classic frozen mixed vegetables can be thawed and dried in the dehydrator in place of the freeze-dried vegetables.

Irwin Reeves
Beaumont, California

PIKES PEAK POTATO SOUP

Total Servings: 3
As Packaged for the Trail: 3 servings
Weight per Serving: About 4 ounces
Preparation Time on the Trail: 15 minutes
Challenge Level: Easy

V-LO

½ cup instant potato flakes

½ cup instant dry whole milk

¼ cup whole wheat flour

1 tablespoon dried minced chives

1 teaspoon dried parsley flakes

¾ teaspoon salt

8-ounce cheddar cheese block

4 cups water, added on the trail

Preparation at Home:
1. Combine potato flakes, dry milk, flour, chives, parsley, and salt in a pint-size ziplock bag.
2. Carry cheese block separately.

Preparation on the Trail:
1. To prepare all 3 servings, bring 4 cups water to a boil in cook pot and add potato mix. Stir well and reduce heat.
2. Slice cheese block into small cubes.
3. After a few minutes, potato soup will have thickened. At that point, add cheese cubes to the pot.
4. Stir until cheese has fully melted, then serve.

Required Equipment on the Trail:
Cook pot

Christine and Tim Conners
Statesboro, Georgia

Nutrition Information per Serving:
Calories: 450
Protein: 25 g
Fat: 29 g
Carbohydrates: 23 g
Fiber: 2 g
Sodium: 1,170 mg
Cholesterol: 93 mg

DOCTARI'S TUNA CASSEROLE

Total Servings: 4
As Packaged for the Trail: 1 serving
Weight per Serving: About 4 ounces
Preparation Time on the Trail: 15 minutes
Challenge Level: Easy

Preparation at Home:
1. In medium-size cook pot, bring 3 cups water to a boil. Slowly add rice.
2. Reduce heat, cover, and simmer rice for about 45 minutes, until tender.
3. Add tuna, condensed soup, peas, and broccoli to the rice and stir. Simmer for about 5 minutes.
4. Next add parsley and mushrooms to the pot, stir, and continue to simmer for an additional 10 minutes.
5. Stir cheese into rice mixture until cheese melts.
6. Remove pot from stove and set aside to cool.
7. Pour about 2 cups casserole onto each of 4 drying trays, then dehydrate.
8. Once casserole is dry, place contents from each tray into separate pint-size ziplock bags. Break any clumps into smaller pieces.

Preparation on the Trail:
1. To prepare 1 serving, bring 1 cup water to a boil in cook pot.
2. Add contents from a single bag of casserole mix to the cook pot.
3. Stir casserole until rehydrated and heated through, about 10 minutes. Add additional water in small quantities if needed.

Gary "Doctari" Adams
Cincinnati, Ohio

3 cups water

1½ cups basmati rice, rinsed

2 (5-ounce) cans water-packed tuna, drained

1 (10.75-ounce) can condensed cream of mushroom soup

1 (16-ounce) package frozen sweet peas, thawed

1 (14-ounce) package frozen chopped broccoli, thawed

2 tablespoons dried parsley flakes

8 ounces fresh mushrooms, chopped

¼ cup shredded cheddar cheese

Optional: ground cayenne pepper to taste

1 cup water per serving, added on the trail

Required Equipment on the Trail:
Cook pot

Nutrition Information per Serving:
Calories: 510
Protein: 34 g
Fat: 10 g
Carbohydrates: 73 g
Fiber: 9 g
Sodium: 1,080 mg
Cholesterol: 42 mg

PACKER'S PEA SOUP

V

Total Servings: 4
As Packaged for the Trail: 1 serving
Weight per Serving: About 4 ounces
Preparation Time on the Trail: 15 minutes
Challenge Level: Easy

9 cups water

1 pound dried split green peas

4 tablespoons olive oil

4 cloves garlic, minced

1½ cups diced carrots

1½ cups peeled and diced sweet potatoes

1 cup chopped onion

1 cup chopped celery

1 teaspoon ground marjoram

2 teaspoons dried basil

1 teaspoon ground cumin

3 cubes vegetable bouillon

Optional: salt to taste

¼ cup brewer's yeast

2 cups water per serving, added on the trail

Required Equipment on the Trail:
Cook pot

Nutrition Information per Serving:
Calories: 680
Protein: 33 g
Fat: 16 g
Carbohydrates: 107 g
Fiber: 23 g
Sodium: 850 mg
Cholesterol: 0 mg

Preparation at Home:

1. Pour 9 cups water into a large pot, add peas, then bring water to a boil.

2. Lower heat and simmer the peas for 1 hour, then skim off foam.

3. While peas simmer, warm oil in frying pan over medium heat and sauté the garlic, carrots, sweet potatoes, onion, and celery.

4. Add marjoram, basil, cumin, crumbled bouillon cubes, and optional salt to the pan, stir, then continue to cook for 2 more minutes.

5. Add carrot mixture to the peas in the pot along with the brewer's yeast.

6. Simmer pea soup for an additional hour. Once soup is thick and vegetables tender, remove pot from heat and allow to cool.

7. Transfer soup to a blender or food processor and blend until smooth.

8. Transfer about 1¾ cups soup to each of 4 lined drying trays. Dehydrate.

9. Once thoroughly dried, pulse contents from each tray individually in food processor until it becomes a fine powder.

10. Pack contents from each tray into a pint-size ziplock bag.

Preparation on the Trail:

1. To prepare 1 serving, bring 2 cups water to a boil in a cook pot.

2. Add contents from a single bag of pea soup.

3. Stir well, remove soup from heat, allow to rest for a few minutes, then serve.

Ann Marshall
Port Orchard, Washington

HOTTER-THAN-THE-MOJAVE CHILI

Total Servings: 4
As Packaged for the Trail: 1 serving
Weight per Serving: About 4 ounces
Preparation Time on the Trail: 15 minutes
Challenge Level: Moderate

Nutrition Information per Serving:
Calories: 470
Protein: 42 g
Fat: 6 g
Carbohydrates: 61 g
Fiber: 18 g
Sodium: 1,150 mg
Cholesterol: 70 mg

Preparation at Home:
1. Brown ground beef in a frying pan until no trace of pink remains. Do not burn.
2. Drain then rinse beef in a colander under hot water to remove more fat. Pat dry with paper towels.
3. In a large pot, combine ground beef with all remaining ingredients, including 1 cup water. Stir.
4. Cook chili at a simmer until tender, stirring occasionally.
5. Remove chili from stove and allow to cool.
6. Spread about 2 cups chili onto each of 4 lined drying trays, then dehydrate. Ensure that the chili is thoroughly dry.
7. Transfer contents from each tray into a separate pint-size ziplock bag, breaking chili leather into small pieces in the process.

Preparation on the Trail:
1. To prepare 1 serving, add 1½ cups water to cook pot along with contents from a single bag of chili.
2. Stir, bring chili to a boil, then immediately reduce heat to a simmer.
3. Continue to cook and occasionally stir until chili mix is fully rehydrated, about 10 minutes, being careful to prevent chili from burning.

Brian Guldberg
Bozeman, Montana

1 pound lean ground beef

1 (28-ounce) can diced petite cut tomatoes

2 (6-ounce) cans tomato paste

1 rounded tablespoon chili powder

1½ teaspoons cumin seed

1 tablespoon ground mustard

1 tablespoon garlic powder

1½ teaspoons ground cayenne pepper

1 tablespoon honey

2 tablespoons low-sodium soy sauce

1 medium onion, diced

1 medium bell pepper, diced

1 cup chopped mushrooms

2 (15-ounce) cans pinto beans, drained and rinsed

1 cup water, added at home

1½ cups water per serving, added on the trail

Required Equipment on the Trail:
Cook pot

NIGHT-AFTER-NIGHT BEAN SOUP

Total Servings: 4
As Packaged for the Trail: 1 serving
Weight per Serving: About 4 ounces
Preparation Time on the Trail: 15 minutes
Challenge Level: Easy

"I prepared this recipe every night on a thirty-five-day hike along the Pacific Crest Trail and never grew tired of it."

1 pound dry bean mix

1 (16-ounce) package frozen classic mixed vegetables, thawed

1 pound fresh Roma tomatoes, chopped

1 pound brown onions, chopped

2 teaspoons garlic powder

2 tablespoons Mrs. Dash Original Seasoning Blend

4 (3-ounce) packages ramen noodles, seasoning packet only (any flavor)

3 cups water per serving, added on the trail

Preparation at Home:

1. Soak beans in water overnight in a large pot.
2. Drain beans, add fresh water to the pot, then boil until beans become soft. Drain and rinse.
3. Spread cooked beans evenly on drying trays and rehydrate.
4. Dry mixed vegetables, tomatoes, and onions in a dehydrator.
5. Combine dried beans and vegetables in a large bowl and mix well.
6. Place about 1½ cups of dried bean-vegetable mixture into each of 4 (1-pint) ziplock bags.
7. Add ½ teaspoon garlic powder, 1½ teaspoons Mrs. Dash seasoning, and contents of 1 package noodle seasoning (but not the noodles) to each bag of bean-vegetable mixture.

Preparation on the Trail:

1. To prepare 1 serving, combine 3 cups water with contents of 1 bag bean-vegetable mixture in a cook pot. Stir and bring water to a boil.
2. Cover pot and simmer for 10 to 15 minutes until vegetables become soft.

Option: The bean-vegetable mixture can also be rehydrated using cold water over several hours, providing a no-cook option.

Save the noodles from the ramen packets for Pesto Pasta and Roman Hills Ramen, also in this book.

Pulsing the beans and vegetables in a food processor following drying will considerably lessen rehydrating and cooking time on the trail.

Required Equipment on the Trail:
Cook pot with lid

Nutrition Information per Serving:
Calories: 340
Protein: 28 g
Fat: 1 g
Carbohydrates: 90 g
Fiber: 31 g
Sodium: 1,320 mg
Cholesterol: 1 mg

Marion Davison
Apple Valley, California

Authors' Note:
Having trouble with, er, regularity? Well, look no further than this recipe for fiber. Holy smokes.

Photo by Ted Ayers

CAMPO CORN CHOWDER

Total Servings: 4
As Packaged for the Trail: 1 serving
Weight per Serving: About 4 ounces
Preparation Time on the Trail: 15 minutes (plus 1 hour to rehydrate)
Challenge Level: Easy

V-LO

"Campo, California, is the small town closest to the southern terminus of the Pacific Crest Trail. If you ever find yourself near the terminus of a long trail, stop by the terminal marker if only to experience the aura of the place. You'll find it worth the effort."

5 Yukon Gold potatoes

4 cups 2-percent milk

1 large onion, chopped

2 cloves garlic, minced

1 tablespoon butter

1/2 teaspoon dried oregano

1 dash dried sage

1 teaspoon salt

1/2 teaspoon ground black pepper

1/2 teaspoon dried thyme

2 cubes vegetable bouillon

4 cups frozen corn, thawed

1 bell pepper, chopped

1/2 cup minced scallions

2 cups water per serving, added on the trail

Required Equipment on the Trail:
Cook pot

Nutrition Information per Serving:
Calories: 500
Protein: 16 g
Fat: 8 g
Carbohydrates: 91 g
Fiber: 8 g
Sodium: 1,220 mg
Cholesterol: 27 mg

Preparation at Home:
1. Boil potatoes in a pot of water, then drain, peel, and cube.
2. Bring milk to a low boil in a large pot then add potatoes, onion, garlic, butter, and all the seasonings and bouillon.
3. Cover pot, then simmer for 15 minutes, stirring occasionally.
4. Add corn, bell pepper, and scallions to the pot. Cook until vegetables are tender.
5. Remove pot from heat and allow chowder to cool.
6. Puree chowder in a blender until smooth.
7. Pour about 2 1/4 cups chowder onto each of 4 lined drying trays.
8. Dehydrate chowder into brittle sheets.
9. Transfer contents from each tray into a separate quart-size ziplock freezer bag, breaking dried chowder into small pieces in the process.

Preparation on the Trail:
1. To prepare 1 serving, add 2 cups water to the contents of a bag of chowder 1 hour before dinner.
2. Reseal the bag, knead contents, then place bag in a safe location until dinner.
3. At dinnertime, pour chowder into cook pot, bring to a boil, then reduce heat to a simmer.
4. Continue to cook chowder until fully rehydrated and smooth, about 5 to 10 minutes.

Christine and Tim Conners
Statesboro, Georgia

FOREST BULGUR PILAF

Total Servings: 2
As Packaged for the Trail: 2 servings
Weight per Serving: About 4 ounces
Preparation Time on the Trail: 30 minutes
Challenge Level: Easy

V-LO

Preparation at Home:
1. Blanch carrot and zucchini in boiling water.
2. Dry carrot, zucchini, hash browns, and tomatoes on lined dehydrator trays.
3. Combine dried vegetables with dry buttermilk, bulgur, and contents of soup packet in a quart-size ziplock bag.
4. Pack optional ingredients separately.

Preparation on the Trail:
1. To prepare both servings, bring 2 1/2 cups water to a boil in a cook pot.
2. Add contents from bag of bulgur mix to boiling water. Reduce heat.
3. Cover pot and simmer for about 15 minutes, or until bulgur is soft and the water absorbed.
4. Remove pot from heat and stir in optional cheese and spices.

Ron and Karen Forest
Manitou Springs, Colorado

1 carrot, diced

1 medium zucchini, diced

1/4 cup frozen regular shredded hash browns, thawed

3 Roma tomatoes, chopped

2 tablespoons instant dry buttermilk

1 cup bulgur wheat

1 (1.2-ounce) packet Lipton Savory Herb and Garlic soup mix

Optional: grated Parmesan cheese and Mrs. Dash Extra Spicy Seasoning Blend

2 1/2 cups water, added on the trail

Required Equipment on the Trail:
Cook pot with lid

Nutrition Information per Serving:
Calories: 390
Protein: 14 g
Fat: 1 g
Carbohydrates: 86 g
Fiber: 11 g
Sodium: 1,240 mg
Cholesterol: 4 mg

TORNGAT MOUNTAIN COUSCOUS

Total Servings: 5
As Packaged for the Trail: 1 serving
Weight per Serving: About 4 ounces
Preparation Time on the Trail: 15 minutes
Challenge Level: Easy

V

7 cups water, divided

1½ cups dried lentils

3 tablespoons olive oil

1 large onion, diced

1 green chili pepper, minced

1 pound sweet potatoes, peeled and diced

1 tablespoon curry powder

1 teaspoon ground cumin

2 tablespoons grated fresh ginger root

1 small head cauliflower, diced

2 bell peppers, diced

10 ounces fresh spinach, chopped

3 tablespoons fresh lemon juice

2 teaspoons salt

1¼ cups instant whole wheat couscous

2 cups water per serving, added on the trail

Required Equipment on the Trail:
Cook pot with lid

Preparation at Home:

1. Bring 5 cups water to a boil in medium-size pot. Add lentils, then reduce heat. Simmer for about 30 minutes.

2. In a very large pan or wok, warm oil over medium-high heat and sauté onion and chili pepper for a couple of minutes.

3. Add sweet potatoes, curry powder, cumin, and ginger to the pan. Continue to sauté for several additional minutes.

4. Add 2 cups water to the pan along with cauliflower and bell peppers. Cover pan and simmer for about 10 minutes, until cauliflower becomes tender.

5. Allow lentils to cool after cooking. Puree lentils, along with their cooking liquid, in a blender.

6. Stir chopped spinach, lentil puree, lemon juice, and salt into the pan of vegetables.

7. Simmer vegetables briefly, until spinach has just wilted. Remove pan from heat and allow to cool.

8. Pour about 2 cups vegetable mix onto each of 5 lined dehydrator trays, and dehydrate.

9. Once dry, place contents of each dehydrator tray into a separate pint-size ziplock bag.

10. Add ¼ cup couscous to each bag of dried vegetables.

Preparation on the Trail:

1. To prepare a single serving, bring 2 cups water to a boil in cook pot.
2. Add contents from 1 bag vegetable-couscous mixture to boiling water and stir.
3. Continue to cook until vegetables reconstitute, about 5 minutes.
4. Remove from heat, cover, and allow to rest until couscous is fully rehydrated, about 5 more minutes.
5. Stir, then serve.

Nutrition Information per Serving:
Calories: 550
Protein: 34 g
Fat: 9 g
Carbohydrates: 87 g
Fiber: 21 g
Sodium: 1,050 mg
Cholesterol: 0 mg

Debbie Higgins and Peter Sandiford,
"The Canadians"
Quebec, Canada

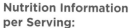

SUGARLAND MOUNTAIN PASTA PRIMAVERA

V-LO

Total Servings: 2
As Packaged for the Trail: 2 servings
Weight per Serving: About 4 ounces
Preparation Time on the Trail: 30 minutes
Challenge Level: Easy

1 (16-ounce) package
frozen Italian-style
vegetable blend, thawed

2 tablespoons dried
onion flakes

1 (4.3-ounce) package
Lipton Alfredo Pasta
Sides

²/₃ cup instant dry
nonfat milk

¼ teaspoon garlic salt

½ teaspoon dried
oregano

2 tablespoons olive oil

Optional: grated
Parmesan cheese

3½ cups water, added
on the trail

**Required Equipment on
the Trail:**
Cook pot with lid

**Nutrition Information
per Serving:**
Calories: 510
Protein: 19 g
Fat: 18 g
Carbohydrates: 63 g
Fiber: 7 g
Sodium: 1,140 mg
Cholesterol: 20 mg

Preparation at Home:

1. Thoroughly dry vegetable blend in a
   dehydrator.
2. Combine dried vegetables with onion flakes
   in a pint-size ziplock bag.
3. Pour contents of Alfredo pasta package
   into a pint-size ziplock bag and add dry
   milk, garlic salt, and oregano.
4. Pack oil and optional Parmesan cheese
   separately for the trail.

Preparation on the Trail:

1. To prepare both servings, add 3½ cups
   water to cook pot along with the dried
   vegetable mix.
2. Bring pot to boiling, then reduce heat to
   a simmer. Cover and cook vegetables for
   about 6 minutes.
3. Add contents of bag containing the
   Alfredo pasta mix to the pot along with 2
   tablespoons olive oil. Stir.
4. Continue to cook at a simmer, stirring often,
   until noodles and vegetables are tender,
   about 10 minutes.
5. Top with Parmesan cheese if desired and
   serve.

Bill Griffin
Elkin, North Carolina

AT

FOOL HOLLOW FETTUCCINE ALFREDO

Total Servings: 2
As Packaged for the Trail: 2 servings
Weight per Serving: About 4 ounces
Preparation Time on the Trail: 1 hour
Challenge Level: Easy

Preparation at Home:
1. Dry chicken, peas, and carrots in a dehydrator.
2. Combine dried chicken and vegetables with seasoning mix from the Pasta Roni package, dry milk, and Butter Buds in a quart-size ziplock freezer bag.
3. Pour noodles from Pasta Roni package into a pint-size ziplock bag.

Preparation on the Trail:
1. To prepare both servings, add 3 cups water to the vegetable-chicken mixture in the bag.
2. Reseal the bag and set aside for about 30 minutes to rehydrate.
3. Pour rehydrated vegetable-chicken mixture into cook pot and bring to a boil.
4. Reduce heat to simmer and continue to cook for an additional 5 minutes or until chicken and vegetables are tender.
5. Add noodles from the pasta bag to the pot and continue to cook over low heat for 5 to 10 minutes, until pasta is al dente, stirring frequently.
6. Do not overcook. The sauce for the noodles will be thin at this point. That's normal. Remove pot from heat and let stand for 3 to 5 minutes for sauce to thicken, then serve.

Option: This recipe can be prepared without the chicken for a vegetarian option.

Katie Salyer Cox
Tucson, Arizona

1 (7-ounce) foil pouch chicken

1/4 pound frozen peas, thawed

1/4 pound carrots, grated and blanched

1 (4.7-ounce) package Pasta Roni Fettuccine Alfredo

2 tablespoons instant dry nonfat milk

1 tablespoon Butter Buds

3 cups water, added on the trail

Required Equipment on the Trail:
Cook pot

Nutrition Information per Serving:
Calories: 380
Protein: 35 g
Fat: 7 g
Carbohydrates: 54 g
Fiber: 3 g
Sodium: 1,420 mg
Cholesterol: 45 mg

OLYMPUS SUSHI

Total Servings: 2
As Packaged for the Trail: 2 servings
Weight per Serving: About 4 ounces
Preparation Time on the Trail: 45 minutes
Challenge Level: Difficult

2 sheets nori seaweed

2 tablespoons tamanoi sushinoko (powdered sushi seasoning)

1 tablespoon furikake or gomasio (sesame seeds and seasoning with nori flakes)

1 (3.5-ounce) pouch boil-in-bag jasmine rice

1 (2.5-ounce) foil pouch water-packed tuna or salmon

Optional: dried tofu, dried mushrooms, soy sauce packet, salt

4 cups water, added on the trail

Required Equipment on the Trail:
Cook pot

Nutrition Information per Serving:
Calories: 260
Protein: 11 g
Fat: 10 g
Carbohydrates: 56 g
Fiber: 2 g
Sodium: 1,530 mg
Cholesterol: 15 mg

Preparation at Home:

1. Seal seaweed sheets flat in a gallon-size ziplock bag.

2. In a snack-size ziplock bag, combine sushi seasoning and furikake or gomasio seasoning.

3. Pack rice pouch, fish pouch, and any optional items separately.

Preparation on the Trail:

1. To prepare both servings, leave rice in its cooking pouch and boil it in 4 cups water for about 10 minutes along with optional dried tofu or dried mushrooms.

2. Drain water from pot, open rice pouch, and pour rice into pot. Cool rice by spreading it out in the pot and fanning it by hand or with the pot lid.

3. Once rice is no longer hot, sprinkle with seasoning blend. Mix well, being careful not to mash the rice.

4. Lay 1 square sheet of nori on top of the gallon-size bag placed on a flat surface, dull side of the nori sheet facing up.

5. Place half of the rice mixture onto the nori sheet and spread to cover most of the surface.

6. Dividing the tuna or salmon in half, flake some of the fish onto the rice mixture along a line near an edge of the nori.

7. Being sure to reserve plenty for the second sushi roll, also spread some of the fish and seasoning over the rice.

8. Using the plastic bag as a base, roll the bag along with the sushi into a cylinder, being sure not to wrap the plastic into the sushi roll.
9. Wet the final edge of the nori, then apply gentle pressure through the plastic bag to seal the whole roll.
10. Cut roll into slices using a very sharp, thin knife. Or eat it like a wrap sandwich. Garnish with optional soy sauce or salt.
11. Repeat steps 4 through 10 to make the second sushi roll.

If the nori sheets crumble, place all ingredients in a pot or bowl. This is called *chirashi*, which means "scattered sushi."

Curt "The Titanium Chef" White
Forks, Washington

PCT

TREE FROG SOUP WITH RATTLESNAKE

Total Servings: 1
As Packaged for the Trail: 1 serving
Weight per Serving: About 5 ounces
Preparation Time on the Trail: 15 minutes
Challenge Level: Easy

"I'm just kidding. No critters are used in this recipe. I just call it that because it's green and lumpy. Though it may not sound like much, Tree Frog Soup with Rattlesnake kept me moving during my long hike on the PCT. Before I had it for the first time, I was ready to hitchhike back to civilization and eat in a restaurant every day for the rest of my life."

1 (1.8-ounce) package Near East Split Pea Soup mix

1 (3-ounce) foil pouch Spam Single Classic

1 cup water, added on the trail

Required Equipment on the Trail:
Cook pot

Nutrition Information per Serving:
Calories: 410
Protein: 27 g
Fat: 17 g
Carbohydrates: 35 g
Fiber: 8 g
Sodium: 1,330 mg
Cholesterol: 55 mg

Preparation at Home:
1. Pour dried soup mix into a pint-size ziplock bag.
2. Carry Spam pouch separately.

Preparation on the Trail:
1. To prepare 1 serving, chop Spam into small pieces.
2. Bring 1 cup water to a boil in a cook pot.
3. Add soup mix and Spam to pot and stir for a couple of minutes, until soup mix is reconstituted.

Mark "Crawls with Bears" Davis
San Francisco, California

GARD'S GLACIER SPAGHETTI

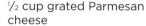

Total Servings: 2
As Packaged for the Trail: 2 servings
Weight per Serving: About 5 ounces
Preparation Time on the Trail: 15 minutes
Challenge Level: Easy

Preparation at Home:
1. Package Parmesan cheese, garlic powder, onion powder, Bac-Os, salt, and black pepper in a pint-size ziplock bag.
2. Break spaghetti noodles and pack in a separate pint-size ziplock bag.
3. Carry oil in a small container.

Preparation on the Trail:
1. To prepare both servings, bring 3 cups water to a boil, then cook spaghetti noodles until al dente, about 10 minutes.
2. Drain any remaining water from the noodles, then thoroughly stir in 1 tablespoon olive oil and the Parmesan cheese mixture before serving.

Dan Gard
Missoula, Montana

½ cup grated Parmesan cheese

2 teaspoons garlic powder

1 teaspoon onion powder

2 tablespoons Bac-Os

1 dash salt

½ teaspoon ground black pepper

6 ounces spaghetti noodles

1 tablespoon olive oil

3 cups water, added on the trail

Required Equipment on the Trail:
Cook pot

Nutrition Information per Serving:
Calories: 490
Protein: 21 g
Fat: 15 g
Carbohydrates: 66 g
Fiber: 2 g
Sodium: 580 mg
Cholesterol: 20 mg

PESTO PASTA

V-LO

Total Servings: 2
As Packaged for the Trail: 2 servings
Weight per Serving: About 5 ounces
Preparation Time on the Trail: 15 minutes
Challenge Level: Easy

2 (3-ounce) packages ramen noodles, seasoning packets removed

1 tablespoon Parmesan cheese powder

1/4 cup pine nuts

1 (1.2-ounce) package Knorr Creamy Pesto Sauce Mix

3 tablespoons olive oil

Optional: dried olives, dried capers, dried pimento, onion powder, red pepper flakes, sardines, anchovies

3 cups water, added on the trail

Required Equipment on the Trail:
Cook pot

Nutrition Information per Serving:
Calories: 700
Protein: 15 g
Fat: 43 g
Carbohydrates: 64 g
Fiber: 3 g
Sodium: 1,700 mg
Cholesterol: 3 mg

Preparation at Home:

1. Pack ramen noodles in a quart-size ziplock bag. Do not include the ramen seasoning packets; they aren't needed for this recipe.

2. Combine cheese powder and pine nuts in a snack-size ziplock bag.

3. Transfer pesto sauce mix to a pint-size ziplock bag.

4. Pack oil and optional toppings separately.

Preparation on the Trail:

1. Rehydrate any optional dried toppings in a small amount of water.

2. To prepare both servings, bring 3 cups water to a boil, then add ramen noodles.

3. Cook noodles until tender, just a few moments. Drain any remaining water from the pot.

4. Add 3 tablespoons olive oil to the pesto mix in the bag. Knead contents into a paste.

5. Pour pesto paste over noodles in the pot. Stir to coat the noodles.

6. Sprinkle cheese–pine nut mix and optional ingredients over the noodles, then serve.

Curt "The Titanium Chef" White
Forks, Washington

CASCADE VALLEY CHICKEN AND RICE

Total Servings: 2
As Packaged for the Trail: 2 servings
Weight per Serving: About 5 ounces
Preparation Time on the Trail: 15 minutes
Challenge Level: Easy

"This recipe is a quick and easy staple. I can cook it in the dark, snow, wind, and rain. Cleanup is simple because there is no oil or sauce used. I prepare it on nearly every backpacking trip."

Preparation at Home:
1. Dry chicken and peas in a dehydrator.
2. Combine dried chicken, peas, and unwrapped bouillon cubes in a pint-size ziplock bag.
3. Pack rice separately in a quart-size ziplock bag.
4. Carry optional oil in a small container.

Preparation on the Trail:
1. To prepare both servings, bring 2 1/2 cups water to a boil in a cook pot, then add dried chicken-pea mix.
2. Cook chicken and peas for about 1 minute, stirring often. Be sure the bouillon cubes completely dissolve.
3. Add rice and stir well. Remove pot from heat and cover.
4. Let pot rest for about 10 minutes, until rice fully rehydrates. Stir in optional 1 tablespoon olive oil.

Option: *If weight isn't a concern, and to avoid dehydrating, substitute 1/4 cup freeze-dried peas for the dried frozen peas and carry a 7-ounce chicken foil pack in lieu of the dried canned chicken. On the trail, slightly reduce the water in the cook pot.*

Ann Marshall
Port Orchard, Washington

1 (5-ounce) can water-packed chunk chicken, drained

4 ounces frozen peas, thawed

2 regular-size cubes chicken bouillon

2 cups instant brown rice

Optional: 1 tablespoon olive oil

2 1/2 cups water, added on the trail

Required Equipment on the Trail:
Cook pot with lid

Nutrition Information per Serving:
Calories: 450
Protein: 15 g
Fat: 4 g
Carbohydrates: 92 g
Fiber: 6 g
Sodium: 1,110 mg
Cholesterol: 8 mg

OZARK BURRITOS

Total Servings: 2 (1 burrito per serving)
As Packaged for the Trail: 2 servings
Weight per Serving: About 5 ounces
Preparation Time on the Trail: 15 minutes
Challenge Level: Easy

V-LO

1 (15-ounce) can low-sodium kidney beans, rinsed and drained

1 cup picante sauce

2 ounces cheddar cheese, from block

2 medium-size whole-wheat tortillas

1 cup water, added on the trail

Required Equipment on the Trail:
Cook pot

Nutrition Information per Serving:
Calories: 450
Protein: 25 g
Fat: 9 g
Carbohydrates: 67 g
Fiber: 18 g
Sodium: 1,700 mg
Cholesterol: 20 mg

Preparation at Home:
1. Dry beans and picante sauce in a dehydrator.
2. Crumble dried picante sauce into small pieces.
3. Combine dried beans and picante sauce in a pint-size ziplock bag.
4. Pack cheese and tortillas separately for the trail.

Preparation on the Trail:
1. To prepare both servings, bring 1 cup water to a boil in a cook pot, then add the dried bean-picante mixture.
2. Reduce heat to a simmer, stirring frequently, until beans fully rehydrate, about 10 minutes.
3. Remove bean mixture from heat, then evenly divide over 2 tortillas.
4. Add small, thin slices of cheese to each tortilla, then roll like a burrito and serve.

It is normal for many kinds of beans to crumble when dried and, once rehydrated, take on the consistency of refried beans.

Craig "Smitty" Smith
Springfield, Missouri

SWEET WENATCHEE RICE DISH

Total Servings: 2
As Packaged for the Trail: 2 servings
Weight per Serving: About 5 ounces
Preparation Time on the Trail: 15 minutes
Challenge Level: Easy

V-LO

"This recipe is easy to prepare, filling, and great tasting—perfect for backpacking. It's one of my favorites, and I never become tired of it. I ate it often during my thru hike of the North Country Trail."

Preparation at Home:
1. Combine all dry ingredients in a quart-size ziplock bag.
2. Package oil separately for the trail.

Preparation on the Trail:
1. To prepare both servings, bring 1 1/2 cups water to a boil in a cook pot.
2. Add rice mixture to the pot along with 2 tablespoons olive oil. Stir well.
3. Reduce heat to a simmer and cook rice mixture for 5 minutes, stirring occasionally.

Lou Ann Fellows
Grand Canyon, Arizona

1/4 cup raisins
1/2 cup diced dried apples
1/4 teaspoon salt
1/2 teaspoon allspice
1/4 cup instant dry nonfat milk
1/2 cup chopped walnuts
1 cup instant brown rice
2 tablespoons olive oil
1 1/2 cups water, added on the trail

Required Equipment on the Trail:
Cook pot

Nutrition Information per Serving:
Calories: 640
Protein: 19 g
Fat: 31 g
Carbohydrates: 61 g
Fiber: 6 g
Sodium: 440 mg
Cholesterol: 2 mg

CASCADE STEW

Total Servings: 2
As Packaged for the Trail: 2 servings
Weight per Serving: About 5 ounces
Preparation Time on the Trail: 15 minutes
Challenge Level: Easy

1 pound potatoes,
boiled, skinned, and cut
into small pieces

1 pound fresh carrots,
peeled, boiled, and
chopped

1 pound Roma tomatoes,
chopped

1 ounce Armour Sliced
Dried Beef

3 tablespoons dried
onion flakes

1/2 cup instant potato
flakes

5 cups water, added on
the trail

**Required Equipment on
the Trail:**
Cook pot

**Nutrition Information
per Serving:**
Calories: 430
Protein: 14 g
Fat: 1 g
Carbohydrates: 104 g
Fiber: 9 g
Sodium: 1,410 mg
Cholesterol: 21 mg

Preparation at Home:
1. Dry potatoes, carrots, tomatoes, and
   Armour beef in a dehydrator.
2. Break dried beef into small pieces and
   combine with other dehydrated ingredients
   as well as onion flakes in a quart-size
   ziplock bag.
3. Pack potato flakes separately for the trail.

Preparation on the Trail:
1. To prepare both servings, add contents of
   beef-vegetable mixture to 5 cups water in
   cook pot.
2. Bring water to a boil, stirring frequently, for
   about 10 minutes or until vegetables are
   fully rehydrated.
3. Remove pot from heat, add potato flakes,
   stir, then serve.

Ann Marshall
Port Orchard, Washington

*"A food dehydrator is very helpful for making backpack-
ing meals. When I arrive in camp, I add a little water to
my dried vegetables and meats and allow them to soak
and rehydrate while I enjoy the afternoon. By dinnertime, my food is tender and ready to add to the meal."*

—*Ursula Brower*
South Lake Tahoe, California

OUTDOOR PESTO TORTELLINI

Total Servings: 3
As Packaged for the Trail: 3 servings
Weight per Serving: About 5 ounces
Preparation Time on the Trail: 15 minutes (plus 1 hour to rehydrate)
Challenge Level: Easy

V-LO

Preparation at Home:
1. Cut Roma tomatoes through the core into ¼-inch-thick slices.
2. Dry sliced tomatoes and chopped mushrooms, olives, and bell pepper in a dehydrator.
3. Package dried vegetables in a quart-size ziplock bag.
4. Add contents of pesto sauce package along with garlic powder, Parmesan cheese, and any optional ingredients to vegetable bag.
5. Pack oil and tortellini separately for the trail.

Preparation on the Trail:
1. About an hour before dinner, prepare all 3 servings by adding ½ cup water to the bag with the pesto-vegetable mixture.
2. Reseal bag, knead contents, then place in a safe location until dinner.
3. At dinnertime, bring a cook pot of water to a boil and cook tortellini until tender, about 10 minutes.
4. Drain water from pot and add rehydrated pesto-vegetable sauce and oil to the tortellini.
5. Return pot to low heat and stir for a few moments before serving.

Jeffrey Hare
Citrus Heights, California

Authors' Note:
Outdoor Pesto Tortellini was the recipe showcased on the cover of the first edition of Lipsmackin' Backpackin'. *It's awesome!*

4 ounces Roma tomatoes

4 ounces fresh mushrooms, chopped

1 (2.25-ounce) can sliced black olives, drained and chopped

1 bell pepper, chopped

1 (1.2-ounce) package Knorr Creamy Pesto Sauce Mix

2 teaspoons garlic powder

2 tablespoons grated Parmesan cheese

¼ cup olive oil

1 (8-ounce) package Barilla Three-Cheese Tortellini

Optional: pepperoni, jerky, pine nuts

½ cup water, added to pesto mix on the trail, plus additional for boiling tortellini

Required Equipment on the Trail:
Cook pot

Nutrition Information per Serving:
Calories: 590
Protein: 19 g
Fat: 25 g
Carbohydrates: 74 g
Fiber: 8 g
Sodium: 1,580 mg
Cholesterol: 9 mg

BALLOU'S TURKEY SPAGHETTI

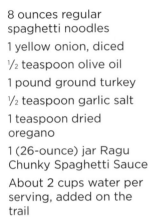

Total Servings: 4
As Packaged for the Trail: 1 serving
Weight per Serving: About 5 ounces
Preparation Time on the Trail: 15 minutes
Challenge Level: Easy

8 ounces regular spaghetti noodles

1 yellow onion, diced

½ teaspoon olive oil

1 pound ground turkey

½ teaspoon garlic salt

1 teaspoon dried oregano

1 (26-ounce) jar Ragu Chunky Spaghetti Sauce

About 2 cups water per serving, added on the trail

Required Equipment on the Trail:
Cook pot

Nutrition Information per Serving:
Calories: 540
Protein: 31 g
Fat: 16 g
Carbohydrates: 73 g
Fiber: 7 g
Sodium: 1,060 mg
Cholesterol: 90 mg

Preparation at Home:

1. Break spaghetti noodles into smaller pieces, then boil in a large pot until al dente.

2. Drain noodles and set aside. Do not remove them from the pot.

3. In a large frying pan, sauté onion in oil until translucent.

4. Add ground turkey, garlic salt, and oregano to the pan and continue to cook until turkey is no longer pink.

5. Drain excess fat from the pan.

6. Return pan to the stove and add spaghetti sauce. Stir well for a minute or so, then remove from heat.

7. Add sauce mixture to the pot containing the spaghetti and stir well.

8. Spread spaghetti-sauce mixture evenly over 2 lightly oiled baking pans.

9. Place both pans on the middle racks of the oven set at its lowest temperature. Leave the oven door slightly ajar while the spaghetti dries.

10. Once spaghetti is brittle throughout, remove from oven and allow to cool.

11. Evenly divide each sheet of dried spaghetti mixture into 2 servings, for 4 servings total.

12. Break the spaghetti apart into smaller pieces, packing each serving in separate quart-size ziplock bags.

Preparation on the Trail:

1. To prepare a single serving, pour contents of 1 bag spaghetti-sauce mixture into cook pot and add just enough water to cover the spaghetti. About 2 cups water should be enough, but be careful not to add too much.

2. Warm over low heat for about 10 minutes, until the sauce is reconstituted, adding more water if required. The spaghetti is ready to serve once heated through.

Presoaking the spaghetti-sauce mixture can help speed cooking at high altitudes.

The spaghetti-sauce mixture can also be dried in a food dehydrator. While drying, break the spaghetti apart by hand every couple of hours to facilitate even drying.

Bob Ballou
Minden, Nevada

BEN'S CHICKEN AND CHEESE

Total Servings: 2
As Packaged for the Trail: 2 servings
Weight per Serving: About 5 ounces
Preparation Time on the Trail: 30 minutes
Challenge Level: Moderate

1 (5-ounce) can water-packed chunk chicken, drained

1 (7.25-ounce) package Kraft Macaroni and Cheese Dinner

2 tablespoons instant dry buttermilk

1 tablespoon olive oil

¼ cup water, added on the trail, plus 4 cups water for cooking noodles

Required Equipment on the Trail:
Cook pot

Nutrition Information per Serving:
Calories: 750
Protein: 28 g
Fat: 12 g
Carbohydrates: 74 g
Fiber: 1 g
Sodium: 1,150 mg
Cholesterol: 74 mg

Preparation at Home:
1. Break apart chunks of chicken and thoroughly dry in a dehydrator.
2. Pack dried chicken in a pint-size ziplock bag.
3. In a separate pint-size ziplock bag, combine cheese powder from package of macaroni and cheese along with instant dry buttermilk.
4. Pack macaroni noodles and olive oil separately for the trail.

Preparation on the Trail:
1. To prepare both servings, add ¼ cup water to bag of dried chicken.
2. Reseal chicken bag and set aside to rehydrate while bringing about 4 cups water to a boil in a cook pot.
3. Cook noodles until tender, about 10 minutes, then drain water.
4. Reduce heat to low and return pot to the stove.
5. Add cheese-buttermilk mixture, olive oil, and chicken to the noodles.
6. Stir and continue to cook on low for a few minutes, until heated through.

Option: To avoid the need to use a dehydrator, and if weight isn't an issue, carry a pouch of chicken instead of the dehydrated meat.

Ben York
Alpine, California

THE HONEYMOONER'S CHEESY RAMEN

Total Servings: 1
As Packaged for the Trail: 1 serving
Weight per Serving: About 6 ounces
Preparation Time on the Trail: 15 minutes
Challenge Level: Easy

Preparation at Home:
Package ramen noodles and cheese separately for the trail.

Preparation on the Trail:
1. To prepare 1 serving, bring 2 cups water to a boil in a cook pot.
2. Add noodles to boiling water and cook until soft, a few minutes. Reduce heat to low.
3. Add contents of ramen spice packet to noodles and stir.
4. Cut cheese into smaller pieces and add to hot noodles.
5. Stir noodles constantly, until cheese melts. Remove from heat and serve.

Dan and Tina "The Honeymooners"
Breedlove
Eudora, Kansas

1 (3-ounce) package ramen noodles, with seasoning packet

3-ounce block cheese, cut from larger block (your choice)

2 cups water, added on the trail

Required Equipment on the Trail:
Cook pot

Nutrition Information per Serving:
Calories: 640
Protein: 31 g
Fat: 30 g
Carbohydrates: 61 g
Fiber: 0 g
Sodium: 1,080 mg
Cholesterol: 29 mg

TAMALE PIE FOR UNGRATEFUL WAIFS

Total Servings: 3
As Packaged for the Trail: 1 serving
Weight per Serving: About 5 ounces
Preparation Time on the Trail: 45 minutes
Challenge Level: Moderate

"My hiking group sometimes refers to my tamale pie as 'tamale mush' or 'tamale gruel,' because the texture appears to come straight out of Oliver Twist's orphanage kitchen. While making such comments about my recipe, they nonetheless gobble it up and ask for seconds. Those ungrateful waifs!"

½ teaspoon ground black pepper

½ teaspoon dried sage

¼ teaspoon dried thyme

¼ teaspoon allspice

¼ teaspoon paprika

1 pound lean ground sirloin

1 (14-ounce) can whole pitted olives, drained and halved

1 (15-ounce) can kidney beans, drained and rinsed

2 (4-ounce) cans water-packed diced chilies, drained

2 Roma tomatoes, chopped

1 cup masa harina (corn flour)

1 tablespoon chili powder

¼ teaspoon ground cumin

1 (1-ounce) packet Lipton Recipe Secrets Onion Soup and Dip Mix

2⅓ cups water per serving, added on the trail

Preparation at Home:

1. Combine black pepper, sage, thyme, allspice, paprika, and ground sirloin in a hot frying pan and thoroughly brown the meat, stirring often.

2. Evenly spread browned meat over paper towels. Add another layer of paper towels over the top of the meat.

3. Place a cutting board over the top layer of paper towels and press down to squeeze fat from the sirloin.

4. Spread sirloin over lined trays and dehydrate until the meat has the consistency of bacon bits.

5. Dry olives, kidney beans, chilies, and tomatoes in a dehydrator.

6. Combine all ingredients from dehydrator in a medium-size bowl, mix well, then evenly divide into 3 pint-size ziplock storage bags, about 1 cup sirloin mixture each. Label each bag of sirloin mixture "Tamale Pie A."

7. Using the same bowl, combine masa harina, chili powder, cumin, and contents of the onion soup packet.

8. Divide the masa harina mixture evenly into 3 pint-size ziplock storage bags, about ⅓ cup mix each. Label each of the bags of masa harina mixture "Tamale Pie B."

Preparation on the Trail:

1. To prepare a single serving, about 30 minutes before dinner combine 2 cups water in a cook pot with the contents of a single bag labeled "Tamale Pie A." Stir and set aside.
2. At dinnertime, add contents of a single bag labeled "Tamale Pie B" to the pot, along with another 1/3 cup water. Stir.
3. Heat tamale mixture slowly over low flame, stirring continuously until thick.
4. Remove pot from heat, cover, and let rest for about 5 minutes. The pie will have the consistency of porridge once ready to serve.

Pam Coz-Hill
Visalia, California

Required Equipment on the Trail:
Cook pot with lid

Nutrition Information per Serving:
Calories: 660
Protein: 43 g
Fat: 31 g
Carbohydrates: 70 g
Fiber: 16 g
Sodium: 1,720 mg
Cholesterol: 93 mg

BACKPACK POT PIE

Total Servings: 3
As Packaged for the Trail: 1 serving
Weight per Serving: About 5 ounces
Preparation Time on the Trail: 1 hour
Challenge Level: Moderate

Pot Pie A Bag

2 (5-ounce) cans water-packed chunk chicken, drained

1 (16-ounce) package frozen classic mixed vegetables

8 ounces fresh sliced mushrooms

1 tablespoon dried minced onion

1/2 teaspoon granulated garlic

1 tablespoon Italian seasoning blend

1 teaspoon dried parsley

2 tablespoons instant dry buttermilk

1 (0.6-ounce) packet Lipton Cup-A-Soup Cream of Chicken

Pot Pie B Bag

2 cups Bisquick Heart Smart pancake mix

1/4 cup water per serving, added on the trail, plus several cups extra for boiling chicken-vegetable mixture

Preparation at Home:

1. Thoroughly dry chicken, vegetable mix, and mushrooms in a dehydrator.

2. In a medium-size bowl, combine dried chicken, vegetables, and mushrooms and the remaining Bag A ingredients. Stir well.

3. Evenly divide contents of the bowl among 3 (1-pint) ziplock bags and label each "Pot Pie A."

4. Divide Bisquick mix among 3 separate pint-size ziplock bags, about 2/3 cups each. Label each of these bags "Pot Pie B."

Preparation on the Trail:

1. To prepare a single serving, pour contents of 1 bag labeled "Pot Pie A" into a cook pot, then add water until the mix is covered to a depth of about 1 inch.

2. Set cook pot aside for about 30 minutes while chicken and vegetables rehydrate.

3. Add 1/4 cup water to the Bisquick mix in 1 bag labeled "Pot Pie B."

4. Reseal "Pot Pie B" bag and knead contents until it becomes a consistently uniform dough.

5. Bring chicken-vegetables mixture to a boil, then reduce heat to a simmer for 5 to 10 minutes. Add or drain water as required, keeping in mind that a small amount of liquid will be required to finish the cooking.
6. Snip a large corner from bottom of the "Pot Pie B" bag and squeeze dough evenly over chicken-vegetables mixture, smoothing the dough out afterward.
7. Cover the pot and continue to simmer until Bisquick bakes through, about 10 minutes.

Option: Try Lipton Cup-a-Soup Broccoli and Cheese flavor in place of the Cream of Chicken.

Pam Coz-Hill
Visalia, California

Required Equipment on the Trail:
Cook pot with lid

Nutrition Information per Serving:
Calories: 560
Protein: 30 g
Fat: 16 g
Carbohydrates: 82 g
Fiber: 7 g
Sodium: 1,840 mg
Cholesterol: 70 mg

BROWN RICE BANZAI

Total Servings: 1
As Packaged for the Trail: 1 serving
Weight per Serving: About 6 ounces
Preparation Time on the Trail: 15 minutes
Challenge Level: Easy

1 (16-ounce) package frozen stir fry-style vegetables, thawed

1 cup instant brown rice

1 clove garlic, unpeeled

1/4 cup teriyaki sauce

2 1/2 cups water, added on the trail

Required Equipment on the Trail:
Cook pot with lid

Nutrition Information per Serving:
Calories: 610
Protein: 15 g
Fat: 3 g
Carbohydrates: 133 g
Fiber: 9 g
Sodium: 1,890 mg
Cholesterol: 0 mg

Preparation at Home:
1. Dry vegetables in a dehydrator.
2. Combine dried vegetables, rice, and unpeeled garlic clove in a pint-size ziplock bag.
3. Pack teriyaki sauce separately for the trail.

Preparation on the Trail:
1. To prepare a single serving, bring 2 1/2 cups water to a boil in cook pot.
2. Peel and chop garlic, then combine with rice-vegetable mixture and teriyaki sauce in the pot. Stir.
3. Cover pot and remove from heat. Allow pot to rest for about 10 minutes while vegetables and rice rehydrate, then serve.

Craig "Smitty" Smith
Springfield, Missouri

CROOKED RIVER CORN CHOWDER

Total Servings: 1
As Packaged for the Trail: 1 serving
Weight per Serving: About 6 ounces
Preparation Time on the Trail: 15 minutes
Challenge Level: Easy

Preparation at Home:
Combine all dry ingredients in a quart-size ziplock bag.

Preparation on the Trail:
1. To prepare 1 serving, add 2 cups water to a cook pot along with the chowder mix. Stir.
2. Bring pot to a boil, then immediately reduce heat. Simmer until the corn softens, about 10 minutes, stirring occasionally, then serve.

Christine and Tim Conners
Statesboro, Georgia

¾ cup freeze-dried corn

½ cup instant potato flakes

½ cup instant dry whole milk

¼ teaspoon ground white pepper

¼ teaspoon dried dill weed

1 tablespoon dried chives

1 tablespoon Butter Buds

1 tablespoon dried minced onion

1 regular-size cube chicken bouillon

2 cups water, added on the trail

Required Equipment on the Trail:
Cook pot

Nutrition Information per Serving:
Calories: 550
Protein: 44 g
Fat: 16 g
Carbohydrates: 82 g
Fiber: 5 g
Sodium: 1,340 mg
Cholesterol: 60 mg

CLIMBER'S COLCANNON

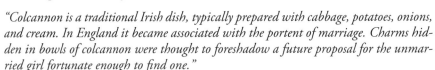

Total Servings: 1
As Packaged for the Trail: 1 serving
Weight per Serving: About 6 ounces
Preparation Time on the Trail: 15 minutes
Challenge Level: Easy

"Colcannon is a traditional Irish dish, typically prepared with cabbage, potatoes, onions, and cream. In England it became associated with the portent of marriage. Charms hidden in bowls of colcannon were thought to foreshadow a future proposal for the unmarried girl fortunate enough to find one."

3 cups coleslaw vegetable mix

2 tablespoons dried onion flakes

1 cup instant potato flakes

½ cup instant dry whole milk

1 dash salt

1 dash ground black pepper

Optional: 1 pinch mace, 1 tablespoon bacon bits, and 1 tablespoon Butter Buds

2 cups water, added on the trail

Required Equipment on the Trail:
Cook pot with lid

Nutrition Information per Serving:
Calories: 640
Protein: 24 g
Fat: 16 g
Carbohydrates: 101 g
Fiber: 10 g
Sodium: 650 mg
Cholesterol: 61 mg

Preparation at Home:
1. Blanch coleslaw mixture in boiling water for 2 minutes, then drain.
2. Transfer coleslaw to a dehydrator tray and dry thoroughly, occasionally breaking up any clumps.
3. Transfer dried coleslaw to a pint-size ziplock bag and add onion flakes.
4. Combine potato flakes, dry milk, and seasonings in a second pint-size ziplock bag.
5. Carry optional bacon bits and Butter Buds separately.

Preparation on the Trail:
1. To prepare 1 serving, add 2 cups water to cook pot along with the coleslaw mixture.
2. Bring to a boil, then reduce heat to a simmer. Continue to cook, stirring occasionally, for 5 minutes.
3. Blend the potato mixture into the cooked coleslaw.
4. Remove pot from heat, cover, and let rest for several minutes before topping with optional bacon bits and Butter Buds.

Option: A 1.25-ounce individually wrapped mini block of cream cheese, added immediately before the pot is removed from the heat, adds a creamy texture more akin to traditional colcannon recipes. However, as with any soft cheese, the unrefrigerated shelf life of cream cheese is fairly short, making this option practical only within a day or two of the trailhead.

Ken Harbison
Rochester, New York

SPEEDY SPAGHETTI

Total Servings: 2
As Packaged for the Trail: 2 servings
Weight per Serving: About 6 ounces
Preparation Time on the Trail: 15 minutes (plus 1 hour to rehydrate)
Challenge Level: Easy

Preparation at Home:
1. Dry all vegetables in a dehydrator.
2. Dehydrate spaghetti sauce on lined trays until sauce has the texture of leather.
3. Pulverize dried sauce in a food processor.
4. Break angel hair pasta into small lengths, then boil until al dente.
5. Dry pasta in a dehydrator, occasionally breaking apart clumps for even drying.
6. Fry ground sirloin until no trace of pink remains. Do not overcook.
7. Transfer sirloin onto paper towels to absorb excess fat, then transfer to a colander and rinse under hot water to remove more oil.
8. Thoroughly dry sirloin in a dehydrator until hard like gravel.
9. Package dried vegetables, spaghetti sauce, and sirloin in gallon-size ziplock freezer bag.
10. Pack angel hair pasta separately in a pint-size ziplock bag.

Preparation on the Trail:
1. To prepare both servings, about an hour before dinner, add 4 cups water to bag containing the sauce-vegetable-sirloin mixture.
2. Reseal the bag and place in a safe place until dinner.
3. When time to eat, bring 2 1/2 cups water to a boil in a cook pot, then add pasta.
4. Stir pasta for 2 to 3 minutes, until al dente, adding additional water if necessary to prevent scorching. Lower heat, then drain any remaining water.
5. Return pot to the flame and immediately add rehydrated sauce mixture. Stir constantly until heated through, then serve.

1 (8-ounce) can French-cut green beans, drained

1 (2.25-ounce) can sliced black olives, drained

1 small onion, diced

8 ounces fresh mushrooms, diced

1 (24-ounce) jar Prego Garden Spaghetti Sauce

6 ounces angel hair pasta

1/2 pound ground sirloin

6 1/2 cups water, divided, added on the trail

Required Equipment on the Trail:
Cook pot

Nutrition Information per Serving:
Calories: 750
Protein: 47 g
Fat: 14 g
Carbohydrates: 111 g
Fiber: 12 g
Sodium: 1,710 mg
Cholesterol: 70 mg

Pam Coz-Hill
Visalia, California

SMITTY'S FAVORITE SPAGHETTI

Total Servings: 2
As Packaged for the Trail: 2 servings
Weight per Serving: About 6 ounces
Preparation Time on the Trail: 15 minutes
Challenge Level: Easy

V

"I fix this meal every time I go out on the trail. It's my favorite."

2 ½ pounds Roma tomatoes

½ pound angel hair pasta

2 cloves garlic, unpeeled

½ cup regular TVP

Optional: ¼ cup grated Parmesan cheese and 1 tablespoon olive oil

1 (1.37-ounce) package McCormick Spaghetti Sauce Mix

4 cups water, added on the trail

Required Equipment on the Trail:
Cook pot

Nutrition Information per Serving:
Calories: 670
Protein: 32 g
Fat: 4 g
Carbohydrates: 127 g
Fiber: 11 g
Sodium: 1,100 mg
Cholesterol: 0 mg

Preparation at Home:
1. Cut Roma tomatoes through the core into ¼-inch-thick slices.
2. Dry tomatoes in a dehydrator.
3. Pack dried tomatoes, pasta, unpeeled garlic cloves, TVP, and optional Parmesan cheese in a quart-size ziplock bag.
4. Carry spaghetti sauce package separately.
5. Pack optional olive oil in a small container.

Preparation on the Trail:
1. To prepare both servings, remove garlic cloves from the ziplock bag, peel, and mince.
2. Add garlic to cook pot, along with 4 cups water. Bring to a boil.
3. Add tomato-pasta mixture and optional 1 tablespoon olive oil to boiling water, stirring often.
4. After a couple of minutes, add contents of spaghetti sauce package to the pot and stir until sauce mix is thoroughly dissolved.
5. The dish is ready to serve once tomatoes and TVP are fully rehydrated, about 5 to 10 minutes after adding to the boiling water.

Option: To make a feast, serve with toasted hard rolls and, for dessert, a few cookies followed by coffee with honey and cinnamon.

Craig "Smitty" Smith
Springfield, Missouri

CROCKET'S TEX-MEX CHICKEN

Total Servings: 2
As Packaged for the Trail: 2 servings
Weight per Serving: About 6 ounces
Preparation Time on the Trail: 15 minutes
Challenge Level: Easy

Preparation at Home:
1. Shred chicken with a fork and combine and toss with tomatoes and chilies in a small bowl.
2. Dry chicken mixture in a dehydrator, then pack in a pint-size ziplock bag.
3. Break tortilla chips into smaller pieces, then place in a second pint-size ziplock bag.
4. Combine flour, chili powder, and cumin in a snack-size ziplock bag.
5. Carry block cheese separately.

Preparation on the Trail:
1. To prepare both servings, bring 2 cups water to a boil along with the chicken mixture. Reduce heat and simmer for about 8 minutes.
2. Cut cheese block into small cubes, then add to the pot along with the flour-spice mixture and tortilla chips.
3. Stir constantly until sauce thickens, about 3 minutes, then serve.

Option: For a milder flavor, substitute some or all of the pepper jack cheese with cheddar or regular jack cheese.

Ken Harbison
Rochester, New York

1 (7-ounce) foil pouch chicken

1 (14-ounce) can no-salt-added diced tomatoes, drained

1 (4-ounce) can green chilies, drained

4 ounces corn tortilla chips

2 tablespoons all-purpose flour

1 teaspoon chili powder

1 teaspoon ground cumin

4-ounce block pepper jack cheese, cut from larger block

2 cups water, added on the trail

Required Equipment on the Trail:
Cook pot

Nutrition Information per Serving:
Calories: 680
Protein: 39 g
Fat: 29 g
Carbohydrates: 54 g
Fiber: 7 g
Sodium: 1,150 mg
Cholesterol: 120 mg

MOUNTAINEER'S TUNA STROGANOFF

Total Servings: 2
As Packaged for the Trail: 2 servings
Weight per Serving: About 6 ounces
Preparation Time on the Trail: 15 minutes
Challenge Level: Easy

"Versions of this recipe have been popular for years on trips sponsored by the Rochester Winter Mountaineering Society."

1 (4.9-ounce) package Whole Grain Hamburger Helper Stroganoff

3 tablespoons dried mushrooms

½ cup instant dry whole milk

1 (3-ounce) foil pouch water-packed tuna

3-ounce block sharp cheddar cheese, cut from larger block

2 tablespoons sliced almonds, toasted

2 cups water, added on the trail

Required Equipment on the Trail:
Cook pot with lid

Nutrition Information per Serving:
Calories: 520
Protein: 34 g
Fat: 17 g
Carbohydrates: 55 g
Fiber: 3 g
Sodium: 1,250 mg
Cholesterol: 70 mg

Preparation at Home:

1. Add 2 tablespoons mix from the stroganoff sauce packet to a quart-size ziplock bag.

2. To the same ziplock bag, add the stroganoff noodles, dried mushrooms, and dry milk.

3. Carry tuna pouch, block cheese, and almonds separately.

Preparation on the Trail:

1. To prepare both servings, cut cheese into small cubes

2. Bring 2 cups water to a boil along with the noodle mix, tuna, and cubed cheese. Reduce heat and stir.

3. Cover and simmer for 10 to 15 minutes, stirring regularly, until noodles are tender.

4. Top with almonds, then serve.

Jack Freeman
Glens Falls, New York

MOUNTAIN OF THE SLEEPING LADY CURRIED CHICKEN

Total Servings: 3
As Packaged for the Trail: 3 servings
Weight per Serving: About 6 ounces
Preparation Time on the Trail: 15 minutes
Challenge Level: Easy

"The 'Mountain of the Sleeping Lady' is the nickname for Doi Nang Non, a connected line of peaks in the Chiang Rai province of Thailand. In the shape of a woman sleeping on her back, legend says the mountains are the remains of a beautiful lady who went searching for her wayward husband before finally falling in the fields and dying of a broken heart . . . Well, try to enjoy your dinner anyway!"

Preparation at Home:
1. Combine uncooked rice, curry paste, ketchup, and lime juice in a medium-size bowl.
2. Toss ingredients in bowl until rice is uniformly coated, then spread on a lined dehydrator tray.
3. Dry rice mix, then package in a pint-size ziplock bag along with the scalloped potatoes. Note that the sauce mix from the box of scalloped potatoes isn't used in this recipe.
4. Pack coconut in a snack-size ziplock bag and carry chicken pouch separately.

Preparation on the Trail:
1. To prepare all 3 servings, combine all ingredients in a pot along with 3 1/2 cups water.
2. Bring contents of pot to a boil, stir, then reduce heat to a simmer.
3. Cover pot and continue to cook until potatoes rehydrate, about 15 minutes.

Ken Harbison
Rochester, New York

1 cup instant brown rice

1 tablespoon Thai Kitchen Red Curry Paste

1 tablespoon ketchup

1 tablespoon lime juice

2 ounces Betty Crocker instant scalloped potatoes

1/4 cup sweetened shredded coconut

1 (7-ounce) foil pouch chicken

3 1/2 cups water, added on the trail

Required Equipment on the Trail:
Cook pot with lid

Nutrition Information per Serving:
Calories: 440
Protein: 22 g
Fat: 7 g
Carbohydrates: 68 g
Fiber: 5 g
Sodium: 390 mg
Cholesterol: 53 mg

SMOKY MOUNTAIN CHILI

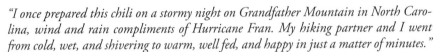

Total Servings: 2
As Packaged for the Trail: 2 servings
Weight per Serving: About 6 ounces
Preparation Time on the Trail: 15 minutes
Challenge Level: Moderate

V

"I once prepared this chili on a stormy night on Grandfather Mountain in North Carolina, wind and rain compliments of Hurricane Fran. My hiking partner and I went from cold, wet, and shivering to warm, well fed, and happy in just a matter of minutes."

1 (15-ounce) can reduced-sodium kidney beans, drained and rinsed

1 (15-ounce) can reduced-sodium pinto beans, drained and rinsed

1 cup Pace Thick and Chunky salsa

1 cup Bob's Red Mill regular TVP

1 tablespoon chili powder

1 teaspoon brown sugar

Optional: block cheddar cheese and tortilla chips

5 cups water, added on the trail

Required Equipment on the Trail:
Cook pot

Nutrition Information per Serving:
Calories: 560
Protein: 47 g
Fat: 1 g
Carbohydrates: 99 g
Fiber: 37 g
Sodium: 1,660 mg
Cholesterol: 0 mg

Preparation at Home:
1. Dry beans in a dehydrator until crumbly.
2. Dehydrate salsa on lined trays until it breaks easily.
3. Combine dehydrated ingredients along with textured vegetable protein (TVP), chili powder, and brown sugar in a quart-size ziplock bag.
4. Package optional ingredients separately for the trail.

Preparation on the Trail:
1. To prepare both servings, add contents of chili bag to 5 cups boiling water.
2. Stir chili, then reduce heat to a simmer.
3. Continue to cook for about 15 minutes, until beans and TVP fully rehydrate, stirring often. If your stove is incapable of maintaining a low simmer, plan to hold the pot above the flame to prevent charring.
4. Serve with optional cheese and tortilla chips.

> This chili becomes quite thick over the flame. It may be necessary to add a little more water during the later stages of cooking to prevent scorching.

Martha Manzano
Falls Church, Virginia

JAPANESE ENERGY SOUP

Total Servings: 1
As Packaged for the Trail: 1 serving
Weight per Serving: About 7 ounces
Preparation Time on the Trail: 15 minutes
Challenge Level: Easy

Preparation at Home:
1. Pack tuna and tofu soup mix in their original packaging.
2. Combine crumbled sushi nori and brown rice in a pint-size ziplock bag.

Preparation on the Trail:
1. To prepare 1 serving, bring 2 1/2 cups water to a boil in a cook pot.
2. Add tuna, tofu soup mix, and contents of the bag containing the rice mixture to the hot water.
3. Maintain a full boil, stirring frequently, until rice is softened, about 10 minutes.

Option: The tuna can also be dried in a dehydrator, saving about 1 1/2 ounces per serving.

Julia Vogel
Pasadena, California

1 (2.5-ounce) foil pouch water-packed tuna

1 (0.35-ounce) packet Kikkoman Instant Tofu Miso Soup mix

2 sheets sushi nori (dried seaweed), crumbled

1 cup Minute Brown Rice

2 1/2 cups water, added on the trail

Required Equipment on the Trail:
Cook pot

Nutrition Information per Serving:
Calories: 440
Protein: 27 g
Fat: 6 g
Carbohydrates: 74 g
Fiber: 6 g
Sodium: 980 mg
Cholesterol: 40 mg

THRU-HIKER VEGGIE SPAGHETTI

Total Servings: 3
As Packaged for the Trail: 1 serving
Weight per Serving: About 6 ounces
Preparation Time on the Trail: 15 minutes (plus 1 hour to rehydrate)
Challenge Level: Easy

V-LO

"I had this meal two out of every three nights on my 1996 thru hike of the Pacific Crest Trail and always looked forward to it."

1 (26-ounce) jar vegetarian spaghetti sauce

1/4 cup chopped bell pepper

1/4 cup dried onion flakes

1/2 tablespoon olive oil

1 (16-ounce) bag frozen classic mixed vegetables, thawed

3/4 cup grated Parmesan cheese

12 ounces angel hair pasta

3 cups water per serving, added on the trail

Required Equipment on the Trail:
Cook pot

Nutrition Information per Serving:
Calories: 710
Protein: 30 g
Fat: 14 g
Carbohydrates: 116 g
Fiber: 7 g
Sodium: 1,600 mg
Cholesterol: 16 mg

Preparation at Home:

1. Simmer spaghetti sauce in a medium-size saucepan.

2. In a large frying pan, sauté bell pepper and onion flakes in olive oil until soft, then add mixed vegetables. Stir.

3. Once vegetables are cooked through, add the vegetable blend to the simmering sauce. Stir well and remove saucepan from heat. Let cool.

4. Puree sauce mixture in blender or food processor until no lumps remain.

5. Ladle 1 1/4-cup portions of sauce onto each of 3 lined drying trays.

6. Dry sauce in a dehydrator until it has the consistency of tough leather.

7. Pulse each tray of dehydrated sauce for a few seconds in a food processor to break it into small pieces.

8. Transfer each serving of dehydrated sauce to a small bowl and allow to cool thoroughly. Package each serving into a separate quart-size ziplock freezer bag.

9. Add 1/4 cup Parmesan cheese to each bag of dehydrated sauce.

10. Evenly divide the angel hair pasta into 3 servings. Store each in a separate pint-size ziplock bag.

Preparation on the Trail:

1. To prepare a single serving, about an hour before dinner, add 1¼ cups water to a bag containing the dehydrated sauce.
2. Reseal the bag and place in a safe place until dinner.
3. When time to eat, bring 1¾ cups water to a boil in a cook pot.
4. Break a single serving of angel hair pasta into smaller pieces and add to the pot.
5. Stir pasta for 2 to 3 minutes, until al dente. Lower heat and drain remaining water.
6. Return pot to the flame and add rehydrated sauce. Stir constantly until heated through, then serve.

> Learn to tweak the amount of water used to boil the pasta so that no water remains once the pasta is finished cooking. This simplifies the process and requires less filtered water for cooking, especially important in trail environments where water is scarce.

Diane King
Somers, Connecticut

SHEPHERD'S PIE

Total Servings: 2
As Packaged for the Trail: 2 servings
Weight per Serving: About 6 ounces
Preparation Time on the Trail: 30 minutes
Challenge Level: Moderate

2 ounces Ground Beef Gravel (see recipe in this book)

1 cup Just Peas brand freeze-dried peas

1 pinch ground cayenne pepper

1 (0.87-ounce) package McCormick Brown Gravy Mix

1⅓ cups instant Hungry Jack Mashed Potatoes

¼ teaspoon garlic powder

¼ cup instant dry whole milk

Optional: 1 tablespoon Butter Buds

2-ounce block cheddar cheese, cut from larger block

3½ cups water, divided, added on the trail

Required Equipment on the Trail:
Cook pot with lid

Nutrition Information per Serving:
Calories: 740
Protein: 47 g
Fat: 30 g
Carbohydrates: 69 g
Fiber: 5 g
Sodium: 1,130 mg
Cholesterol: 52 mg

Preparation at Home:

1. Combine dried beef, peas, cayenne, and contents of gravy mix package in a quart-size ziplock bag.

2. In another quart-size ziplock freezer bag, combine potatoes, garlic powder, dry milk, and optional Butter Buds.

3. Carry block cheese separately.

Preparation on the Trail:

1. To prepare both servings, bring 2 cups water to a boil in a cook pot.

2. Brace ziplock bag containing the potato mixture and pour hot water into the bag.

3. Add 1½ cups cold water to the pot along with the beef mixture.

4. Heat beef mixture to a boil while stirring, then reduce heat to a simmer. Cover and continue to cook for about 5 to 10 minutes or until beef fully rehydrates.

5. Remove pot from stove.

6. Carefully seal bag containing potato mixture, then knead to eliminate clumps.

7. Spread rehydrated potatoes in a layer over the beef mixture.

8. Slice cheese block into thin pieces, then evenly spread over the potatoes.

9. Cover the pot and serve once cheese melts.

Option: A vegetarian version can be made by substituting 6 ounces MorningStar Farms Meal Starters Grillers Recipe Crumbles for the dried ground beef and a 0.7-ounce package of Hain Vegetarian Brown Gravy Mix for the McCormick Brown Gravy Mix. Dehydrate crumbles prior to packing for the trail. Preparation on trail remains the same.

Ken Harbison
Rochester, New York

CAROLINA SPICE RICE

Total Servings: 1
As Packaged for the Trail: 1 serving
Weight per Serving: About 7 ounces
Preparation Time on the Trail: 15 minutes
Challenge Level: Easy

Preparation at Home:
   Pack rice, soy sauce, and Slim Jim separately for the trail.

Preparation on the Trail:
1. To prepare 1 serving, bring 2 cups water to a boil in cook pot.
2. Cook the rice in its boil bag, with pot covered, for about 10 minutes.
3. Remove rice bag, drain the pot, and pour the cooked rice from the bag back into the pot.
4. Cut Slim Jim into small pieces and add to the pot along with soy sauce. Stir and serve.

Jim Hoeferlin
Charlotte, North Carolina

1 (3.5-ounce) package Boil–in-Bag Success Whole Grain Brown Rice

2 tablespoons low-sodium soy sauce

1 (0.97-ounce) stick Slim Jim Beef Jerky

2 cups water, added on the trail

Required Equipment on the Trail:
Cook pot with lid

Nutrition Information per Serving:
Calories: 470
Protein: 16 g
Fat: 15 g
Carbohydrates: 70 g
Fiber: 4 g
Sodium: 1,580 mg
Cholesterol: 15 mg

BROWER'S BAC-O SPUDS

Total Servings: 2
As Packaged for the Trail: 2 servings
Weight per Serving: About 6 ounces
Preparation Time on the Trail: 30 minutes (plus 1 hour to rehydrate)
Challenge Level: Moderate

"This is a basic recipe I've used for years. It's very filling and has just the right amount of salt to quench that craving."

1 (5-ounce) can chicken, drained

4 ounces frozen classic mixed vegetables, thawed

1 (0.87-ounce) package McCormick Low-Sodium Brown Gravy Mix

1½ cups instant potato flakes

⅓ cup instant dry nonfat milk

1 (0.5-ounce) individual packet Butter Buds

1 teaspoon dried parsley

1 teaspoon dried onion

½ teaspoon ground black pepper

½ cup Betty Crocker Bac-Os

4¼ cups water, divided, added on the trail

Preparation at Home:

1. Dry chicken and vegetables in a dehydrator.
2. Seal dried chicken and vegetables in a pint-size ziplock freezer bag.
3. Carry gravy mix in its original package.
4. Combine remaining dry ingredients in a separate quart-size ziplock bag.

Preparation on the Trail:

1. To prepare both servings, about an hour before dinner, begin rehydrating the dried chicken and vegetables by adding about ¼ cup water to the bag.
2. Seal bag and place in a safe place until dinner.
3. At dinnertime, prepare 2 servings by first making the gravy, slowly combining contents of the gravy mix with 1 cup water in a cook pot over low heat.
4. Bring gravy to a boil, then return heat to low for 1 minute, stirring constantly.
5. Pour gravy into a cup or bowl and set aside. Pot does not require rinsing before the next step.
6. Combine 3 cups water and the rehydrating chicken and vegetables in the cook pot.
7. Bring mixture to a boil, then add contents of bag containing the potato mixture. Stir well.
8. Remove pot from heat once spuds thicken, gradually stirring in a little extra water if potatoes are too thick.
9. Pour gravy, previously set aside, over potatoes before serving.

Option: One-quarter cup freeze-dried vegetable blend can be used in place of the dehydrated vegetables in this recipe.

Ursula Brower
South Lake Tahoe, California

Required Equipment on the Trail:
Cook pot

Cup or bowl

Nutrition Information per Serving:
Calories: 560
Protein: 39 g
Fat: 9 g
Carbohydrates: 78 g
Fiber: 4 g
Sodium: 1,480 mg
Cholesterol: 55 mg

"Most of my hiking is in the Sierra Nevada, where the temperature drops quickly once the sun sets. I always boil a little extra water when cooking dinner and use it to prepare a cup of instant soup while the main course is cooking. It makes a great appetizer while taking the chill away!"

—*Ursula Brower*
South Lake Tahoe, California

VERMILION VALLEY VEGETABLE SOUP

Total Servings: 2
As Packaged for the Trail: 2 servings
Weight per Serving: About 7 ounces
Preparation Time on the Trail: 15 minutes
Challenge Level: Easy

V

1 (1-ounce) packet Lipton Recipe Secrets Vegetable Soup and Dip Mix

¼ cup dried mushrooms

½ cup freeze-dried Just Peas brand freeze-dried peas

½ cup freeze-dried Just Corn brand freeze-dried corn

1 (3-ounce) package ramen noodles, seasoning packet removed

¼ cup instant potato flakes

1 tablespoon dried onion flakes

¼ teaspoon ground black pepper

1 teaspoon garlic powder

4 cups water, added on the trail

Required Equipment on the Trail:
Cook pot

Nutrition Information per Serving:
Calories: 390
Protein: 14 g
Fat: 2 g
Carbohydrates: 66 g
Fiber: 6 g
Sodium: 1,110 mg
Cholesterol: 0 mg

Preparation at Home:
Combine all dry ingredients in a quart-size ziplock bag.

Preparation on the Trail:
1. To prepare both servings, bring 4 cups water to a boil in a cook pot.
2. Empty ingredients from ziplock bag into the pot, reduce heat to a simmer, and stir often, until vegetables are tender, about 10 minutes.

Save ramen noodle seasoning packet for "Night-After-Night Bean Soup," also in this book.

Jeffrey Hare
Citrus Heights, California

Authors' Note:
Special thanks to Ken Harbison for reworking the original recipe from the first edition to reduce sodium content per serving.

"I add 4 ounces of corn elbow pasta to my dehydrated meals for even more energy." —Steve "Switchback" Fuquay

Las Vegas, Nevada

INDIAN LEMON CHICKEN AND COUSCOUS

Total Servings: 2
As Packaged for the Trail: 2 servings
Weight per Serving: About 7 ounces
Preparation Time on the Trail: 15 minutes
Challenge Level: Easy

"Great tasting food is worth its weight."

Preparation at Home:
1. Combine spices and bouillon cube in a snack-size ziplock bag.
2. Carry chicken pouch and couscous separately.

Preparation on the Trail:
1. To prepare both servings, bring 1½ cups water to boil in a cook pot along with the spices and bouillon cube.
2. Add chicken and couscous to the pot, stir, then return to a boil.
3. Cover pot, remove from heat, and allow to rest for about 5 minutes. Stir, then serve.

> You can prepare your own curry powder by combining equal amounts of ground cayenne, fenugreek, garlic powder, ground mustard seed, and turmeric.

Margaret Reek
Churchville, New York

1 tablespoon curry powder

¼ teaspoon ginger powder

1 dash ground fennel

¼ teaspoon dried lemon peel

1 regular-size cube chicken bouillon

1 (7-ounce) foil pouch chicken

1 cup instant couscous

1½ cups water, added on the trail

Required Equipment on the Trail:
Cook pot with lid

Nutrition Information per Serving:
Calories: 450
Protein: 49 g
Fat: 5 g
Carbohydrates: 65 g
Fiber: 4 g
Sodium: 1,120 mg
Cholesterol: 80 mg

LASSEN VOLCANIC ERUPTION CHILI

Total Servings: 2
As Packaged for the Trail: 2 servings
Weight per Serving: About 7 ounces
Preparation Time on the Trail: 15 minutes (plus 1 hour to rehydrate)
Challenge Level: Easy

½ pound lean ground beef

8 Roma tomatoes

3 cayenne or jalapeño peppers, chopped

1 bell pepper, sliced in thin strips

2 (15-ounce) cans reduced-sodium black beans, drained and rinsed

1 (1.25-ounce) package McCormick Reduced-Sodium Chili Seasoning

3½ cups water, added on the trail

Required Equipment on the Trail:
Cook pot

Nutrition Information per Serving:
Calories: 660
Protein: 45 g
Fat: 13 g
Carbohydrates: 79 g
Fiber: 14 g
Sodium: 930 mg
Cholesterol: 96 mg

Preparation at Home:
1. Thoroughly brown ground beef in a frying pan; drain the fat.
2. Rinse beef under hot water in a colander.
3. Dehydrate beef until thoroughly dry like gravel.
4. Slice tomato through the core into ¼-inch-thick slices.
5. Dry tomatoes, hot peppers, bell peppers, and beans in a dehydrator.
6. Combine all dehydrated ingredients in a gallon-size ziplock freezer bag.
7. Carry package of chili seasoning separately.

Preparation on the Trail:
1. To prepare both servings, about an hour before dinner, add 3½ cups water to dehydrated ingredients.
2. Reseal bag, knead contents, and place in safe place.
3. At dinnertime, pour rehydrated ingredients into a cook pot along with contents of the chili seasoning packet.
4. Warm thoroughly over low heat, then serve.

Craig "Smitty" Smith
Springfield, Missouri

STILLWATER SWEET AND SOUR RICE

Total Servings: 3
As Packaged for the Trail: 3 servings
Weight per Serving: About 7 ounces
Preparation Time on the Trail: 15 minutes
Challenge Level: Easy

Preparation at Home:
1. Combine all dry ingredients in a quart-size ziplock bag.
2. Carry chicken pouch separately.

Preparation on the Trail:
1. To prepare all 3 servings, bring 3 cups water to a boil in a pot.
2. Add rice mixture and chicken, then continue boiling for about 5 minutes, stirring occasionally.

Ken Harbison
Rochester, New York

1½ cups instant rice

½ cup Just Carrots brand freeze-dried carrots

½ cup candied pineapple tidbits, chopped

¼ cup dried bell pepper flakes

2 tablespoons dried minced onion

¼ cup sun-dried tomato, chopped

2 tablespoons brown sugar

1 (0.75-ounce) packet Sun Bird or Sun Luck brand Sweet-and-Sour Seasoning Mix

1 (7-ounce) foil pouch chicken

3 cups water, added on the trail

Required Equipment on the Trail:
Cook pot

Nutrition Information per Serving:
Calories: 420
Protein: 25 g
Fat: 3 g
Carbohydrates: 77 g
Fiber: 2 g
Sodium: 610 mg
Cholesterol: 53 mg

THANKSGIVING ON THE TRAIL

Total Servings: 3
As Packaged for the Trail: 3 servings
Weight per Serving: About 7 ounces
Preparation Time on the Trail: 15 minutes
Challenge Level: Easy

1 (4-ounce) package Idahoan Loaded Baked Flavored Mashed Potatoes

¼ cup instant dry whole milk

½ cup dried herbed stuffing mix (your choice)

¾ cup Craisins

1 (7-ounce) foil pouch chicken

1 teaspoon olive oil

2⅓ cups water, added on the trail

Required Equipment on the Trail:
Cook pot

Nutrition Information per Serving:
Calories: 440
Protein: 23 g
Fat: 14 g
Carbohydrates: 62 g
Fiber: 4 g
Sodium: 1,170 mg
Cholesterol: 63 mg

Preparation at Home:
1. Combine potato flakes, dry milk, stuffing mix, and Craisins in a quart-size ziplock bag.
2. Carry chicken pouch and olive oil separately.

Preparation on the Trail:
1. To prepare all 3 servings, bring 2⅓ cups water to a boil in a cook pot, then add 1 teaspoon olive oil. Remove pot from heat.
2. Immediately add dry ingredients to the pot and stir well.
3. Crumble chicken into pot and stir. Allow to rest for a few minutes before serving.

Chad Kinsey
Mount Airy, Georgia

JAMMIN' JAMBALAYA

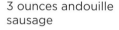

Total Servings: 3
As Packaged for the Trail: 1 serving
Weight per Serving: About 7 ounces
Preparation Time on the Trail: 15 minutes
Challenge Level: Easy

"With jambalaya, the signature dish of Louisiana, hot spice and rice are essential."

Preparation at Home:

1. Slice sausage thinly and break chicken into small pieces.
2. Combine sausage, chicken, shrimp, bell pepper, celery, onion, tomato sauce, Worcestershire sauce, and Cajun seasoning in a medium-size cook pot.
3. Cook jambalaya until heated through, adding a small amount of water if necessary to prevent burning.
4. Evenly spread jambalaya onto 3 lined dehydrator trays, about 1 heaping cup to each tray. Thoroughly dry until crumbly.
5. Package contents from each tray into a separate pint-size ziplock bag.
6. Add 1/2 cup rice to each of the 3 bags.

Preparation on the Trail:

1. To prepare 1 serving, add 2 cups water to a cook pot and then pour ingredients from 1 of the ziplock bags into the pot and bring to a boil. Stir.
2. Cover pot, reduce heat, and simmer until rice is fully rehydrated, about 15 minutes.

Ken Harbison
Rochester, New York

3 ounces andouille sausage

1 (10-ounce) can water-packed chunk chicken, undrained

1 (4-ounce) can tiny shrimp, undrained

1 bell pepper, diced

1 stalk celery, diced

1 medium onion, diced

1 (8-ounce) can low-sodium tomato sauce

1 tablespoon Worcestershire sauce

1 teaspoon Cajun seasoning

1 1/2 cups instant brown rice

2 cups water per serving, added on the trail

Required Equipment on the Trail:
Cook pot with lid

Nutrition Information per Serving:
Calories: 740
Protein: 44 g
Fat: 24 g
Carbohydrates: 89 g
Fiber: 6 g
Sodium: 1,240 mg
Cholesterol: 195 mg

CHICKEN CASHEW CURRY

Total Servings: 3
As Packaged for the Trail: 3 servings
Weight per Serving: About 7 ounces
Preparation Time on the Trail: 15 minutes
Challenge Level: Easy

1 (7-ounce) foil pouch chicken

½ cup roasted cashew pieces

½ cup dried mango, chopped

½ cup freeze-dried peas or carrots

1 tablespoon curry powder

1 teaspoon chicken bouillon granules

1 cup instant brown rice

⅓ cup instant dry whole milk

2½ cups water, added on the trail

Required Equipment on the Trail:
Cook pot with lid

Nutrition Information per Serving:
Calories: 550
Protein: 31 g
Fat: 13 g
Carbohydrates: 85 g
Fiber: 7 g
Sodium: 690 mg
Cholesterol: 54 mg

Preparation at Home:
1. Pack chicken pouch and cashews separately.
2. Combine remaining dry ingredients in a quart-size ziplock bag.

Preparation on the Trail:
1. To prepare all 3 servings, add 2½ cups water to cook pot along with the rice mixture and chicken.
2. Bring to a boil, then reduce heat to a simmer. Stir, cover, and continue to cook until rice is tender, about 12 minutes.
3. Stir in cashew pieces, then serve.

Option: Raisins or dried apricots can be substituted for the mango.

Ken Harbison
Rochester, New York

TALLULAH GORGE TORTELLINI

Total Servings: 3
As Packaged for the Trail: 3 servings
Weight per Serving: About 7 ounces
Preparation Time on the Trail: 15 minutes
Challenge Level: Easy

V-LO

Preparation at Home:
Pack Boboli sauce and tortellini separately for the trail.

Preparation on the Trail:
1. To prepare all 3 servings, add Boboli sauce to 4 cups water in a cook pot and bring to a boil.
2. Add tortellini and continue boiling for about 10 minutes, or until pasta softens.

Christine and Tim Conners
Statesboro, Georgia

2 (5-ounce) packets Boboli pizza sauce

1 (12-ounce) package Barilla dry cheese tortellini

4 cups water, added on the trail

Required Equipment on the Trail:
Cook pot

Nutrition Information per Serving:
Calories: 490
Protein: 17 g
Fat: 16 g
Carbohydrates: 71 g
Fiber: 4 g
Sodium: 1,240 mg
Cholesterol: 71 mg

TRAVELIN' TAGLIARINI

Total Servings: 4
As Packaged for the Trail: 1 serving
Weight per Serving: About 7 ounces
Preparation Time on the Trail: 15 minutes
Challenge Level: Easy

"Tagliarini was popular during the Great Depression as an inexpensive, nutritious comfort food, often served by churches and soup kitchens. Sounds like perfect backpacking food as well!"

1 onion, diced

1 teaspoon chopped garlic

1 pound lean ground beef

1 teaspoon olive oil

1 bell pepper, diced

2 cups frozen corn, thawed

1 (6-ounce) can sliced olives, drained

1 (24-ounce) jar marinara sauce

1 tablespoon chili powder

1 teaspoon dried oregano

8 ounces spaghetti noodles

4 (0.8-ounce) sticks cheddar cheese

2¼ cups water per serving, added on the trail

Preparation at Home:

1. In a skillet over medium heat, fry onion, garlic, and ground beef in olive oil, breaking up the hamburger into small pieces while cooking.

2. Once the onions are soft and no pink remains in the beef, add bell pepper, corn, olives, marinara sauce, and spices.

3. Continue to cook until simmering, then remove from heat. Cover and set aside to cool.

4. Evenly divide tagliarnini among 4 lined dehydrator trays, then thoroughly dry.

5. Package dried contents from each tray in a separate pint-size ziplock bag.

6. Divide spaghetti noodles evenly among 4 snack-size ziplock bags.

7. Do not remove stick cheese from its packaging. Carry separately.

Preparation on the Trail:
1. To prepare a single serving, add beef mixture from a pint-size ziplock bag into a cook pot with 2 ¼ cups water, then heat to boiling.
2. Stir in noodles from a single snack-size ziplock bag. Cover pot, reduce heat, and simmer until noodles are tender, about 12 minutes.
3. Remove pot from stove, slice 1 cheese stick into ½-inch pieces, then add to pot.
4. Allow cheese to melt into the mix, then serve.

Ken Harbison
Rochester, New York

Required Equipment on the Trail:
Cook pot with lid

Nutrition Information per Serving:
Calories: 930
Protein: 65 g
Fat: 43 g
Carbohydrates: 64 g
Fiber: 9 g
Sodium: 1,350 mg
Cholesterol: 185 mg

Don't substitute flat noodles, such as fettuccini, for the pasta. Flat noodles tend to stick to each other, then fail to cook properly on the trail.

MICHIGAN SALMON FETTUCCINE

Total Servings: 2
As Packaged for the Trail: 2 servings
Weight per Serving: About 7 ounces
Preparation Time on the Trail: 45 minutes
Challenge Level: Easy

2 (6-ounce) cans no-salt-added salmon, drained

2 (4.4-ounce) packages Knorr Pasta Sides Alfredo

1 (0.5-ounce) individual packet Butter Buds

⅓ cup instant dry nonfat milk

3 cups water, added on the trail

Required Equipment on the Trail:
Cook pot

Nutrition Information per Serving:
Calories: 620
Protein: 49 g
Fat: 23 g
Carbohydrates: 55 g
Fiber: 1 g
Sodium: 1,530 mg
Cholesterol: 177 mg

Preparation at Home:
1. Thoroughly dry salmon in a dehydrator and pack it in a pint-size ziplock freezer bag.
2. In a second pint-size ziplock bag, add Alfredo noodle mix, Butter Buds, and instant dry milk.

Preparation on the Trail:
1. To prepare both servings, put dried salmon into 3 cups water in a cook pot and allow to rest for 30 minutes to rehydrate.
2. Bring water to a boil, then add noodle mix from the second ziplock bag. Stir.
3. Reduce heat to low and continue to cook, stirring often, for 5 minutes. Add more water, a little at a time, if necessary to prevent noodles from drying out.

Option: If weight isn't a concern, salmon can be carried in foil pouches, bypassing the need for dehydrating the canned salmon. For this option, use a little less water when cooking on the trail.

> Packaged salmon comes in a variety of types and sizes. An exact amount isn't critical to the success of this recipe. Whatever the quantity used, look for low-salt brands.

Joan Young
Scottville, Michigan

BACKPACKER'S POTLUCK

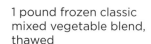

Total Servings: 2
As Packaged for the Trail: 2 servings
Weight per Serving: About 7 ounces
Preparation Time on the Trail: 45 minutes
Challenge Level: Easy

"This recipe, courtesy of the Daily Gazette of Schenectady, New York, was adapted from an article about backpacking food published in the Schenectady Gazette several decades ago. The article described Backpacker's Potluck as 'a delicious trail dinner idea, an easy stew to prepare in the wild.'"

Preparation at Home:
1. Dry vegetables and chicken in a dehydrator.
2. Combine dried vegetables, dried chicken, rice, contents of onion soup mix packet, and cayenne pepper in a quart-size ziplock bag.
3. Pack oil separately for the trail.

Preparation on the Trail:
1. To prepare both servings, combine 1 tablespoon olive oil, contents from ziplock bag, and 3 cups water in a cook pot. Stir.
2. Allow pot to rest for 30 minutes while contents rehydrate.
3. Bring contents of pot to a boil for 10 minutes or until vegetables soften, stirring often. Lower flame temperature as water is fully absorbed.

David and Sandra Geisinger
Schenectady, New York

1 pound frozen classic mixed vegetable blend, thawed

1 (5-ounce) can water-packed chunk chicken

2 cups instant brown rice

1 (1-ounce) packet Lipton Recipe Secrets Onion Soup and Dip Mix

1 dash ground cayenne pepper

1 tablespoon olive oil

3 cups water, added on the trail

Required Equipment on the Trail:
Cook pot

Nutrition Information per Serving:
Calories: 720
Protein: 31 g
Fat: 16 g
Carbohydrates: 122 g
Fiber: 12 g
Sodium: 1,520 mg
Cholesterol: 43 mg

TRAIL OVEN PIZZA TO GO

Total Servings: 2
As Packaged for the Trail: 2 servings
Weight per Serving: About 7 ounces
Preparation Time on the Trail: 45 minutes
Challenge Level: Moderate

V-LO

"I firmly believe that the weight of food is less important than the quality and taste, and that spending a little more time cooking is a small sacrifice for a great meal. As an example, this recipe produces a pizza that any reputable pizzeria would envy!"

1 (16.17-ounce) package Chef Boyardee Cheese Pizza Maker

Optional toppings: ground beef gravel, pepperoni, jerky, dried onions, bell peppers, tomatoes, zucchini, pineapple, mushrooms

1-ounce block mozzarella cheese, cut from larger block

1 tablespoon olive oil

A little more than 1 cup water, added on the trail

Required Equipment on the Trail:
Pack oven and small oven bag

Cook pot with lid

Nutrition Information per Serving:
Calories: 710
Protein: 19 g
Fat: 25 g
Carbohydrates: 48 g
Fiber: 6 g
Sodium: 1,580 mg
Cholesterol: 20 mg

Preparation at Home:

1. Place crust mix and unopened cheese packet from Pizza Maker kit into a quart-size ziplock bag.

2. Dry pizza sauce from Pizza Maker kit on lined dehydrator tray.

3. Tear dried sauce into small pieces.

4. Pack dried sauce in a pint-size ziplock freezer bag. Place any optional ingredients with the dried sauce.

5. Package mozzarella and oil separately for the trail.

Preparation on the Trail:

1. Remove cheese packet from the crust mix bag.

2. To prepare both servings, add ⅔ cup warm water to crust mix bag along with 1 tablespoon olive oil. Seal bag and knead dough for a couple of minutes.

3. Set dough bag aside in a warm location such as a sunny spot or inside your jacket and allow dough to rise for at least 5 minutes.

4. Add ½ cup water to sauce bag, slightly more water if rehydrating other toppings. Seal bag, knead contents for a few moments, then set aside for about 10 minutes. (If reconstituting optional toppings, rehydrating may take an hour or more.)

5. Form pizza dough into a disk, then place in the bottom of an oven bag.

6. Add rehydrated sauce mix to the top of pizza dough.
7. Slice mozzarella cheese into thin pieces and evenly lay over sauce. Pour contents of cheese packet over the sauce as well.
8. Bake pizza in pack oven until crust dough is cooked through and cheese has melted, about 15 minutes.
9. Divide baked pizza in half, then serve.

Jeffrey Hare
Citrus Heights, California

Options: *To reduce mess while eating, dough can be folded before baking into a type of calzone.*

If weight isn't a concern, the dehydrating step can be avoided by carrying sauce in its original container.

WHITE TRASH PASTA

Total Servings: 1
As Packaged for the Trail: 1 serving
Weight per Serving: About 8 ounces
Preparation Time on the Trail: 15 minutes
Challenge Level: Easy

V-LO

"This recipe works great if you are looking for dinners that don't require too much thought or cash. I've never grown tired of eating White Trash Pasta, maybe because I was raised on casseroles from Good Housekeeping *magazine!"*

1 (16-ounce) bag frozen broccoli, thawed

1 (5.7-ounce) package Knorr Pasta Sides Cheddar Broccoli

¼ cup instant brown rice

2¼ cups water, added on the trail

Required Equipment on the Trail:
Cook pot

Nutrition Information per Serving:
Calories: 810
Protein: 33 g
Fat: 7 g
Carbohydrates: 161 g
Fiber: 16 g
Sodium: 1,710 mg
Cholesterol: 5 mg

Preparation at Home:
1. Chop broccoli into small pieces, then dry in a dehydrator.
2. Combine broccoli and remaining dry ingredients in a quart-size ziplock bag.

Preparation on the Trail:
1. To prepare 1 serving, add ingredients from ziplock bag to 2¼ cups water in a cook pot, then bring to a boil.
2. Stir then reduce heat to a simmer.
3. Continue to cook for 5 to 10 minutes, until broccoli is rehydrated.

Craig Giffen
Portland, Oregon

"I sometimes realize that the food in my pack may not last until the next resupply. So I build a 'gleaner's bag.' To the bag I donate a couple of uncooked spoonfuls of food per meal. Then once I run out of my planned meals, I divide the contents of the gleaner's bag by the number of days remaining to town."

—*Will "The Green Ghost" O'Daix*
Indianapolis, Indiana

SUNDOWN SAUSAGE DELIGHT

Total Servings: 2
As Packaged for the Trail: 2 servings
Weight per Serving: About 8 ounces
Preparation Time on the Trail: 15 minutes
Challenge Level: Easy

Preparation at Home:
1. Combine all dry ingredients, including optional cayenne pepper, in a quart-size ziplock bag.
2. Pack sausage separately for the trail.

Preparation on the Trail:
1. To prepare both servings, slice sausage into small pieces.
2. Bring 2 1/4 cups water to a boil in a cook pot.
3. Add sliced sausage and contents from bag of rice mixture to boiling water. Stir and reduce heat.
4. Cover pot and simmer for about 10 minutes, until rice is soft.

Securely wrap the open end of a sausage log when on the trail to prevent premature spoilage.

Cathy Czachorowski
Torrington, Connecticut

1 1/2 cups instant brown rice

2 teaspoons McCormick Perfect Pinch Roasted Garlic & Bell Pepper Seasoning

9 sun-dried tomatoes, chopped

1 cube vegetable bouillon

2 bay leaves, chopped into small pieces

1/2 teaspoon paprika

1/4 teaspoon ground black pepper

1 dash turmeric

1/2 teaspoon dried thyme

1/2 teaspoon dried oregano

Optional: ground cayenne pepper to taste

2 ounces summer sausage

2 1/4 cups water, added on the trail

Required Equipment on the Trail:
Cook pot with lid

Nutrition Information per Serving:
Calories: 440
Protein: 13 g
Fat: 12 g
Carbohydrates: 72 g
Fiber: 5 g
Sodium: 1,090 mg
Cholesterol: 20 mg

TAHOE CHICKEN CURRY

Total Servings: 2
As Packaged for the Trail: 2 servings
Weight per Serving: About 8 ounces
Preparation Time on the Trail: 15 minutes
Challenge Level: Easy

3 (5-ounce) cans water-packed chunk chicken, drained

1/2 pound frozen peas, thawed

1 1/2 cups instant brown rice

1 1/2 teaspoons curry powder

1/4 teaspoon ground black pepper

1/2 cup unsalted cashew halves

1/2 cup raisins

2 regular-size cubes chicken bouillon

2 cups water, added on the trail

Required Equipment on the Trail:
Cook pot with lid

Nutrition Information per Serving:
Calories: 770
Protein: 40 g
Fat: 22 g
Carbohydrates: 119 g
Fiber: 8 g
Sodium: 1,290 mg
Cholesterol: 75 mg

Preparation at Home:
1. Dry chicken and peas in a dehydrator.
2. Combine dried chicken, peas, and remaining dry ingredients, including unwrapped bouillon cubes, in a quart-size ziplock bag.

Preparation on the Trail:
1. To prepare both servings, bring 2 cups water to a boil in a cook pot, then add dried chicken mixture.
2. Cook chicken curry for about 1 minute, stirring often.
3. Remove pot from stove, cover, and allow to rest for 5 to 10 minutes, until rice is tender.

Ursula Brower
South Lake Tahoe, California

CELEBRATION DINNER

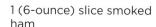

Total Servings: 2
As Packaged for the Trail: 2 servings
Weight per Serving: About 8 ounces
Preparation Time on the Trail: 15 minutes
Challenge Level: Easy

"This meal is a real treat after a few weeks on the trail. It's easy to make and very tasty. We prepare it when we need to reward ourselves. Just the thing to lift the spirits when feeling dreary and lethargic."

Preparation at Home:
1. Slice ham into small pieces.
2. Thoroughly dry ham and peas in a dehydrator.
3. Combine dried ham, peas, and noodles in quart-size ziplock bag.
4. Pack cheese separately for the trail.

Preparation on the Trail:
1. To prepare both servings, bring 3 cups water to a boil in a cook pot.
2. Add ham mixture to the pot. Stir, reduce heat to a simmer, then continue to cook until noodles are tender and meat begins to soften, about 10 minutes.
3. Remove pot from the stove, stir in Parmesan cheese, then serve.

Option: *To avoid the need to dry any of the ingredients, and if weight isn't an issue, use 2 (3-ounce) pouches of Spam singles and 1 cup freeze-dried peas in place of the ham and frozen peas.*

Chris Woodall
Simpsonville, South Carolina

1 (6-ounce) slice smoked ham

3 cups frozen peas, thawed

6 ounces macaroni or egg noodles

1 cup grated Parmesan cheese

3 cups water, added on the trail

Required Equipment on the Trail:
Cook pot

Nutrition Information per Serving:
Calories: 570
Protein: 47 g
Fat: 15 g
Carbohydrates: 40 g
Fiber: 7 g
Sodium: 1,860 mg
Cholesterol: 85 mg

BOB 'N' BUG'S SPANISH RICE FIESTA

Total Servings: 2
As Packaged for the Trail: 2 servings
Weight per Serving: About 8 ounces
Preparation Time on the Trail: 15 minutes
Challenge Level: Easy

V

1 (16-ounce) jar low-sodium salsa

1 (7-ounce) package Fantastic Foods Refried Beans

2 cups instant brown rice

Optional: 2 tablespoons grated Parmesan cheese

4 cups water, added on the trail

Required Equipment on the Trail:
Cook pot

Nutrition Information per Serving:
Calories: 780
Protein: 31 g
Fat: 6 g
Carbohydrates: 149 g
Fiber: 29 g
Sodium: 1,230 mg
Cholesterol: 0 mg

Preparation at Home:
1. Dry salsa on a lined dehydrator tray.
2. Tear dried salsa into small pieces, then package in a pint-size ziplock bag.
3. Combine refried beans, rice, and optional cheese in a quart-size ziplock bag.

Preparation on the Trail:
1. To prepare both servings, combine 4 cups water and dried salsa in a cook pot.
2. Bring water to a boil, stirring occasionally.
3. Add bean mixture to boiling water and stir. Reduce heat to a simmer, then continue to cook for about 5 minutes before serving.

Option: Prepare burritos by serving this Spanish rice on tortillas.

*Bob and Joy "Bob 'n' Bug" Turner
Coeur d'Alene, Idaho*

BEARTOWN COUSCOUS

Total Servings: 2
As Packaged for the Trail: 2 servings
Weight per Serving: About 8 ounces
Preparation Time on the Trail: 15 minutes
Challenge Level: Easy

V

"Couscous looks like millet but is actually a form of pasta; and it cooks much faster than spaghetti."

Preparation at Home:
1. Dry onion, bell pepper, and cooked carrots in a dehydrator.
2. Combine dried vegetables in a pint-size ziplock bag.
3. Add couscous, salt, brown sugar, and curry powder to a quart-size ziplock bag.

Preparation on the Trail:
1. To prepare both servings, add vegetable mixture to 2¼ cups water in a cook pot and bring to a boil. Stir.
2. Lower heat to a simmer and continue to cook until vegetables rehydrate, about 5 minutes.
3. Add couscous mixture to the pot, stir, and return to a boil.
4. Immediately remove pot from heat, cover, and allow to rest for about 5 to 10 minutes, until couscous becomes soft.

Rick Bombaci
Enterprise, Oregon

1 large onion, diced

1 bell pepper, chopped

2 large carrots, thinly sliced and cooked

2 cups instant whole wheat couscous

½ teaspoon salt

2 tablespoons brown sugar

2 tablespoons curry powder

2¼ cups water, added on the trail

Required Equipment on the Trail:
Cook pot with lid

Nutrition Information per Serving:
Calories: 840
Protein: 28 g
Fat: 5 g
Carbohydrates: 174 g
Fiber: 29 g
Sodium: 1,250 mg
Cholesterol: 0 mg

TRAIL THAI STIR FRY

Total Servings: 2
As Packaged for the Trail: 2 servings
Weight per Serving: About 8 ounces
Preparation Time on the Trail: 15 minutes
Challenge Level: Easy

V

1 (5.5-ounce) package Tofurky "turkey" slices

1 (8-ounce) can French-cut green beans, drained

1/4 ounce dried shiitake mushrooms, chopped

1/4 cup peanuts, chopped

Optional: 2 tablespoons whole egg powder

1 (9-ounce) package Thai Kitchen Pad Thai Noodle Kit

2 tablespoons peanut oil

2 1/2 cups water, added on the trail

Required Equipment on the Trail:
Cook pot with lid

Nutrition Information per Serving:
Calories: 850
Protein: 35 g
Fat: 34 g
Carbohydrates: 105 g
Fiber: 7 g
Sodium: 1,220 mg
Cholesterol: 0 mg

Preparation at Home:

1. Slice Tofurky and green beans into small pieces, then dehydrate.
2. Combine dried Tofurky, green beans, mushrooms, peanuts, and optional egg powder in a pint-size ziplock bag.
3. Remove noodles and seasoning packet from the noodle kit. Pack the noodles in a quart-size ziplock bag along with unopened seasoning packet.
4. Pack oil separately for the trail.

Preparation on the Trail:

1. To prepare both servings, add Tofurky mixture to 2 1/2 cups water in a cook pot.
2. Bring water to a boil, stir, then reduce heat to a simmer. Cover pot and continue to cook for about 8 minutes.
3. Add noodles to pot and continue to cook, stirring often, about 5 more minutes or until noodles are soft and water is fully absorbed.
4. Add contents of seasoning packet and 2 tablespoons peanut oil to the noodles, then toss for a minute or so before removing pot from stove and serving.

Joan Frazier
Rochester, New York

THE COUSCOUS BURRITO OF THE MIGHTY SAN GABRIELS

Total Servings: 3 (2 burritos per serving)
As Packaged for the Trail: 1 serving
Weight per Serving: About 8 ounces
Preparation Time on the Trail: 15 minutes
Challenge Level: Easy

V-LO

"This is one of my favorites. Lightweight, easy to prepare, lots of carbs, and surprisingly hearty. The perfect meal on the trail!"

Preparation at Home:
1. In a small bowl, combine couscous with contents of taco seasoning package.
2. Evenly divide couscous mixture among 3 (1-pint) ziplock bags, about 1/2 cup each.
3. Pack tortillas, hot sauce, and block cheese separately for the trail.

Preparation on the Trail:
1. To prepare 1 serving, bring 1/2 cup water to a boil in a cook pot, then add contents from a single bag of couscous mixture.
2. Reduce heat to a simmer, stirring frequently until couscous fully rehydrates, about 5 to 10 minutes.
3. Remove couscous mixture from heat and evenly divide over 2 tortillas.
4. Add hot sauce from a single packet (about 1/2 teaspoon) to each tortilla along with small, thin slices of cheese.
5. Roll each tortilla like a burrito and serve.

1 1/2 cups instant couscous

1 (1-ounce) package Lawry's Taco Seasoning

6 medium-size flour tortillas

6 hot sauce packets or 3 teaspoons hot sauce

3-ounce block cheddar cheese, cut from larger block

1/2 cup water per serving, added on the trail

Required Equipment on the Trail:
Cook pot

Nutrition Information per Serving:
Calories: 780
Protein: 21 g
Fat: 13 g
Carbohydrates: 137 g
Fiber: 13 g
Sodium: 1,400 mg
Cholesterol: 10 mg

Tortillas carry well when packed against the relatively flat, shoulder strap-side wall of the inside of a backpack.

Kevin Corcoran
Palmdale, California

KATAHDIN TAMALE PIE

V-LO

Total Servings: 2
As Packaged for the Trail: 2 servings
Weight per Serving: About 8 ounces
Preparation Time on the Trail: 30 minutes
Challenge Level: Moderate

6 ounces MorningStar Farms Grillers Recipe Crumbles

1 cup frozen corn, thawed

1 green bell pepper, diced

¼ cup (about half of a 6-ounce can) no-salt-added tomato paste

3 tablespoons dried onion flakes

1 tablespoon chili powder

¼ teaspoon crushed red pepper

1 teaspoon cornstarch

1 (8.26-ounce) package Krusteaz One Step corn muffin mix

3⅓ cups water, divided, added on the trail

Required Equipment on the Trail:
Cook pot with lid

Preparation at Home:

1. Dry MorningStar Farm Crumbles in a dehydrator.
2. Combine corn, bell pepper, and tomato paste in a small bowl.
3. Evenly spread vegetable mixture on a lined drying tray and dehydrate.
4. Combine dehydrated ingredients along with onion flakes, chili powder, red pepper, and cornstarch in a pint-size ziplock bag.
5. Repackage corn muffin mix in a quart-size ziplock bag.

Preparation on the Trail:

1. To prepare both servings, pour entire vegetable-seasoning mixture into a cook pot along with 3 cups water. Stir.
2. Bring water to a boil, stirring often, for about 3 minutes, or until vegetables soften. Temporarily remove pot from heat.
3. Add ⅓ cup water to bag of corn muffin mix. Reseal, then knead contents to form a smooth batter.
4. Cut a small corner from the bottom of the batter bag and squeeze contents evenly over the top of the ingredients in the pot. Do not stir!
5. Set heat to very low, return cook pot to the flame, cover, and allow to steam for at least 10 minutes. Again, refrain from stirring.
6. The tamale pie is ready to serve once a knife blade inserted into the corn bread comes out clean.

Keep a close eye on the flame temperature for the final steps to keep the pie from burning. If your stove won't throttle to a very low setting, hold the pot off the flame while the corn bread steams.

Nutrition Information per Serving:
Calories: 720
Protein: 27 g
Fat: 16 g
Carbohydrates: 127 g
Fiber: 11 g
Sodium: 1,310 mg
Cholesterol: 45 mg

Walt and Jane Daniels
Mohegan Lake, New York

Authors' Note:
Special thanks to Ken Harbison for reworking Katahdin Tamale Pie from the first edition to recover the lower sodium intent of the Daniels's original recipe.

Photo by Ted Ayers

ITALIAN TRAIL COUSCOUS

Total Servings: 1
As Packaged for the Trail: 1 serving
Weight per Serving: About 9 ounces
Preparation Time on the Trail: 30 minutes
Challenge Level: Easy

V-LO

"I consider this recipe one of my classics. On some outings, I've prepared it nearly every day."

1 (6-ounce) can tomato paste

1 cup instant whole wheat couscous

3 tablespoons grated Parmesan cheese

1 teaspoon Italian seasoning blend

Optional: salt to taste

1 tablespoon olive oil

1 1/2 cups water, added on the trail

Required Equipment on the Trail:
Cook pot

Nutrition Information per Serving:
Calories: 1,020
Protein: 43 g
Fat: 24 g
Carbohydrates: 168 g
Fiber: 11 g
Sodium: 490 mg
Cholesterol: 23 mg

Preparation at Home:
1. Dry tomato paste on a lined dehydrator tray.
2. Break dried tomato paste into small pieces.
3. Combine dried tomato paste with couscous, cheese, Italian seasoning, and optional salt to taste in a pint-size ziplock bag.
4. Pack oil separately for the trail.

Preparation on the Trail:
1. To prepare 1 large serving, pour 1 1/2 cups water in a cook pot along with 1 tablespoon olive oil and the couscous mixture. Stir and let rest for about 20 minutes.
2. Bring pot to a boil, stirring frequently, then reduce heat to a simmer.
3. Continue to stir while couscous finishes cooking, about 5 minutes.

Option: For a sweeter taste, substitute a 5-ounce package pizza sauce for the tomato paste before drying.

The couscous in this recipe will have the consistency of a moist paste once the dish is ready to serve.

Luca de Alfaro
Palo Alto, California

ORIENTAL TAKEOUT

Total Servings: 4
As Packaged for the Trail: 1 serving
Weight per Serving: About 9 ounces
Preparation Time on the Trail: 45 minutes
Challenge Level: Moderate

Preparation at Home:
1. Dry shallots, bok choy, eggplant, carrots, and spinach in a dehydrator.
2. In a large bowl, combine dried vegetables with rice, mushrooms, pork sung, and contents of stir-fry seasoning packets. Toss well.
3. Evenly divide ingredients among 4 (1-quart) ziplock bags, about 2 cups each.

Preparation on the Trail:
1. To prepare a single serving, bring 3 cups water along with contents of 1 bag stir-fry to a boil in a cook pot. Stir.
2. Reduce heat to a simmer, cover pot, and continue cooking until rice begins to become tender, about 20 minutes.
3. Remove pot from heat and let sit, covered, for another 10 minutes or so. Stir once more before serving.

Options: Chicken fu sung or beef jerky can be substituted for the pork sung.

For a vegetarian dish, try substituting 1 cup dehydrated cooked beans for the pork sung, but add an additional ¼ cup water per serving to the pot when on the trail.

Parboiling the rice at home, then drying it, can cut cooking time and fuel consumed on the trail by about two-thirds.

---

1 pound shallots, chopped

1 pound bok choy, chopped

1 pound Asian eggplant, chopped and blanched

1 pound carrots, peeled, chopped, and blanched

1 pound spinach, chopped

3 cups jasmine rice

3 ounces dried mushrooms, chopped

4 ounces pork sung

2 (1-ounce) packets Noh Oriental Stir-Fry Seasoning Mix

3 cups water per serving, added on the trail

Required Equipment on the Trail:
Cook pot with lid

Nutrition Information per Serving:
Calories: 770
Protein: 22 g
Fat: 2 g
Carbohydrates: 174 g
Fiber: 13 g
Sodium: 1,580 mg
Cholesterol: 15 mg

Benedict "Ben Go" Go
Vallejo, California

GROUND BEEF GRAVEL

or

Total Servings: As required
As Packaged for the Trail: As required
Weight per Serving: 1 ounce
Preparation Time on the Trail: Less than 15 minutes
Challenge Level: Easy

"This is a generic recipe for batch drying ground beef for trail use. Dehydrate as much as needed for your upcoming trip, using with any dish that beef might be added to."

High-quality lean
ground beef

Required Equipment on the Trail:
Cook pot or frying pan

Nutrition Information per Serving:
Calories: 100
Protein: 18 g
Fat: 3 g
Carbohydrates: 0 g
Fiber: 0 g
Sodium: 60 mg
Cholesterol: 50 mg

Preparation at Home:
1. Cook beef thoroughly in a frying pan but do not char. Pour off all accumulated grease.
2. If a flavoring sauce, such as soy or Worcestershire, is desired, add it now to taste and continue to cook over low heat until the sauce liquid evaporates.
3. Spread cooked meat over paper towels.
4. Layer more paper towels over the beef, then press down to squeeze out as much fat into the paper towels as possible. *This step is imperative for prolonging the shelf life of the beef once on the trail!*
5. Break apart any remaining clumps of beef so that only very small pieces remain.
6. Thoroughly dry beef on dehydrator trays at a temperature of at least 155°F.
7. Once beef is hard as gravel, allow to cool, then add to other recipes or pack in bulk in sturdy ziplock freezer bags for the trail.

Preparation on the Trail:
Ground beef gravel can be added to most any recipe, provided the dish has adequate moisture for rehydrating the meat, about 1/4 cup water per 1 ounce gravel, and at least 5 minutes of simmer is called for in the preparation steps.

Dried ground beef can serve as a carrier for a variety of oil-free sauces, sparing the inconvenience of packing the liquids separately for the trail. As it does for jerky, the salt in the sauces also helps extend the beef's shelf life on the trail.

Properly dried beef should keep at least a couple of weeks unrefrigerated, provided that it's securely packaged and kept reasonably cool. *Never use dried meat that looks or smells rancid!*

Craig "Smitty" Smith
Springfield, Missouri

NO-DRAWINGS-NEEDED POACHED TROUT

Total Servings: 2
As Packaged for the Trail: 2 servings
Weight per Serving: Less than 1 ounce (for seasoning)
Preparation Time on the Trail: 45 minutes (plus time for fishing)
Challenge Level: Difficult

"Whenever I try to cook trout over the open campfire, I usually end up scorching the skin, drying out the flesh, or undercooking the meat near the backbone. Poached trout is a delicious, lightweight, reliable alternative. This recipe comes from a free-spirit hippie lady whom we met along Idaho's Warm Springs Creek in the 1970s."

¼ teaspoon dried basil

¼ teaspoon dried rosemary

¼ teaspoon dried thyme

¼ teaspoon ground sage

¼ teaspoon salt

¼ teaspoon ground black pepper

1 cube vegetable bouillon

2 freshly caught medium-size trout

Several cups water, added on the trail

Required Equipment on the Trail:
Frying pan with cover

Nutrition Information per Serving:
Calories: 380
Protein: 65 g
Fat: 11 g
Carbohydrates: 0 g
Fiber: 0 g
Sodium: 300 mg
Cholesterol: 188 mg

Preparation at Home:
Combine herbs, spices, and unwrapped bouillon cube in a pint-size ziplock bag.

Preparation on the Trail:
1. To prepare both servings, gut and clean 2 freshly caught trout, leaving skin on.
2. Pour 2 cups water in a frying pan, add spice-herb blend and bouillon cube, and bring water to a boil until bouillon cube dissolves.
3. Add cleaned trout to the pan in a single layer. If fish are too large to fit in the pan, cut to appropriate size. If all the fish won't fit in the pan, cook in batches.
4. Add more water until trout is mostly covered. Return water to a boil, then reduce heat to low.
5. Cover pan and poach fish for 2 minutes.
6. Remove pan from heat and allow to rest, lid on, for 10 minutes, or until flesh is firm (white or light pink, depending on the species) and cooked through to the backbone.
7. Remove fins and their short bones. Skin is good to eat, but can be discarded at this point if desired.

Another telltale sign that trout are ready to serve: The fillets on each side of the backbone can be stripped away with ease.

Roy Tryon
California City, California

GLAZED SPAM FOR FESTIVE OCCASIONS

Total Servings: 1
As Packaged for the Trail: 1 serving
Weight per Serving: About 5 ounces
Preparation Time on the Trail: 15 minutes
Challenge Level: Easy

Preparation at Home:
Pack all ingredients separately for the trail.

Preparation on the Trail:
1. To prepare 1 serving, grease frying pan with 1 tablespoon olive oil, then warm over low heat.
2. Spread sugar evenly over bottom of pan.
3. Lay Spam slices in hot pan. Brown slices on both sides before serving, being careful not to burn the meat.

1 tablespoon olive oil

2 tablespoons brown sugar

1 (3-ounce) foil pouch Spam Single Lite

Required Equipment on the Trail:
Frying pan

Spatula

Nutrition Information per Serving:
Calories: 330
Protein: 14 g
Fat: 22 g
Carbohydrates: 20 g
Fiber: 0 g
Sodium: 860 mg
Cholesterol: 91 mg

> A nonstick pan makes cleanup easier for this recipe.

Christine and Tim Conners
Statesboro, Georgia

"*A friend of mine had a recipe that caused envy among his fellow hikers. He'd place a frozen steak in the top of his pack where it would keep his vegetables cool while it was thawing during the day. He'd then have a sizzling T-bone or rib eye and fresh veggies for dinner while the rest of them ate that freeze-dried stuff.*"

—Valerie York
Alpine, California

AWFUL FALAFEL BURGERS

Total Servings: 4
As Packaged for the Trail: 1 serving
Weight per Serving: About 4 ounces
Preparation Time on the Trail: 15 minutes
Challenge Level: Easy

V-LO

"This is actually a great recipe. 'Why then should the falafel be awful?' you ask. Well, a glance at the fiber content will provide a clue. When packing Awful Falafel Burgers, it's helpful to pack the sense of humor as well because you're gonna need it!"

1 (10-ounce) package Fantastic Foods Falafel

1/4 cup dried onions

1/4 cup grated Parmesan cheese

2 tablespoons olive oil per serving

Optional: pita, bagels, or buns and favorite condiments

1/3 cup water per serving, added on the trail

Required Equipment on the Trail:
Frying pan

Spatula

Nutrition Information per Serving:
Calories: 540
Protein: 18 g
Fat: 34 g
Carbohydrates: 44 g
Fiber: 10 g
Sodium: 650 mg
Cholesterol: 5 mg

Preparation at Home:
1. Combine falafel mixture, onions, and Parmesan cheese in a medium-size bowl.
2. Stir contents in bowl and evenly divide among 4 (1-pint) ziplock bags, about 1/2 cup each.
3. Pack oil and optional bread and condiments separately for the trail.

Preparation on the Trail:
1. To prepare 1 serving, add 1/3 cup water to the falafel mixture in a single bag.
2. Seal bag and knead contents until doughlike and uniform in consistency. Allow to rest for 15 minutes.
3. Grease frying pan with 2 tablespoons olive oil and warm over low heat.
4. Form falafel mixture into 2 burger patties and flatten into the pan. If the pan is too small to hold both patties, cook one at a time.
5. Fry patties until browned on the bottom then flip, cooking the opposite side until browned as well.
6. Enjoy as is, or insert burger patty into optional pita, or place on bagel or bun, adding optional condiments at this time.

Christine and Tim Conners
Statesboro, Georgia

BEAR RIDGE SCRAMBLE

Total Servings: 3 (2 tortillas per serving)
As Packaged for the Trail: 3 servings
Weight per Serving: About 6 ounces
Preparation Time on the Trail: 15 minutes
Challenge Level: Easy

V

Preparation at Home:
1. Repackage Nature Burger mix in a quart-size ziplock bag.
2. Pack tortillas, oil, and optional ingredients separately for the trail.

Preparation on the Trail:
1. To prepare all 3 servings, add 1 1/2 cups water to the bag of Nature Burger mix.
2. Seal bag and knead contents until water has been fully and evenly absorbed.
3. Grease pan with 2 tablespoons olive oil, then warm over low heat.
4. Add burger mix to pan and scramble until heated through.
5. Serve burger scramble on tortillas. Top with optional ingredients.

1 (10-ounce) package Fantastic Foods Nature Burger mix

6 medium-size whole wheat tortillas

2 tablespoons olive oil

Optional: rehydrated dried vegetables or salsa, grated cheese, or condiments

1 1/2 cups water, added on the trail

Required Equipment on the Trail:
Frying pan

Dan and Sara Rufner
San Diego, California

Nutrition Information per Serving:
Calories: 670
Protein: 54 g
Fat: 15 g
Carbohydrates: 98 g
Fiber: 14 g
Sodium: 940 mg
Cholesterol: 0 mg

"I find that foods that may be too flavorful at home are often barely zesty enough on the trail. So I put more kick into my meals by adding a little more spice."

—Steve "Switchback" Fuquay
Las Vegas, Nevada

PIUTE MOUNTAIN PIZZA

Total Servings: 1
As Packaged for the Trail: 1 serving
Weight per Serving: About 6 ounces
Preparation Time on the Trail: 30 minutes
Challenge Level: Easy

V-LO

"The Piute Mountains are a remote and ruggedly beautiful island of greenery, rising up from the surrounding desert, an oasis over which the Pacific Crest Trail passes on its way from the Mojave to the High Sierra. We've spent a lot of time on the PCT in the Piutes, and this recipe is named for an area high on our list of favorite places. Piute Mountain Pizza is amazingly delicious and curbs that universal pizza craving we all seem to develop on long treks!"

1 (5-ounce) packet
Boboli pizza sauce

2 whole wheat pitas

1-ounce block cheddar
cheese, cut from larger
block

1 tablespoon olive oil

Optional: pepperoni,
rehydrated dried
onions, bell peppers,
mushrooms

⅓ cup water, added on
the trail

**Required Equipment on
the Trail:**
Frying pan

**Nutrition Information
per Serving:**
Calories: 630
Protein: 19 g
Fat: 28 g
Carbohydrates: 76 g
Fiber: 6 g
Sodium: 1,480 mg
Cholesterol: 35 mg

Preparation at Home:
1. Dehydrate Boboli on a lined tray until the sauce has the consistency of tough leather.
2. Tear dried sauce into small pieces.
3. Seal dried sauce in a pint-size ziplock bag.
4. Pack pitas, block cheese, and oil separately for the trail.

Preparation on the Trail:
1. To prepare 1 serving, add ⅓ cup water to the dried pizza sauce in the bag.
2. Seal bag and carefully knead for a few minutes to help pizza sauce rehydrate.
3. Slice cheese into small pieces.
4. Create a pocket in each pita, being careful not to tear the pita apart.
5. With the sauce rehydrated, cut a small corner from the bottom of the sauce bag and divide among the pita pockets, squirting the sauce directly from the bag.
6. Divide the cheese and any optional ingredients among the pita pockets.
7. Grease frying pan with 1 tablespoon olive oil and warm over low heat.
8. Place a pita into the hot pan and fry both sides.
9. Serve once cheese melts inside the pita.
10. Repeat steps 8 and 9 for the remaining pita.

*Christine and Tim Conners
Statesboro, Georgia*

MOUNTAIN QUESADILLA

Total Servings: 1
As Packaged for the Trail: 1 serving
Weight per Serving: About 7 ounces

V-LO

Preparation Time on the Trail: 15 minutes (plus 1 hour to rehydrate)
Challenge Level: Moderate

Preparation at Home:
1. Dry mushrooms, onion, and salsa in a dehydrator.
2. Tear dried salsa into small pieces.
3. Combine dried mushrooms, onions, and salsa in pint-size ziplock bag.
4. Pack cheese, tortillas, and oil separately for the trail.

Preparation on the Trail:
1. To prepare 1 serving, about an hour before dinner, add ¼ cup water to the bag of vegetables and salsa.
2. Reseal bag, knead contents, and place in a safe location until dinnertime.
3. Grease frying pan with 1 tablespoon sunflower oil and warm over low heat.
4. Add 1 tortilla to the pan and top with rehydrated salsa mix.
5. Chop cheese into small pieces and distribute over salsa.
6. Cover cheese and salsa with second tortilla.
7. Brown until cheese begins to melt, keeping a close eye so as not to burn the bottom tortilla.
8. Compress top tortilla with spatula, then flip, browning the other tortilla before serving.

8 ounces fresh sliced mushrooms

1 medium onion, chopped

½ cup chunky salsa

1-ounce block provolone cheese, cut from larger block

2 medium-size whole-wheat tortillas

1 tablespoon sunflower oil

¼ cup water, added on the trail

Required Equipment on the Trail:
Frying pan

Spatula

Nutrition Information per Serving:
Calories: 530
Protein: 23 g
Fat: 22 g
Carbohydrates: 40 g
Fiber: 11 g
Sodium: 1,520 mg
Cholesterol: 19 mg

Options: Wild onions make an excellent addition to this quesadilla. Rehydrated olives, tuna, or chicken also work very nicely with this dish.

Joe and Claire "Mongoose and Buttercup" Hageman
Trenton, North Carolina

AT

Breads

FULLER RIDGE GRANOLA FRUIT MUFFINS

V-LO

Total Servings: 12 (1 muffin per serving)
As Packaged for the Trail: Individual servings as required
Weight per Serving: About 2 ounces
Preparation Time on the Trail: None
Challenge Level: Easy

Preparation at Home:
1. Preheat oven to 425°F.
2. Combine flour, sugar, baking powder, salt, granola, and prunes in a large bowl. Stir well.
3. Add oil, egg, and milk to the bowl and stir until all ingredients are moist.
4. Spoon batter into greased muffin tins.
5. Bake for 15 minutes, then remove from oven and allow to cool.
6. Pack muffins in ziplock bags for the trail.
7. Carry optional condiments separately for the trail.

Preparation on the Trail:
Serve a muffin as is or with optional condiments.

These muffins are adequately durable for shorter backpacking trips and are an excellent treat to have waiting for you in your resupply cache on thru-hike treks. They freeze well for long-term storage at home.

Marion Davison
Apple Valley, California

1 cup whole wheat flour

¼ cup granulated sugar

1 tablespoon baking powder

½ teaspoon salt

1 cup uncooked granola

1 cup prunes, chopped

3 tablespoons sunflower oil

1 egg, beaten

1 cup 2-percent milk

Optional: your favorite condiments

Required Equipment on the Trail:
None

Nutrition Information per Serving:
Calories: 170
Protein: 4 g
Fat: 4 g
Carbohydrates: 30 g
Fiber: 2 g
Sodium: 210 mg
Cholesterol: 20 mg

PONY EXPRESS TRAIL BREAD

Total Servings: 16 (1 slice per serving)
As Packaged for the Trail: Individual servings as required
Weight per Serving: About 2 ounces
Preparation Time on the Trail: None
Challenge Level: Easy

V-LO

"This bread packs beautifully. On one occasion, I had some in the saddlebags for a short ride but completely forgot about it. Several days later, on another ride, I rediscovered the bread. It was still in excellent shape and great tasting."

2 cups all-purpose flour

2 cups whole wheat flour

1/3 cup wheat germ

3 tablespoons instant dry nonfat milk

3/4 cup packed brown sugar

1 1/2 teaspoons baking powder

1 1/2 teaspoons salt

3/4 cup water

1/2 cup honey

1/2 cup molasses

1/3 cup sunflower oil

Optional: your favorite condiments

Required Equipment on the Trail:
None

Nutrition Information per Serving:
Calories: 240
Protein: 4 g
Fat: 5 g
Carbohydrates: 50 g
Fiber: 2 g
Sodium: 250 mg
Cholesterol: 1 mg

Preparation at Home:
1. Preheat oven to 300°F.
2. Combine dry ingredients in a large bowl. Stir well.
3. Add remaining ingredients to the bowl and mix until dough is uniformly moist.
4. Pour dough into a greased 8-inch or 9-inch square baking pan.
5. Bake for about an hour, until bread has pulled away from the sides of the pan.
6. Cut warm bread into 16 squares.
7. Allow bread to cool and dry on the countertop, covered only by a paper towel, for 8 to 10 hours.
8. Pack bread in ziplock bags for the trail.
9. Carry optional condiments separately for the trail.

Preparation on the Trail:
Serve a slice of bread as is or with optional condiments.

Pony Express Trail Bread freezes well for long-term storage at home. It also dries well in a dehydrator for extended life on the trail.

Jeff and Chris Wall
Lancaster, California

Authors' Note:
This outstanding recipe has become one of the Conners's favorite energy fixes when we're on the trail.

BANJO BREAD

Total Servings: 24 (1 bar per serving)
As Packaged for the Trail: Individual servings as required
Weight per Serving: About 3 ounces
Preparation Time on the Trail: None
Challenge Level: Easy

V-LO

"I've stored dried Banjo Bread in ziplock bags for six months with no problems. Don't know if it lasts longer than that, because it's always gone by then! It is very dense. But, then again, that's the beauty of it."

Preparation at Home:

1. In a very large bowl, combine oats, flour, baking powder, dry milk, salt, brown sugar, cinnamon, nutmeg, dried fruit, and nuts. Mix thoroughly to eliminate clumps.
2. In a separate bowl, whisk together oil, honey, molasses, and water.
3. Add the wet ingredients to the dry ingredients and fold all together, adding water as needed to produce a spreadable, but still thick, dough.
4. Spread dough at a uniform depth nearly to the edges of a lightly greased cookie sheet.
5. Bake at 300°F for 60 to 70 minutes, then score dough into 24 bars.
6. Reduce oven temperature to its lowest setting and continue baking until bread becomes bone-dry. Alternately, the bread can finish drying in a dehydrator.
7. Set bread squares aside to cool, then pack in ziplock bags for the trail.
8. Carry optional condiments separately.

Preparation on the Trail:

Serve a square as is or with optional condiments.

Required Equipment on the Trail:

None

Chris Counts
Clear Lake City, Texas

3 cups regular oats

4 cups whole wheat flour

2 teaspoons baking powder

$1/2$ cup instant dry whole milk

1 tablespoon salt

1 cup light brown sugar

$1/2$ teaspoon ground cinnamon

$1/2$ teaspoon ground nutmeg

2 cups mixed dried fruit (your favorite), diced

2 cups nuts (your favorite), diced

$1/2$ cup sunflower oil

$3/4$ cup honey

2 tablespoons molasses

2 cups water

Optional: your favorite condiments

Nutrition Information per Serving:
Calories: 340
Protein: 8 g
Fat: 13 g
Carbohydrates: 59 g
Fiber: 6 g
Sodium: 280 mg
Cholesterol: 3 mg

THE CANADIANS' AMAZING TRAPPERS BREAD

Total Servings: 40 (1 slice per serving)
As Packaged for the Trail: Individual servings as required
Weight per Serving: About 3 ounces
Preparation Time on the Trail: None
Challenge Level: Easy

V-LO

"Properly wrapped and stored, this bread will keep for weeks without refrigeration."

2 quarts water

1½ cups raisins

1½ cups currants

3 cups hot water

1 cup brown sugar

1 tablespoon salt

1 cup (2 standard sticks) plus 1 tablespoon butter

1 cup molasses

2 tablespoons granulated sugar

1 cup lukewarm water

2 tablespoons active dry yeast

6 cups whole wheat flour

6 cups all-purpose flour

Optional: your favorite condiments

Required Equipment on the Trail:
None

Nutrition Information per Serving:
Calories: 210
Protein: 4 g
Fat: 10 g
Carbohydrates: 28 g
Fiber: 3 g
Sodium: 100 mg
Cholesterol: 12 mg

Preparation at Home:

1. Bring 2 quarts water to a boil, then add raisins and currants. Cook fruit for 30 minutes, or until raisins become plump. Drain pot and set fruit aside.

2. In a very large bowl, combine hot water, brown sugar, salt, 1 cup butter, and molasses. Stir ingredients until butter melts, then allow to cool until lukewarm.

3. Meanwhile, in a separate small bowl, dissolve granulated sugar in lukewarm water (105°F to 115°F), then sprinkle dry yeast over the sugar mixture.

4. Allow yeast liquid to rest and foam for about 10 minutes before whisking briskly with a fork. Add yeast liquid to molasses mixture and stir.

5. Add the whole wheat flour to the mixture; beat in by hand.

6. Add the now-plumped fruit, along with the all-purpose flour, and blend all ingredients together by hand using a rotating motion.

7. Turn dough onto a lightly floured surface and knead for 8 to 10 minutes.

8. Shape dough into a smooth ball, then place into greased bowl. Rotate dough ball in the bowl to oil the entire surface.

9. Cover greased bowl with a damp cloth, then allow dough to rise in a warm location until it doubles in size, about 2 hours.

10. Punch down the dough, then divide into 4 loaves of roughly equal size. Place each loaf into an 8½ x 4½-inch loaf pan.

11. Cover the 4 pans with a cloth, return to warm location, and allow dough to rise once again until doubled in size, about 1 hour.

12. Preheat oven to 375°F, then bake all 4 loaves simultaneously for 40 to 50 minutes, until a knife inserted into the loaves comes out clean. Do not allow bread to burn.
13. Melt 1 tablespoon butter, then brush tops of the hot loaves with the melted butter.
14. Allow loaves to cool before storing. Or, if ready to pack, cut each loaf into 10 slices and store in ziplock bags. These loaves freeze well for storage.
15. Pack optional condiments for the trail.

Preparation on the Trail: Serve a slice as is or with optional condiments.

Debbie Higgins and Peter Sandiford, " The Canadians" Quebec, Canada

SUTLIFF'S LOGAN BREAD

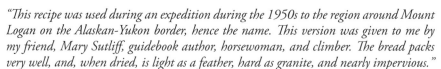

Total Servings: 42 (1 slice per serving)
As Packaged for the Trail: Individual servings as required
Weight per Serving: About 3 ounces
V-LO
Preparation Time on the Trail: None
Challenge Level: Easy

"This recipe was used during an expedition during the 1950s to the region around Mount Logan on the Alaskan-Yukon border, hence the name. This version was given to me by my friend, Mary Sutliff, guidebook author, horsewoman, and climber. The bread packs very well, and, when dried, is light as a feather, hard as granite, and nearly impervious."

1½ cups water

1¾ cups granulated sugar

2 cups applesauce

½ cup molasses

⅔ cup honey

2 cups (4 standard sticks) butter

8 cups whole wheat flour

2⅔ cups all-purpose flour

2 teaspoons baking soda

1 teaspoon baking powder

1 teaspoon ground cloves

1 teaspoon ground nutmeg

Optional: your favorite condiments

Required Equipment on the Trail:
None

Nutrition Information per Serving:
Calories: 250
Protein: 4 g
Fat: 11 g
Carbohydrates: 38 g
Fiber: 3 g
Sodium: 160 mg
Cholesterol: 23 mg

Preparation at Home:
1. Combine water, sugar, applesauce, molasses, honey, and butter in a saucepan and bring to a boil, stirring often. Immediately remove from heat.
2. In a large bowl, combine remaining dry ingredients, then add liquid from the saucepan. Stir well.
3. Preheat oven to 300°F.
4. Evenly divide batter among 3 greased 9⅝ x 5½-inch or 5 greased 8½ x 4½-inch loaf pans.
5. Bake the bread for 1 hour, then set aside to cool before cutting into about 42 slices.
6. Pack bread in ziplock bags for the trail.
7. Carry optional condiments separately.

Preparation on the Trail:
Serve a slice as is or with optional condiments.

Options: *Drying Logan Bread in a dehydrator further improves durability and reduces weight.*

Slicing the bread in strips prior to drying results in a texture and flavor similar to biscotti, excellent for dipping in your cowboy coffee while on the trail!

Ann Marshall
Port Orchard, Washington

TABLE MOUNTAIN ORANGE BREAD

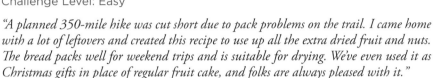

V-LO

Total Servings: 8 (1 slice per serving)
As Packaged for the Trail: Individual servings as required
Weight per Serving: About 5 ounces
Preparation Time on the Trail: None
Challenge Level: Easy

"A planned 350-mile hike was cut short due to pack problems on the trail. I came home with a lot of leftovers and created this recipe to use up all the extra dried fruit and nuts. The bread packs well for weekend trips and is suitable for drying. We've even used it as Christmas gifts in place of regular fruit cake, and folks are always pleased with it."

Preparation at Home:
1. Preheat oven to 350°F.
2. In a large bowl, combine flours, sugar, baking powder, and salt.
3. Add orange juice, milk, oil, and egg to the bowl and mix until well blended.
4. Stir nuts and fruit into the dough.
5. Pour dough into a greased 8 1/2 x 4 1/2-inch loaf pan.
6. Bake for about 65 minutes or until a knife inserted in the center of the loaf comes out clean.
7. Allow loaf to cool before storing. Or, if ready to pack, cut loaf into 8 slices and store in ziplock bags.
8. Pack optional condiments for the trail.

Preparation on the Trail:
Serve a slice as is or with optional condiments.

Option: Use 1 1/4 cups of your favorite dried fruit blend in place of the Sun Maid mixed fruit.

Marion Davison
Apple Valley, California

2 cups whole wheat flour

1 1/2 cups all-purpose flour

3/4 cup granulated sugar

2 teaspoons baking powder

1/2 teaspoon salt

3/4 cup orange juice

1/2 cup 2-percent milk

1/2 cup sunflower oil

1 egg

1/2 cup dry-roasted mixed nuts, chopped

1 (7-ounce) package Sun Maid dried mixed fruit, chopped

Optional: your favorite condiments

Required Equipment on the Trail:
None

Nutrition Information per Serving:
Calories: 510
Protein: 10 g
Fat: 20 g
Carbohydrates: 75 g
Fiber: 6 g
Sodium: 330 mg
Cholesterol: 28 mg

SWISS ALPS BREAD

V-LO

Total Servings: 16 (2 slices per serving)
As Packaged for the Trail: Individual servings as required
Weight per Serving: About 4 ounces
Preparation Time on the Trail: None
Challenge Level: Easy

2 cups milk

1 cup plus 1 teaspoon granulated sugar

1½ cups (3 standard sticks) unsalted butter, cold

1 teaspoon plus 7½ cups all-purpose flour

1 teaspoon warm milk

1 (¼-ounce) package rapid-rise yeast

4 eggs

2 teaspoons vanilla extract

Optional: your favorite condiments

Required Equipment on the Trail:
None

Nutrition Information per Serving:
Calories: 420
Protein: 8 g
Fat: 20 g
Carbohydrates: 56 g
Fiber: 1 g
Sodium: 200 mg
Cholesterol: 95 mg

Preparation at Home:

1. Heat milk in a saucepan until scalded, then immediately remove pan from hot burner.

2. Add 1 cup sugar and the butter to the pan, then stir until butter melts.

3. In a small nonmetallic bowl, combine 1 teaspoon flour, 1 teaspoon sugar, and warm milk, then immediately stir in the yeast. Set bowl aside in warm location.

4. In a large bowl, beat eggs with vanilla extract.

5. Add the scalded milk, yeast mixture, and 7½ cups flour to the egg mixture. Stir well to form a smooth dough.

6. Turn dough onto a lightly floured surface and knead for at least 5 minutes, adding a little more dough if required to prevent sticking.

7. Shape dough into a smooth ball and place into a greased bowl. Rotate dough ball in the bowl to oil the entire surface.

8. Cover greased bowl with a damp cloth, then allow dough to rise in a warm location until it doubles in size, about 2½ to 3 hours.

9. Turn dough onto floured surface again and knead for a few moments, then divide into 4 loaves of equal size.

10. Place each loaf into an 8½ x 4½-inch loaf pan.

11. Cover pans with a cloth, return to warm location, and allow dough to rise for another hour.

12. Preheat oven to 350°F and cover each of the pans with aluminum foil. Bake all 4 loaves simultaneously for 45 minutes, until an inserted knife comes out clean.

13. Allow loaves to cool before storing. Or, if ready to pack, cut each loaf into 8 slices and store in ziplock bags.
14. Pack optional condiments for the trail.

Preparation on the Trail: Serve a couple of slices as is or with optional condiments.

Cathy Czachorowski
Torrington, Connecticut

This bread can be dehydrated to extend storage life and reduce pack weight.

WHOLE-GRAIN TRAIL BREAD MIX

 or

V-LO

Total Servings: 7
As Packaged for the Trail: Individual servings as required
Weight per Serving: About 5 ounces
Preparation Time on the Trail: 15 minutes
Challenge Level: Easy to Moderate

"This is a versatile, basic mix for making several different bread products on the trail."

3 cups all-purpose flour

2 cups whole wheat flour

1/2 cup wheat bran

1 cup wheat germ

2 tablespoons baking powder

1 teaspoon salt

1/2 cup instant dry buttermilk

1-3 tablespoons sunflower oil per serving

For pan bread, biscuits, or dumplings: about 1/3 cup water per serving, added on the trail

For pancakes or tortillas: about 1/2 cup water per serving, added on the trail

Required Equipment on the Trail:
Cook pot with lid, or

Frying pan with cover and spatula

Preparation at Home:
1. Combine all dry ingredients in a large bowl. Mix thoroughly.
2. Evenly divide bread mix into 7 (1-pint) ziplock freezer bags, about 1 cup each.
3. Pack oil separately for the trail.

Preparation on the Trail—Pan Bread or Biscuits:
1. To prepare 1 serving, grease frying pan with 1 tablespoon sunflower oil and warm over low heat.
2. Add about 1/3 cup water and 1 tablespoon sunflower oil to 1 bag bread mix.
3. Reseal bag. Knead contents until smooth.
4. Snip large corner from the bottom of the dough bag and squeeze contents into hot pan, either as individual biscuits or smoothed into a single dough patty.
5. Cover pan until bread has risen and is lightly browned on the pan side.
6. Flip bread, brown the other side, then serve.

Preparation on the Trail—Pancakes or Tortillas:
1. To prepare 1 serving, grease frying pan with 2 tablespoons sunflower oil and warm over low heat.
2. Add about 1/2 cup water and 1 tablespoon sunflower oil to 1 bag bread mix.
3. Reseal bag. Knead contents until smooth.
4. Snip small corner from the bottom of the dough bag and carefully squeeze contents into hot pan, forming either pancakes or, by further smoothing the dough, thin tortillas.
5. Briefly brown both sides before serving.

Preparation on the Trail—Soup Dumplings:
1. To prepare 1 serving, add about ⅓ cup water and 1 tablespoon sunflower oil to 1 bag bread mix.
2. Reseal bag and knead contents into a smooth dough.
3. Snip large corner from the bottom of the dough bag and squeeze contents as individual dough balls into hot soup (prepared separately) in a cook pot.
4. Cover pot and simmer for an additional 2 minutes or until dumplings are thoroughly cooked

Kathleen "The Old Gray Goose" Cutshall Conneaut, Ohio

Nutrition Information per Serving:
Calories: 190
Protein: 8 g
Fat: 2 g plus additional 14 g per tablespoon oil
Carbohydrates: 39 g
Fiber: 4 g
Sodium: 360 mg
Cholesterol: 3 mg

Photo by Wayne Kodama

CHAPATIS INDIAN HERB BREAD

Total Servings: 2
As Packaged for the Trail: 2 servings
Weight per Serving: About 3 ounces
Preparation Time on the Trail: 15 minutes
   (plus about an hour for bread to rise)
Challenge Level: Difficult

V

1 cup all-purpose flour

1/2 teaspoon Italian
seasoning blend

1/2 teaspoon salt

1 tablespoon olive oil

3/8 cup (6 tablespoons)
water, added on the trail

**Required Equipment on
the Trail:**
Frying pan

Spatula

**Nutrition Information
per Serving:**
Calories: 210
Protein: 6 g
Fat: 7 g
Carbohydrates: 44 g
Fiber: 2 g
Sodium: 580 mg
Cholesterol: 0 mg

Preparation at Home:
1. Combine all dry ingredients in a pint-size ziplock freezer bag.
2. Pack oil separately for the trail.

Preparation on the Trail:
1. To prepare both servings, add 3/8 cup (6 tablespoons) water to the bag of bread mix.
2. Reseal bag and knead contents until smooth.
3. Allow bread dough to rest for about an hour, then knead well once again.
4. Grease frying pan with 1 tablespoon olive oil, then warm over low heat.
5. Roll dough until very thin, about the thickness of two credit cards.
6. Immediately place dough in hot pan and fry, flipping occasionally until brown spots appear.

Option: Chapatis is excellent warm with a little peanut butter.

A sturdy cylindrical water bottle serves nicely as a rolling pin for this recipe, and the bottom of a cook pot can work as the rolling surface.

To achieve perfectly thin dough, this recipe requires very close attention to the amount of flour packed for the trail as well as the quantity of water added on the trail. Be sure you'll have the ability, once on the trail, to precisely measure the somewhat odd quantity of water this recipe calls for.

---

*Gary "Doctari" Adams
Cincinnati, Ohio*

BULK-BUILDING BREAD-ON-A-BRANCH

V-LO

Total Servings: 13
As Packaged for the Trail: 1 serving
Weight per Serving: About 3 ounces
Preparation Time on the Trail: 15 minutes
Challenge Level: Moderate

Preparation at Home:
1. Combine all dry ingredients in a large bowl. Mix thoroughly.
2. Evenly divide bread mix into 13 (1-pint) ziplock bags, about 1/2 cup each.

Preparation on the Trail:
1. To prepare a single serving, add 1/4 cup water to 1 bag bread mix.
2. Reseal bag and knead contents to the consistency of pie dough.
3. Form dough into a ribbon and wrap around the peeled end of a smooth branch to form a 6-inch-long "blanket." Seal the end with a flap of dough.
4. Bake bread over a campfire until golden brown, being careful not to burn the dough.
5. Slide or peel from the branch to eat.

> Some shrubs and trees are toxic! Exercise caution when selecting a cooking stick for this recipe.

> Use only branches collected from the ground and, then, only in areas where downed wood is plentiful and gathering is permitted.

Sandy Lee Burns
Prospect, Oregon

1/2 cup whole wheat flour
1/2 cup barley flour
1/2 cup rye flour
1/2 cup oat flour
1 cup all-purpose flour
1/2 cup ground sesame seeds
1/2 cup whole sesame seeds
1/2 cup flaxseed
1/2 cup sunflower seed kernels
1/2 teaspoon salt
2 teaspoons baking powder
1 teaspoon baking soda
1 1/2 cups instant dry nonfat milk
1/2 cup ground rice or wheat germ
1/4 cup water per serving, added on the trail

Required Equipment on the Trail:
Cooking stick, found along trail

Nutrition Information per Serving:
Calories: 230
Protein: 12 g
Fat: 15 g
Carbohydrates: 26 g
Fiber: 5 g
Sodium: 270 mg
Cholesterol: 3 mg

LAZY BOY ROY'S BISCUIT-ON-A-STICK

Total Servings: 2
As Packaged for the Trail: 2 servings
Weight per Serving: About 3 ounces
Preparation Time on the Trail: 15 minutes
Challenge Level: Moderate

V

"This recipe is super-great for older kids, because they can do it themselves and the results are really tasty."

1 cup Bisquick Heart Smart Pancake and Baking Mix

⅓ cup water, added on the trail

Required Equipment on the Trail:
Cooking stick, found along the trail

Nutrition Information per Serving:
Calories: 210
Protein: 5 g
Fat: 9 g
Carbohydrates: 41 g
Fiber: 1 g
Sodium: 510 mg
Cholesterol: 0 mg

Preparation at Home:
Pack Bisquick in a pint-size ziplock bag.

Preparation on the Trail:
1. To prepare both servings, add a little less than ⅓ cup water to the bag of mix.
2. Reseal the bag and knead contents into a stiff dough.
3. Open bag and add dribbles of water to the dough mix. Reseal, then knead to produce a moist, but not runny, texture. Repeat as necessary.
4. Snip a corner from bottom of the dough bag.
5. Squeeze about half the dough evenly onto a cooking stick with one hand while slowly twirling the stick with the other hand in candy-cane fashion.
6. Bake dough over the campfire, while slowly turning the stick, until the biscuit becomes golden brown. Be careful not to burn the dough.
7. Peel biscuit from the branch to eat.
8. Repeat steps 5 through 7 for the second serving.

Options: Try adding Butter Buds, grated cheese, sugar, or instant milk to the dry mix for variety.
The dough can be removed from the bag and directly wrapped around the stick before baking, but a little vegetable oil will be required on your hands to prevent a sticky mess.

Some shrubs and trees are toxic! Exercise caution when selecting a cooking stick for this recipe.

Use only branches collected from the ground and, then, only in areas where downed wood is plentiful and gathering is permitted.

Roy Tryon
California City, California

DAMPER

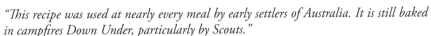

V-LO

Total Servings: 4 (½ loaf per serving)
As Packaged for the Trail: 2 servings
Weight per Serving: About 5 ounces
Preparation Time on the Trail: 45 minutes
Challenge Level: Difficult

"This recipe was used at nearly every meal by early settlers of Australia. It is still baked in campfires Down Under, particularly by Scouts."

1 cup instant dry nonfat milk

1 (½-ounce) packet Butter Buds

2 cups self-rising flour

1 cup whole wheat flour

Optional: handful of raisins or chopped dried fruit; your favorite condiments

½ cup water per loaf, added on the trail

Required Equipment on the Trail:
None

Nutrition Information per Serving:
Calories: 410
Protein: 14 g
Fat: 1 g
Carbohydrates: 85 g
Fiber: 5 g
Sodium: 980 mg
Cholesterol: 3 mg

Preparation at Home:
1. Combine all dry ingredients in a medium-size bowl. Stir well.
2. Divide ingredients evenly into 2 quart-size ziplock bags, about 2 cups in each bag.
3. Pack optional raisins, dried fruit, and condiments separately for the trail.

Preparation on the Trail:
1. To prepare both servings, add ½ cup water to 1 bag bread mix.
2. Reseal the bag and knead contents into a uniform dough.
3. Remove dough from bag and form into a ball.
4. Bury the damper ball directly in the hot coals of a campfire.
5. Bake for 20 to 30 minutes, then insert a knife into the bread ball. Once the knife extracts cleanly, the damper is finished cooking.
6. Very carefully remove damper from coals and trim off burnt exterior.
7. Serve as is or with optional condiments.

Options: The damper ball can also be wrapped in aluminum foil before baking to reduce charring of the crust. It can also be cooked in a covered pan or folded around a branch and roasted like a sausage-on-a-stick over the campfire.

*Geoff O'Hara
Honolulu, Hawaii*

Snacks and Desserts

WATERMELON CANDY

V

Total Servings: 1
As Packaged for the Trail: 1 serving
Weight per Serving: About 1 ounce
Preparation Time on the Trail: None
Challenge Level: Easy

"The best candy around!"

1 pound fresh seedless
watermelon

**Required Equipment on
the Trail:**
None

**Nutrition Information
per Serving:**
Calories: 140
Protein: 3 g
Fat: 2 g
Carbohydrates: 32 g
Fiber: 2 g
Sodium: 20 mg
Cholesterol: 0 mg

Preparation at Home:
1. Slice watermelon into 1-inch cubes.
2. Dehydrate melon until thoroughly dry, then
   package in a ziplock bag for the trail.

Preparation on the Trail:
Just try not to eat it all at once!

The weight of the fresh watermelon is
measured after it has been prepared, i.e.,
with rind removed.

---

*Dan and Sara Rufner
San Diego, California*

YOSEMITE FALLS YOGURT DROPS

V-LO

Total Servings: 1
As Packaged for the Trail: 1 serving
Weight per Serving: About 1 ounce
Preparation Time on the Trail: None
Challenge Level: Easy

Preparation at Home:
1. Drop tablespoon-size dollops of yogurt onto a lined drying tray.
2. Dehydrate yogurt until it is firm and leathery throughout.
3. Package yogurt drops in a snack-size ziplock bag for the trail.

Preparation on the Trail:
Enjoy a bag of yogurt drops as a midday walking snack.

Options: *Try adding finely pureed fresh fruit or flavor extracts to plain yogurt before drying.*

Yogurt can also be dried as a single sheet of "leather" then rolled once dry.

Christine and Tim Conners
Statesboro, Georgia

1 (6-ounce) container vanilla or blended-fruit yogurt

Required Equipment on the Trail:
None

Nutrition Information per Serving:
Calories: 190
Protein: 7 g
Fat: 2 g
Carbohydrates: 35 g
Fiber: 0 g
Sodium: 120 mg
Cholesterol: 10 mg

FUEL FUDGE

Total Servings: 32 (1 bar per serving)
As Packaged for the Trail: 1 serving
Weight per Serving: About 1 ounce
Preparation Time on the Trail: None
Challenge Level: Easy

"I got the idea for this recipe in Maine when a fellow long-distance hiker related how he ate pure butter and grease at bedtime in cold weather to help keep warm during the night. Fuel Fudge is very rich and not for 'recreational' consumption! I eat a small amount late in the day when I really need the energy or on chilly evenings before sliding into the sleeping bag."

1 (16-ounce) jar creamy peanut butter

½ cup hot bacon grease, strained

½ cup honey

3 cups instant dry nonfat milk

2 cups peanuts, crushed

1 cup raisins

1 cup sweetened flaked coconut

Required Equipment on the Trail:
None

Nutrition Information per Serving:
Calories: 250
Protein: 9 g
Fat: 19 g
Carbohydrates: 19 g
Fiber: 3 g
Sodium: 110 mg
Cholesterol: 6 mg

Preparation at Home:
1. Microwave peanut butter for about 1 minute, or until it flows easily.
2. Pour peanut butter into large mixing bowl, then stir in hot bacon grease.
3. Blend honey, dry milk, peanuts, raisins, and coconut into peanut butter mixture.
4. Evenly divide fudge mixture between 2 (8-inch-square) baking pans, spreading to a uniform depth. Set pans aside to cool.
5. Slice fudge in each pan into 16 squares for 32 pieces total, then pack for the trail in small ziplock bags.

Preparation on the Trail:
Serve a bar of Fuel Fudge as a snack during the day or for dessert.

Option: You can use ½ cup pure lard in place of the bacon grease.

Fuel Fudge may turn a bit gloppy after a couple of weeks on the trail, but it will still taste very good. It will keep unrefrigerated for about 4 weeks without spoilage.

John Woodall
Simpsonville, South Carolina

MOUNTAIN LAKES TRAIL FROSTING

Total Servings: 3
As Packaged for the Trail: 1 serving
Weight per Serving: About 1 ounce
Preparation Time on the Trail: Less than 5 minutes
Challenge Level: Easy

V-LO

Preparation at Home:
1. Combine all dry ingredients in a medium-size bowl and stir.
2. Evenly divide dry ingredients among 3 snack-size ziplock bags, about 3 tablespoons frosting in each.
3. Pack oil separately for the trail.

Preparation on the Trail:
1. To prepare a single serving, add 1 teaspoon sunflower oil and 2 teaspoons water to 1 bag frosting mix.
2. Reseal bag and knead mixture until uniformly smooth.
3. Snip small corner from bottom of bag and squeeze frosting over cake or other dessert.

Deborah Brill and Scott "Marty" Place Berkeley, California

1½ teaspoons instant dry buttermilk

5 tablespoons confectioners' sugar

1 teaspoon all-purpose flour

1 single-serving packet hot cocoa mix

3 teaspoons Butter Buds

1 teaspoon sunflower oil per serving

2 teaspoons water per serving, added on the trail

Optional: Spread over Mammoth Lakes Plop Cake (see recipe in this book)

Required Equipment on the Trail:
None

Nutrition Information per Serving:
Calories: 140
Protein: 1 g
Fat: 4 g
Carbohydrates: 26 g
Fiber: 0 g
Sodium: 100 mg
Cholesterol: 1 mg

ROCKY FORK FRUIT LEATHER

Total Servings: 2
As Packaged for the Trail: 1 serving
Weight per Serving: About 2 ounces
Preparation Time on the Trail: None
Challenge Level: Easy

"When I was a boy, my folks had a small plot of land near Rocky Fork Lake in the countryside of southern Ohio. We often camped there in our small trailer to get away from the stress of the city. I loved Rocky Fork, and it was there that I also learned to love the outdoors as well as the fun and fellowship that come with a campfire."

—Tim

2 pounds prepared fresh fruit (your favorite)

1 tablespoon lemon juice

Required Equipment on the Trail:
None

Nutrition Information per Serving (approximate):
Calories: 250
Protein: 5 g
Fat: 2 g
Carbohydrates: 60 g
Fiber: 15 g
Sodium: 10 mg
Cholesterol: 0 mg

Preparation at Home:
1. Add fruit and lemon juice to a blender and puree until smooth.
2. Cover 2 inverted baking sheets with parchment paper and pour puree over each sheet to a depth of no more than about 1/4 inch, leaving at least a 1-inch border between the puree and the edge of each tray.
3. Dry puree in oven at 140°F, or at lowest heat setting if higher than this, until puree becomes leathery, still pliable but losing its stickiness. This can take from 5 to 10 hours.
4. Once dry, set the leather aside to cool, then roll and cut into desired lengths and divide between 2 (1-pint) ziplock bags for the trail.

Preparation on the Trail:
Enjoy a bag of fruit leather during the day while walking along the trail or anytime a healthy snack is desired.

Option: Frozen fruit, thawed, or light-packed canned fruit, drained, can be substituted for the fresh fruit.

The weight of the fresh fruit is measured after it has been prepared, i.e., with skin, rind, seeds, and core removed.

Some fruits, especially when combined, produce a more uniform and pliable leather than others. Experiment with fresh fruits to discover which produce your favorite leathers.

Food dehydrators also produce fine fruit leathers and can be used in place of the oven for this recipe.

Christine and Tim Conners
Statesboro, Georgia

SUPER-DUPER MEGA RICE KRISPIE TREAT

Total Servings: 12 (2 bars per serving)
As Packaged for the Trail: Individual servings as required
Weight per Serving: About 2 ounces
Preparation Time on the Trail: None
Challenge Level: Easy

"My last Super-Duper Mega Rice Krispie Treat had a surface area of 5 square-feet and made for a nice conversation piece."

¼ cup (½ standard stick) butter

40 large marshmallows

6 cups Rice Krispies cereal

1 cup unsalted raw cashew halves

1 cup Ocean Spray Craisins

1 tablespoon vegetable shortening

Required Equipment on the Trail:
None

Nutrition Information per Serving:
Calories: 220
Protein: 2 g
Fat: 16 g
Carbohydrates: 32 g
Fiber: 2 g
Sodium: 30 mg
Cholesterol: 80 mg

Preparation at Home:

1. Place butter in a large microwave-safe bowl and melt in a microwave oven at medium power.
2. Add marshmallows to the bowl in the microwave oven and cook at medium power until marshmallows melt.
3. Remove bowl from oven and stir in Rice Krispies, cashews, and Craisins until well-mixed.
4. While it is still warm and pliable, press mixture into a greased 15¼ x 10¼-inch baking pan.
5. Set pan aside to cool then slice Krispie Treat into 24 bars.
6. Package bars for the trail in ziplock bags.

Preparation on the Trail:
Have a couple of treats for dessert.

Option: Try including peanuts, quick oats, raisins, or dried cranberries in small quantities as well.

*Craig Giffen
Portland, Oregon*

PEANUT BUTTER FUDGE

V-LO

Total Servings: 16 (1 square per serving)
As Packaged for the Trail: Individual servings as required
Weight per Serving: About 2 ounces
Preparation Time on the Trail: None
Challenge Level: Easy

Preparation at Home:
1. Preheat oven to 350°F.
2. Combine oats, condensed milk, salt, and vanilla extract in a medium-size bowl.
3. Stir peanut butter and chocolate chips into oat mixture.
4. Press oat-peanut butter mixture into greased 8-inch-square baking pan.
5. Bake for 30 minutes then set aside to cool.
6. Slice fudge into 16 squares, then package in small ziplock bags for the trail.

Preparation on the Trail:
Have a square of fudge as a snack or for dessert.

Marion Davison
Apple Valley, California

1½ cups quick oats

1 (14-ounce) can sweetened condensed milk

½ teaspoon salt

1 teaspoon vanilla extract

½ cup chunky peanut butter

1 (12-ounce) bag semisweet chocolate chips

Required Equipment on the Trail:
None

Nutrition Information per Serving:
Calories: 260
Protein: 5 g
Fat: 12 g
Carbohydrates: 35 g
Fiber: 1 g
Sodium: 140 mg
Cholesterol: 6 mg

SECRET-TO-SUCCESS COOKIES

Total Servings: 30 (4 cookies per serving)
As Packaged for the Trail: Individual servings as required
Weight per Serving: About 2 ounces
Preparation Time on the Trail: None
Challenge Level: Easy

V-LO

"These cookies were my secret to success when I thru-hiked the Appalachian and Pacific Crest trails. I baked a few thousand before both of my hikes then froze them before having them shipped to me in my food-supply packages. The cookies were a very satisfying treat after dinner, a gift to myself for hiking hard. I also found them to be a very valuable commodity on the trail, useful as capital, gifts, or just a way to make someone happy."

2 cups (4 standard sticks) butter

3 eggs

1½ cups granulated sugar

1½ cups dark brown sugar

4 teaspoons vanilla extract

3 cups all-purpose flour

4 teaspoons baking powder

4 teaspoons ground cinnamon

1 cup wheat bran

3 cups quick oats

1½ cups walnuts, chopped

3 cups semisweet chocolate chips

Required Equipment on the Trail:
None

Nutrition Information per Serving:
Calories: 430
Protein: 8 g
Fat: 24 g
Carbohydrates: 52 g
Fiber: 4 g
Sodium: 120 mg
Cholesterol: 56 mg

Preparation at Home:
1. Preheat oven to 350°F.
2. Combine all ingredients in a very large bowl then blend using a hand mixer. If dough remains runny, add more oats in small quantities until dough firms.
3. Drop teaspoon-size balls of cookie dough on greased baking sheets then bake for 10 to 12 minutes.
4. Set cookies aside to cool before packing in ziplock bags for the trail.

Preparation on the Trail:
Serve 4 cookies to make a satisfying serving.

Option: Raisins can be substituted for the chocolate chips.

*Allmuth "Curly" Perzel
Tolland, Connecticut*

CAMPIN' CANDY BARS

V-LO

Total Servings: 32 (1 bar per serving)
As Packaged for the Trail: Individual servings as required
Weight per Serving: About 2 ounces
Preparation Time on the Trail: None
Challenge Level: Easy

Preparation at Home:

1. In a medium-size microwave-safe bowl, melt chocolate and butterscotch chips in microwave oven at low power then stir in honey.
2. In a large microwave-safe bowl, combine all remaining ingredients then blend in the chocolate-butterscotch mix. Stir well.
3. Pour mixture onto a greased baking sheet, about 10 by 15 inches in size. If batter has cooled and become too stiff to pour, first soften in microwave oven at low power.
4. Allow batter to fully cool then cut into 32 bars.
5. Pack bars in ziplock bags for the trail.

Preparation on the Trail:

One campin' bar makes for a great snack on the trail or in camp at the end of the day.

Jane and Walt Daniels
Mohegan Lake, New York

2 (12-ounce) packages milk chocolate chips

2 (6-ounce) packages butterscotch chips

$\frac{1}{2}$ cup honey

$\frac{1}{2}$ cup dates, chopped

1 cup apricots, chopped

1 cup yellow raisins

$\frac{1}{2}$ cup sweetened shredded coconut

$1\frac{1}{2}$ cups Rice Krispies cereal

$\frac{1}{2}$ cup granola cereal

$\frac{1}{2}$ cup wheat germ

$\frac{1}{2}$ cup unsalted sunflower seed kernels

$\frac{1}{2}$ cup unsalted sesame seeds

$\frac{1}{2}$ cup salted cashews, chopped

Required Equipment on the Trail:
None

Nutrition Information per Serving:
Calories: 270
Protein: 4 g
Fat: 14 g
Carbohydrates: 38 g
Fiber: 2 g
Sodium: 70 mg
Cholesterol: 6 mg

SNACKS FOR TRAIL DOGS (AND TRAIL PEOPLE)

Total Servings: about 100 (1 biscuit per serving)
As Packaged for the Trail: Individual servings as required
Weight per Serving: About 2 ounces
Preparation Time on the Trail: None
Challenge Level: Easy

"I made this wholesome and healthy biscuit recipe for my own dog, Bernadette, and she went from glum and sore-footed to peppy every step for 400 continuous miles. I ate them, too, and they really are nutritious and delicious! – Sandy Lee Burns"

2 cups regular oats

2 cups brown rice

2 cups rolled barley

2 cups rolled rye

2 cups rolled wheat

2 cups rolled triticale

2 cups millet

2 cups cornmeal

1 pound dry bean mix

4 quarts vegetable broth (made without potatoes)

3 cups instant dry whole milk

2 tablespoons salt

15 crushed kelp tablets

1 cup garlic powder

1 cup dried oregano

1/3 cup high-quality bone meal

1 cup shredded carrots

2 cups corn oil

6 cups whole-wheat flour

Preparation at Home:

1. Soak oats, rice, barley, rye, rolled wheat, triticale, millet, cornmeal, and mixed beans overnight in the vegetable broth.

2. Stir instant milk into soaked ingredients and cook in a very large pot over low heat until beans are soft.

3. Remove pot from heat then stir in remaining ingredients. The mix will be very thick and heavy. Set aside to cool for an hour or so.

4. Divide mixture among 4 (15 1/4 x 10 1/4-inch) baking pans, pressing it to a uniform depth of about 1/2 inch. Score into 2 1/2 x 2 1/2-inch squares.

5. Place in oven at 175°F for about 8 hours or until thoroughly dry.

6. Package for the trail in ziplock bags in the quantity required.

Preparation on the Trail:
Feed large dogs 2 biscuits 3 times each day. This should satisfy most of their daily food requirement. Adjust accordingly for your dog's own needs; and don't forget to save a few for yourself.

Experiment using this food at home with your own dogs before hitting the trail for long treks. It is very nutritious and filling, and dogs will benefit from a couple of weeks of adjustment to the new diet.

Use high-quality bone meal, fit for human consumption, and available as a dietary supplement.

Required Equipment on the Trail:
None

Nutrition Information per Serving:
Calories: 150
Protein: 5 g
Fat: 6 g
Carbohydrates: 24 g
Fiber: 4 g
Sodium: 210 mg
Cholesterol: 1 mg

Chuck and Susan Atkinson
Dorris, California

CASCADE CAROB-SEED CANDY

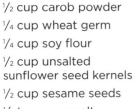

Total Servings: 8 (3 balls per serving)
As Packaged for the Trail: Individual servings as required
Weight per Serving: About 3 ounces
Preparation Time on the Trail: None
Challenge Level: Easy

½ cup carob powder

¼ cup wheat germ

¼ cup soy flour

½ cup unsalted sunflower seed kernels

½ cup sesame seeds

½ teaspoon salt

½ cup honey

½ cup chunky peanut butter

Required Equipment on the Trail:
None

Nutrition Information per Serving:
Calories: 320
Protein: 12 g
Fat: 18 g
Carbohydrates: 33 g
Fiber: 6 g
Sodium: 240 mg
Cholesterol: 0 mg

Preparation at Home:
1. Combine all dry ingredients in a medium-size non-metallic bowl then add honey and peanut butter and blend well. The mixture will be stiff, requiring kneading by hand.
2. Form batter into 24 balls, each with a diameter about that of a quarter.
3. Package candy balls in ziplock bags for the trail.

Preparation on the Trail:
Enjoy a few carob candy balls as a hearty snack during the day while on the trail or after dinner for dessert.

If the batter remains too stiff to mix by hand, warm briefly in the microwave to soften it.

Marion Davison
Apple Valley, California

GOAT ROCK FUDGE

Total Servings: 12 (1 square per serving)
As Packaged for the Trail: Individual servings as required
Weight per Serving: About 3 ounces
Preparation Time on the Trail: None
Challenge Level: Easy

Preparation at Home:
1. Combine milk and sugar in a medium-size cook pot.
2. Bring milk-sugar combination to a boil over medium heat then immediately reduce heat to a simmer. Continue to cook for about 4 minutes, stirring constantly.
3. Remove pan from heat and quickly add marshmallows, peanut butter, and M&Ms. Stir until M&Ms melt.
4. Carefully pour hot fudge into a greased 10 x 7-inch pan. Set aside to cool.
5. Slice fudge into 12 squares then individually package for the trail in small ziplock snack bags.

Preparation on the Trail:
Have a square of fudge as a snack or for dessert.

Kevin "Blue" Hobart
Mount Vernon, Washington

²/₃ cup whole milk

2 cups granulated sugar

³/₄ cup mini marshmallows

2 cups chunky peanut butter

¹/₂ cup regular M&Ms

Required Equipment on the Trail:
None

Nutrition Information per Serving:
Calories: 420
Protein: 12 g
Fat: 24 g
Carbohydrates: 50 g
Fiber: 4 g
Sodium: 220 mg
Cholesterol: 2 mg

GONKY BALLS

Total Servings: 12 (2 Gonky Balls per serving)
As Packaged for the Trail: Individual servings as required
Weight per Serving: About 3 ounces
Preparation Time on the Trail: None
Challenge Level: Easy

V-LO

½ cup (1 standard stick) butter

½ cup 2-percent-fat milk

2 cups granulated sugar

1 teaspoon vanilla extract

3 cups quick oats

1 cup sweetened shredded coconut

2 tablespoons cocoa powder

Required Equipment on the Trail:
None

Nutrition Information per Serving:
Calories: 310
Protein: 4 g
Fat: 11 g
Carbohydrates: 52 g
Fiber: 3 g
Sodium: 90 mg
Cholesterol: 21 mg

Preparation at Home:
1. Melt butter in medium-size sauce pan then stir in milk and sugar.
2. Bring milk mixture to a boil then immediately reduce heat to a simmer.
3. Add vanilla then stir in all remaining ingredients.
4. Remove pan from heat and allow mixture to cool and become sticky.
5. Roll mixture into 24 balls, each about 1-inch in diameter.
6. Package Gonky Balls in small ziplock bags for the trail.

Preparation on the Trail:
Serve a couple of Gonky Balls as a snack or for dessert.

Debbie Higgins and Peter Sandiford,
"The Canadians"
Quebec, Canada

CRABTREE TRAGEDY PUDDING

Total Servings: 2
As Packaged for the Trail: 2 servings
Weight per Serving: About 3 ounces
Preparation Time on the Trail: Less than 15 minutes
Challenge Level: Moderate

V-LO

"A friend of mine named Whiteroot tried this recipe at Crabtree Meadow. Unfortunately, he substituted regular pudding for the instant. He shook and shook the mix for hours with nothing to show for it."

Preparation at Home:
1. Combine dry milk and contents of pudding mix package in a quart-size ziplock freezer bag.
2. Pack optional cookies separately for the trail.

Preparation on the Trail:
1. To prepare both servings, add 2 cups cold water to the pudding mix in the bag.
2. Reseal the bag securely and hold bag tightly by the seal while shaking vigorously for a couple of minutes until pudding thickens. Knead the bag by hand as required to break up clumps.
3. Add optional cookies to the pudding and serve directly from bag or divide between 2 bowls or cups.

Option: *Try substituting other pudding flavors for the vanilla.*

If pudding is slow to congeal and a flowing stream is nearby, place sealed ziplock bag in the cool water to help accelerate the process.

½ cup instant dry whole milk

1 (5.1-ounce) package Jell-O instant vanilla pudding mix

Optional: vanilla wafers or animal cookies

2 cups cold water, added on the trail

Required Equipment on the Trail:
None

Nutrition Information per Serving:
Calories: 420
Protein: 14 g
Fat: 4 g
Carbohydrates: 86 g
Fiber: 0 g
Sodium: 1140 mg
Cholesterol: 15 mg

Diane King
Somers, Connecticut

Authors' Note:
If you've ever been deep in the wilderness for days on end, you can appreciate the magnitude of Whiteroot's tragedy. For crying out loud, always remember Whiteroot and use instant, not regular!

DECADENCE CHOCOLATE PIE

V-LO

Total Servings: 4
As Packaged for the Trail: 4 servings
Weight per Serving: About 3 ounces
Preparation Time on the Trail: Less than 15 minutes
Challenge Level: Moderate

8 Oreo cookies

1 tablespoon chocolate sprinkles

1/2 cup instant dry whole milk

1 (5.9-ounce) package Jell-O Instant Chocolate Pudding Mix

1 1/2 cups cold water, added on the trail

Required Equipment on the Trail:
4 bowls or drinking cups

Nutrition Information per Serving:
Calories: 290
Protein: 5 g
Fat: 7 g
Carbohydrates: 57 g
Fiber: 1 g
Sodium: 750 mg
Cholesterol: 4 mg

Preparation at Home:
1. Place Oreo cookies in a pint-size ziplock freezer bag, seal the bag, then crush cookies by hand.
2. Add sprinkles to the bag.
3. Combine dry milk and contents of pudding mix package in a quart-size ziplock freezer bag.

Preparation on the Trail:
1. To prepare all 4 servings, add 1 1/2 cups cold water to bag containing pudding mix.
2. Reseal the bag securely and hold bag tightly by the seal while shaking vigorously for a couple of minutes until pudding thickens. Knead the bag by hand as required to break up clumps.
3. Snip corner from bottom of pudding bag and squeeze contents into 4 separate cups or bowls.
4. Sprinkle each serving with cookie crumble mixture, then serve.

> Be sure to use cold water! If too warm, the pudding mix won't thicken properly.

Craig "Smitty" Smith
Springfield, Missouri

CDT

Authors' Note:
Think it isn't possible to have decadent food while on the trail? Well, try this recipe and you'll quickly change your mind!

SMITTY'S APRICOT CONFECTION

Total Servings: 2
As Packaged for the Trail: 2 servings
Weight per Serving: About 4 ounces
Preparation Time on the Trail: 5 minutes (plus 6 hours to rehydrate)
Challenge Level: Easy

Preparation at Home:
1. Package apricots in a quart-size ziplock freezer bag.
2. Pack syrup separately for the trail.

Preparation on the Trail:
1. Early in the day, add about 1 cup water to apricots in the ziplock bag.
2. Reseal bag tightly and place in a safe location at the top of your backpack until evening.
3. Once it's time for dessert, drain water from the apricots.
4. Add ¼ cup syrup to the apricots in the ziplock bag, reseal tightly, and shake well for about 1 minute.
5. Evenly divide apricots and syrup between 2 cups or bowls and serve.

1 cup dried apricots
¼ cup apricot syrup
1 cup water, added on the trail

Required Equipment on the Trail:
2 bowls or drinking cups

Nutrition Information per Serving:
Calories: 250
Protein: 3 g
Fat: 0 g
Carbohydrates: 59 g
Fiber: 5 g
Sodium: 7 mg
Cholesterol: 0 mg

Option: Try other fruit and syrup combinations.

Craig "Smitty" Smith
Springfield, Missouri

231

WHITEWATER CHEESECAKE

V-LO

Total Servings: 4
As Packaged for the Trail: 4 servings
Weight per Serving: About 4 ounces
Preparation Time on the Trail: 15 minutes
Challenge Level: Moderate

1 (11-ounce) package Jell-O No-Bake Cheesecake Mix

2 tablespoons granulated sugar

2 tablespoons Butter Buds

2 tablespoons instant dry nonfat milk

1 tablespoon sunflower oil

1³/₄ cups water, divided, added on the trail

Required Equipment on the Trail:
4 bowls or drinking cups

Nutrition Information per Serving:
Calories: 370
Protein: 8 g
Fat: 8 g
Carbohydrates: 68 g
Fiber: 2 g
Sodium: 670 mg
Cholesterol: 8 mg

Preparation at Home:
1. Remove both pouches from the cheesecake mix package.
2. Combine cheesecake crust mix with sugar and Butter Buds in a pint-size ziplock bag.
3. In a quart-size ziplock freezer bag, combine cheesecake filling mix with dry milk.
4. Pack oil separately for the trail.

Preparation on the Trail:
1. To prepare all 4 servings, add ¹/₄ cup water and 1 tablespoon sunflower oil to the bag of cheesecake crust mix.
2. Reseal the bag and knead contents until uniformly moist.
3. Divide crust mixture evenly, pressing the crust into the bottom of 4 cups or bowls.
4. Add 1¹/₂ cups cold water to the bag containing the cheesecake filling mix.
5. Reseal bag tightly and knead contents to eliminate lumps, then shake bag for about 3 minutes, until cheesecake filling congeals.
6. Cut corner from the bottom of the bag of filling mix and squeeze over the crusts, dividing filling evenly.
7. Allow cheesecake to rest a few minutes to further congeal before serving.

> The water added to the filling mix on the trail must not be warm, otherwise the filling may not congeal properly.

Ed Acheson
Cincinnati, Ohio

HANGING-BY-YOUR-BOOTS UPSIDE-DOWN CAKE

Total Servings: 4
As Packaged for the Trail: 4 servings
Weight per Serving: About 3 ounces
Preparation Time on the Trail: 45 minutes
Challenge Level: Moderate

V

Preparation at Home:
1. Pack pineapple pieces in a snack-size ziplock bag.
2. Combine Bisquick mix and granulated sugar in a pint-size ziplock bag.
3. Pack brown sugar separately for the trail.

Preparation on the Trail:
1. To prepare all 4 servings, add ⅓ cup water to the Bisquick mixture in the bag.
2. Reseal bag and knead dough until uniformly moist. Set aside.
3. Bring 1 cup water to a boil in a cook pot; pour into a drinking cup or bowl.
4. Add dried pineapple to hot water and set aside for at least 20 minutes to rehydrate.
5. Pour rehydrated pineapple, with water, into cook pot and place over low heat, simmering for 10 minutes.
6. Sprinkle brown sugar over pineapple in the pot, but *do not* stir.
7. Snip corner from bottom of dough bag and squeeze over the brown sugar and pineapple. Dough will be gooey and will naturally spread over pineapple.
8. Cover pot and steam on low heat for about 10 minutes, being careful not to burn the cake. Serve once an inserted knife comes out clean.

4 slices dried pineapple, chopped

1 cup Bisquick Heart Smart Pancake and Baking Mix

1 tablespoon granulated sugar

¼ cup brown sugar

1⅓ cups water, added on the trail

Required Equipment on the Trail:
Bowl or drinking cup

Cook pot with lid

Nutrition Information per Serving:
Calories: 200
Protein: 3 g
Fat: 5 g
Carbohydrates: 36 g
Fiber: 1 g
Sodium: 320 mg
Cholesterol: 0 mg

Option: Try substituting other types of dried fruit for the pineapple.

Walt and Jane Daniels
Mohegan Lake, New York

YELLOW WORMS

Total Servings: 1
As Packaged for the Trail: 1 serving
Weight per Serving: About 4 ounces
Preparation Time on the Trail: 15 minutes
Challenge Level: Moderate

V

1 tablespoon all-purpose flour

1 rounded tablespoon lemonade mix

1 (3-ounce) package ramen noodles, seasoning packet removed

2 cups plus 2 tablespoons water, added on the trail

Required Equipment on the Trail:
Cook pot

Nutrition Information per Serving:
Calories: 390
Protein: 10 g
Fat: 3 g
Carbohydrates: 80 g
Fiber: 0 g
Sodium: 670 mg
Cholesterol: 0 mg

Preparation at Home:
1. Combine flour and lemonade mix in a snack-size ziplock bag.
2. Pack noodles separately for the trail.

Preparation on the Trail:
1. Boil ramen noodles in a cook pot with 2 cups water.
2. Remove pot from stove and drain noodles, reserving, if possible, the hot cooking water for cleanup of the sticky utensils.
3. Add 2 tablespoons water to the lemonade mixture in the bag and knead contents until smooth.
4. Drizzle lemonade mixture over the noodles in the pot, then toss and serve.

Option: Try ½ tablespoon lemon juice or ½ tablespoon lemon rind shavings, along with a little sugar, in place of the lemonade mix.

Will "The Green Ghost" O'Daix
Indianapolis, Indiana

"Know the capabilities and limitations of your pack stove before hitting the trail. I once tried a new cooking method on a stove with the fuel container just below the burner. After it had been operating for a long time at a high setting, the stove exploded! Thankfully, no one was hurt, but the trip was ruined."

—Jeffrey Hare
Citrus Heights, California

TIMBERLAND BLACKBERRY CRISP

Total Servings: 2
As Packaged for the Trail: 2 servings
Weight per Serving: About 7 ounces
Preparation Time on the Trail: 15 minutes
Challenge Level: Easy

V

Preparation at Home:
1. Evenly spread pie filling on a lined dehydrator tray and dry into a leather.
2. Pack fruit leather and granola in separate pint-size ziplock bags.

Preparation on the Trail:
1. To prepare both servings, tear fruit leather into small pieces and add to 1 cup water in a cook pot.
2. Bring water to a boil, then reduce heat to a simmer, stirring constantly until fruit rehydrates, about 10 minutes.
3. Remove pot from heat. Sprinkle granola over the blackberry filling, then serve.

Option: Substitute your favorite fruit flavor for the blackberry.

1 (21-ounce) can Comstock Premium Blackberry Pie Filling

1 cup granola cereal

1 cup water, added on the trail

Required Equipment on the Trail:
Cook pot

Nutrition Information per Serving:
Calories: 650
Protein: 9 g
Fat: 15 g
Carbohydrates: 117 g
Fiber: 6 g
Sodium: 70 mg
Cholesterol: 0 mg

Unlike some other types of pie filling, Comstock Premium dehydrates well, presumably due to the absence of high fructose corn syrup, which seems to inhibit the drying process.

Leslie Anderson
Harrison, Arkansas

MOUNTAIN STORM CHOCOLATE GLOP

Total Servings: 1
As Packaged for the Trail: 1 serving
Weight per Serving: About 2 ounces
Preparation Time on the Trail: 15 minutes
Challenge Level: Easy

V-LO

"We once prepared this recipe high in the Sierra Nevada as the first storm of winter came roaring in: a great-tasting treat that helped take the edge off some really rough weather."

2 single-serving packets hot cocoa mix

1 tablespoon sunflower oil

1 tablespoon water, added on the trail

Required Equipment on the Trail:
Cup or bowl

Nonstick frying pan

Nutrition Information per Serving:
Calories: 360
Protein: 2 g
Fat: 20 g
Carbohydrates: 46 g
Fiber: 1 g
Sodium: 360 mg
Cholesterol: 5 mg

Preparation at Home:
1. Pack cocoa mix in its original packaging for the trail.
2. Carry oil separately for the trail.

Preparation on the Trail:
1. To prepare 1 serving, add 1 tablespoon water to cocoa mix in a cup or bowl. Stir well.
2. Grease a frying pan with 1 tablespoon sunflower oil and warm over low heat.
3. Add cocoa mixture to frying pan and stir often until it achieves the consistency of taffy.
4. Serve straight from the pan.

> Avoid using a pan without nonstick coating for this recipe, unless you don't mind the prospect of scrubbing your cookware until your fingers bleed!

Christine and Tim Conners
Statesboro, Georgia

"I've found that a small plastic pot scrapper is indispensable for my trail cooking. Many of my backpacking trips take place in the desert, where water is scarce. The pot scrapper often removes all the encrusted remains so that only a small splash of water is needed to finish the cleaning job."

—Pam Coz-Hill
Visalia, California

MAMMOTH LAKES PLOP CAKE

Total Servings: 3
As Packaged for the Trail: 1 serving
Weight per Serving: About 3 ounces
Preparation Time on the Trail: 15 minutes
Challenge Level: Moderate

V-LO

"When we were given the recipe for Mountain Lakes Trail Frosting (also in this book), we knew a trail cake recipe would be a great companion for it. So we got busy, and plop cake was the result. This fun recipe gets its name from one of our favorite fun places, the town of Mammoth Lakes in the High Sierra."

Preparation at Home:
1. Combine all dry ingredients in a medium-size bowl and stir.
2. Evenly divide dry ingredients among 3 (1-pint) ziplock bags, about 1/2 cup mixture in each.
3. Pack oil separately for the trail.

Preparation on the Trail:
1. To prepare a single serving, grease frying pan with 1 tablespoon sunflower oil and warm over low heat.
2. Add about 3 tablespoons water to the flour mixture in the bag.
3. Reseal bag and knead contents until batter is uniformly moist. It should have a thick consistency, but add a little more water if batter appears too dry.
4. Plop cake batter into the hot pan, press down with a spatula, and fry each side until cooked through.
5. Remove from heat and allow cake to cool for a few minutes. Cover with optional frosting.

Christine and Tim Conners
Statesboro, Georgia

1 cup cake flour

1/4 cup granulated sugar

1 tablespoon whole egg powder

1/2 teaspoon baking soda

1/2 teaspoon baking powder

3 tablespoons Butter Buds

1 tablespoon sunflower oil per serving

3 tablespoons water per serving, added on the trail

Optional: Top with Mountain Lakes Trail Frosting (see recipe in this book)

Required Equipment on the Trail:
Frying pan

Spatula

Nutrition Information per Serving:
Calories: 400
Protein: 4 g
Fat: 15 g
Carbohydrates: 58 g
Fiber: 1 g
Sodium: 480 mg
Cholesterol: 25 mg

SUNSET BAGEL

Total Servings: 1
As Packaged for the Trail: 1 serving
Weight per Serving: About 4 ounces
Preparation Time on the Trail: Less than 15 minutes
Challenge Level: Easy

"I finish nearly every dinner with a toasted bagel, using my pot lid as the toaster. Quick, delicious, and the envy of all!"

1 bagel

1 tablespoon sunflower oil

Optional: salt to taste

Required Equipment on the Trail:
Frying pan

Nutrition Information per Serving:
Calories: 380
Protein: 10 g
Fat: 14 g
Carbohydrates: 51 g
Fiber: 3 g
Sodium: 480 mg
Cholesterol: 0 mg

Preparation at Home:
Pack bagel, oil, and optional salt separately for the trail.

Preparation on the Trail:
1. To prepare a single serving, slice bagel in half.
2. Pour about ½ tablespoon sunflower oil on each side of bagel halves and warm in frying pan over medium heat until toasted.
3. Sprinkle bagel with optional salt before serving.

Authors' Note:
Rick's original recipe called for butter instead of oil. Butter is a great-tasting option, but it can spoil rapidly on the trail unless carried in sealed single-serving condiment-type packets. Unfortunately, rugged aseptic butter packets are increasingly difficult to find.

Rick Bombaci
Enterprise, Oregon

CHOCOLATE BANANA CHIPS

V-LO

Total Servings: 1
As Packaged for the Trail: 1 serving
Weight per Serving: About 5 ounces
Preparation Time on the Trail: 15 minutes
Challenge Level: Easy

Preparation at Home:
1. Combine banana chips, walnuts, and chocolate chips in a pint-size ziplock bag.
2. Pack oil separately for the trail.

Preparation on the Trail:
1. To prepare 1 serving, grease a frying pan with 2 tablespoons sunflower oil and warm over low heat.
2. Add banana mixture to the hot pan and fry until chocolate melts.
3. Remove pan from heat and allow to cool for a few minutes before serving.

Option: A packet of hot cocoa mix can be carried in place of the chocolate chips. Then, on the trail, use 2 teaspoons water to make a cocoa paste before adding to the pan with the other ingredients.

Chet J. Fromm
Port Orange, Florida

½ cup dried banana chips
¼ cup walnuts, chopped
¼ cup chocolate chips
2 tablespoons sunflower oil

Required Equipment on the Trail:
Frying pan

Nutrition Information per Serving:
Calories: 850
Protein: 8 g
Fat: 53 g
Carbohydrates: 50 g
Fiber: 1 g
Sodium: 30 mg
Cholesterol: 1 mg

BURIED FOREST TRAIL FUDGE

Total Servings: 2
As Packaged for the Trail: 2 servings
Weight per Serving: About 5 ounces
Preparation Time on the Trail: 15 minutes
Challenge Level: Easy

"This recipe is made using ingredients we found in our packs prior to resupply."

½ cup quick oats

2 tablespoons instant dry buttermilk

3 tablespoons brown sugar

1 single-serving packet hot cocoa mix

¼ cup regular M&Ms

4 large marshmallows, chopped into small pieces

3 tablespoons Butter Buds

2 tablespoons chunky peanut butter

3 tablespoons peanut oil

3 tablespoons water, added on the trail

Required Equipment on the Trail:
Nonstick frying pan

Nutrition Information per Serving:
Calories: 780
Protein: 11 g
Fat: 36 g
Carbohydrates: 101 g
Fiber: 4 g
Sodium: 520 mg
Cholesterol: 8 mg

Preparation at Home:
1. Combine oats, dry buttermilk, brown sugar, hot cocoa mix, and M&Ms in a pint-size ziplock freezer bag.
2. In a snack-size ziplock bag, combine chopped marshmallows and Butter Buds.
3. Pack peanut butter and oil separately for the trail.

Preparation on the Trail:
1. To prepare both servings, heat marshmallow mixture, 2 tablespoons peanut butter, and 3 tablespoons peanut oil in a frying pan over low heat until marshmallows are melted, stirring continuously.
2. Add oat mixture to the pan along with 3 tablespoons water, stirring again until all ingredients are well blended into a soft fudge.
3. Remove from heat and allow to cool for a few minutes before serving.

Option: A single-serving packet of regular instant oatmeal can be used in place of the quick oats.

> The fudge becomes very thick, but don't expect it to solidify. Plan to eat it with a spoon.

> A nonstick frying pan is highly recommended for this very gooey recipe.

Deborah Brill and Scott
"Marty" Place
Berkeley, California

CLEAR CREEK CINNAMON CHIPS

Total Servings: 2
As Packaged for the Trail: 2 servings
Weight per Serving: About 5 ounces
Preparation Time on the Trail: 15 minutes
Challenge Level: Moderate

V

"The title? We fell in love along the Clear Creek Trail in California's Piute Mountains!"

Preparation at Home:
1. Combine cinnamon and sugar in a gallon-size ziplock bag.
2. Pack tortillas and oil separately for the trail.

Preparation on the Trail:
1. To prepare both servings, warm ¼ cup sunflower oil over medium heat in a frying pan.
2. Slice tortillas into wedges, about 8 to 12 each.
3. In batches, so as not to overcrowd the pan, fry tortillas in hot oil for a brief period before flipping.
4. Carefully remove chips from oil and allow to cool before adding to the bag of cinnamon-sugar.
5. Seal and shake ziplock bag to thoroughly coat chips. Eat chips straight from the bag.

½ tablespoon ground cinnamon

2 tablespoons granulated sugar

2 medium-size flour tortillas

¼ cup sunflower oil

Required Equipment on the Trail:
Frying pan

Spatula

Nutrition Information per Serving:
Calories: 580
Protein: 5 g
Fat: 43 g
Carbohydrates: 50 g
Fiber: 3 g
Sodium: 350 mg
Cholesterol: 0 mg

Be sure to use a large ziplock bag for this recipe, because the extra volume is necessary for shaking and coating the chips while on the trail.

Christine and Tim Conners
Statesboro, Georgia

 PCT **AT**

CACHE PEAK CRUMBLES

Total Servings: 2
As Packaged for the Trail: 2 servings
Weight per Serving: About 5 ounces
Preparation Time on the Trail: 15 minutes
Challenge Level: Moderate

v

"If you have many miles under your feet, a sweet tooth, and a little extra oil, it's definitely time for sweet and greasy donut crumbles! We named this recipe after a prominent peak near the town of Tehachapi in the Southern Sierra. On its eastern flanks, the Pacific Crest Trail fights its way through an aggressive defense of chaparral. It's incredibly beautiful and rugged country."

1 cup Bisquick Heart Smart pancake mix

¼ cup granulated sugar

⅓ cup peanut oil

⅓ cup water, added on the trail

Required Equipment on the Trail:
Frying pan

Spatula

Nutrition Information per Serving:
Calories: 625
Protein: 5 g
Fat: 40 g
Carbohydrates: 66 g
Fiber: 1 g
Sodium: 510 mg
Cholesterol: 0 mg

Preparation at Home:
1. Combine Bisquick and sugar in a quart-size ziplock bag.
2. Pack oil separately for the trail.

Preparation on the Trail:
1. To prepare both servings, warm ⅓ cup peanut oil over medium heat in a frying pan.
2. Add ⅓ cup water to the Bisquick mix in the bag.
3. Reseal bag and knead contents until most of the lumps are eliminated.
4. Snip a corner from bottom of the bag and carefully squeeze batter into the pan.
5. Scramble the dough as you would eggs, covering all dough with hot oil, continuing to flip and scramble to prevent burning.
6. The crumbles are ready to serve once they become slightly crispy.

> Hot oil takes a long time to cool, so exercise caution when eating the hot crumbles straight from the pan immediately following cooking.

Christine and Tim Conners
Statesboro, Georgia

Drinks

BORDER-TO-BORDER
BERRY MILKSHAKE

Total Servings: 6
As Packaged for the Trail: 6 servings
Weight per Serving: About 2 ounces
Preparation Time on the Trail: Less than 5 minutes
Challenge Level: Easy

V-LO

"I found this recipe, and even a bag containing its ingredients, in a hiker box along the Pacific Crest Trail."

2 ounces dried
blueberries

1 cup dried banana chips

½ cup instant dry
buttermilk

½ cup instant dry whole
milk

1 cup cold water per
serving, added on the
trail

**Required Equipment on
the Trail:**
Drinking cup

**Nutrition Information
per Serving:**
Calories: 190
Protein: 5 g
Fat: 10 g
Carbohydrates: 22 g
Fiber: 3 g
Sodium: 70 mg
Cholesterol: 13 mg

Preparation at Home:
1. Add dried blueberries and banana chips to
   a blender and pulse until both become a
   fine powder.
2. Combine powdered fruit with dry
   buttermilk and dry whole milk in a pint-size
   ziplock freezer bag.

Preparation on the Trail:
To prepare a single serving, add about ¼
cup milkshake powder to 1 cup cold water,
then stir, mixing well.

Options: You can use a 1-pound bag frozen berries,
any variety, in place of the dried blueberries by drying in a dehydrator.

*Try adding some berry milkshake to your favor-
ite cereal instead of milk.*

*Mark Morse
Anza, California*

244

GLACIER ICE SLURPY

Total Servings: 1
As Packaged for the Trail: 1 serving
Weight per Serving: About 3 ounces
Preparation Time on the Trail: Minutes
Challenge Level: Moderate

Preparation at Home:
Pack Kool-Aid Drink Mix in a pint-size ziplock freezer bag for the trail.

Preparation on the Trail:
1. To prepare 1 serving, add 2 cups water to a quart-size water bottle.
2. Pour Kool-Aid drink mix into water bottle. Seal bottle and shake well.
3. Add snow to fill the remainder of the bottle. Shake well and serve.

> To avoid illness, caution must be exercised when identifying your snow source.
> Only use snow that is fresh fallen and clean. If in doubt, don't use it!

Kurt Thompson
San Ramon, California

½ cup instant sweetened Kool-Aid Drink Mix (your favorite flavor)

2 cups water, added on the trail

2 cups fresh, clean snow, added on the trail

Required Equipment on the Trail:
Quart-size wide-mouth water bottle

Nutrition Information per Serving:
Calories: 240
Protein: 0 g
Fat: 0 g
Carbohydrates: 64 g
Fiber: 0 g
Sodium: 0 mg
Cholesterol: 0 mg

SAND CANYON PINE NEEDLE TEA

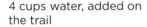

Total Servings: 4
As Packaged for the Trail: 4 servings
Weight per Serving: 0 ounces (all ingredients found on trail)
Preparation Time on the Trail: 30 minutes
Challenge Level: Moderate

V

4 cups water, added on the trail

½ cup fresh-picked pine needles, added on the trail

Required Equipment on the Trail:
Cook pot with lid

Nutrition Information per Serving:
Calories: 5
Protein: 0 g
Fat: 0 g
Carbohydrates: 0 g
Fiber: 0 g
Sodium: 5 mg
Cholesterol: 0 mg

Preparation at Home:
None required. All ingredients are found along the trail.

Preparation on the Trail:
1. To prepare all 4 servings, bring 4 cups water to a boil in cook pot.
2. Remove pot from stove, then add about ½ cup fresh-picked pine needles to the hot water.
3. Cover pot and set aside. Allow needles to steep for about 20 minutes.
4. Scoop pine needles from tea with a fork, then serve.

Caution!
Yew leaves, similar in appearance to pine needles, are toxic to humans and should never be used in pine needle tea. Ponderosa pine needles and Australian pine needles are thought to cause health problems in farm and domestic animals and are not recommended for use by humans. As with all wild fruits or vegetables, be certain of what you're picking before consuming anything!

Pine needle tea is very high in vitamin C.

*Griff and Christine Corpening
Tehachapi, California*

SHERPA TEA MIX

Total Servings: 12
As Packaged for the Trail: 6 servings per ziplock bag
Weight per Serving: Less than 1 ounce
Preparation Time on the Trail: 5 minutes
Challenge Level: Easy

V-LO

Preparation at Home:
1. Combine all dry ingredients in a small bowl and mix well.
2. Evenly divide ingredients between 2 (1-pint) ziplock bags. Each bag will make 6 servings.

Preparation on the Trail:
1. To prepare a single serving, heat 1 cup water in a cook pot. Pour hot water into a drinking cup.
2. Add 3 heaping tablespoons tea mix; stir well.

Ann Marshall
Port Orchard, Washington

2 cups instant dry nonfat milk

⅓ cup granulated sugar

2 tablespoons instant sweetened iced tea mix with lemon

1 cup water per serving, added on the trail

Required Equipment on the Trail:
Cook pot

Nutrition Information per Serving:
Calories: 70
Protein: 4 g
Fat: 0 g
Carbohydrates: 13 g
Fiber: 0 g
Sodium: 60 mg
Cholesterol: 23 mg

BEAR MOUNTAIN MOCHA

Total Servings: 20
As Packaged for the Trail: 10 servings per ziplock bag
Weight per Serving: Less than 1 ounce
Preparation Time on the Trail: 5 minutes
Challenge Level: Easy

V-LO

"Named for the wonderful mountain on which we used to live in the Tehachapi Range of California."

1 cup powdered nondiary creamer

1 cup instant coffee

½ cup granulated sugar

1 single-serving packet hot cocoa mix

¾ teaspoon ground cinnamon

1 cup water per serving, added on the trail

Required Equipment on the Trail:
Cook pot

Nutrition Information per Serving:
Calories: 50
Protein: 0 g
Fat: 2 g
Carbohydrates: 11 g
Fiber: 0 g
Sodium: 20 mg
Cholesterol: 1 mg

Preparation at Home:
1. Combine all dry ingredients in a small bowl and mix well.
2. Evenly divide ingredients between 2 (1-pint) ziplock bags. Each bag will make 10 servings.

Preparation on the Trail:
1. To prepare a single serving, heat 1 cup water in a cook pot. Pour hot water into a drinking cup.
2. Add 2 tablespoons mocha mix to hot water; stir well.

*Christine and Tim Conners
Statesboro, Georgia*

 PCT **AT**

RUSSIAN TEA MIX

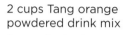

V

Total Servings: 32
As Packaged for the Trail: 8 servings per ziplock bag
Weight per Serving: Less than 1 ounce
Preparation Time on the Trail: 5 minutes
Challenge Level: Easy

Preparation at Home:
1. Combine all dry ingredients in a medium-size bowl; mix well.
2. Divide ingredients evenly among 4 (1-pint) ziplock bags. Each bag will make 8 servings.

Preparation on the Trail:
1. To prepare a single serving, heat 1 cup water in a cook pot. Pour hot water into a drinking cup.
2. Add 2 tablespoons tea mix to hot water; stir well.
3. If a little zing is desired, throw in a few optional Red Hots candies and stir.

Kathleen "The Old Gray Goose" Cutshall
Conneaut, Ohio

2 cups Tang orange powdered drink mix

2 cups instant sweetened iced tea mix

2 teaspoons ground cinnamon

1 teaspoon allspice

1 teaspoon ground cloves

Optional: Red Hots candies

1 cup water per serving, added on the trail

Required Equipment on the Trail:
Cook pot

Nutrition Information per Serving:
Calories: 90
Protein: 0 g
Fat: 0 g
Carbohydrates: 22 g
Fiber: 0 g
Sodium: 20 mg
Cholesterol: 0 mg

VASQUEZ TEA MIX

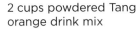

Total Servings: 72
As Packaged for the Trail: 8 servings per ziplock bag
Weight per Serving: Less than 1 ounce
Preparation Time on the Trail: 5 minutes
Challenge Level: Easy

V

2 cups powdered Tang orange drink mix

1/2 cup instant sweetened iced tea mix

1/2 cup instant sweetened lemonade mix

1 1/2 cups granulated sugar

1 teaspoon ground cinnamon

1/2 teaspoon ground cloves

1 cup water per serving, added on the trail

Required Equipment on the Trail:
Cook pot

Nutrition Information per Serving:
Calories: 40
Protein: 0 g
Fat: 0 g
Carbohydrates: 10 g
Fiber: 0 g
Sodium: 5 mg
Cholesterol: 0 mg

Preparation at Home:
1. Combine all dry ingredients in a medium-size bowl and stir well.
2. Evenly divide tea mix among 9 (1-pint) ziplock bags, adding about 1/2 cup mix to each. Each bag will make 8 servings.

Preparation on the Trail:
1. To prepare a single serving, heat 1 cup water in a cook pot. Pour hot water into a drinking cup.
2. Add 1 tablespoon tea mix to hot water; stir well.

Option: The mix makes a great cup of cold tea as well.

Peg Spry
Agua Dulce, California

PICKAX PETE'S COWBOY COFFEE

Total Servings: 4
As Packaged for the Trail: 4 servings
Weight per Serving: Less than 1 ounce
Preparation Time on the Trail: 15 minutes
Challenge Level: Easy

"I normally make a pot of coffee every three or four days while on the trail. One morning, north of Stevens Pass along the Pacific Crest, I was joined by two hikers, Craig and Curtis, and I offered to share a pot of cowboy coffee. I was brewing Starbucks in place of my usual generic brand, and the aroma was great. 'Well, we aren't coffee drinkers,' came the reply, 'but since you're making a pot . . .' It was a tactical mistake. From there to Canada, I could hardly get those guys on the trail each morning without a cup of my coffee."

Preparation at Home:
Pack ground coffee in a pint-size ziplock bag for the trail.

Preparation on the Trail:
1. To prepare all 4 servings, float coffee grounds over 4 cups cold water in a cook pot to form a thick mat.
2. Momentarily bring water to a boil over high heat, then remove pot from the stove.
3. Add a splash of cold water to help settle any grounds that remain floating on the surface.
4. Carefully scoop coffee from the top of the liquid to avoid disturbing the settled grounds (unless you enjoy some chew to your drink).

Option: *Experiment with different grinds, roasts, strengths, beans, and boiling times to find your perfect cup.*

½ cup coffee grounds, medium grind

4 cups water, added on the trail

Required Equipment on the Trail:
Cook pot

Nutrition Information per Serving:
Calories: 2
Protein: 0 g
Fat: 0 g
Carbohydrates: 0 g
Fiber: 0 g
Sodium: 5 mg
Cholesterol: 0 mg

When disposing of used coffee grinds, burying them in a proper cat hole should pose no issue to most local environments along the trail. Hike friendly and don't scatter used grinds over the surface of the soil. And be prepared to pack out the waste when traveling through sensitive areas.

Pete "Pickax Pete" Fish
Ventura, California

BURNT RANCH CINNAMON COFFEE

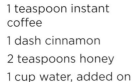

Total Servings: 1
As Packaged for the Trail: 1 serving
Weight per Serving: About 1 ounce
Preparation Time on the Trail: 5 minutes
Challenge Level: Easy

V

1 teaspoon instant coffee

1 dash cinnamon

2 teaspoons honey

1 cup water, added on the trail

Required Equipment on the Trail:
Cook pot

Nutrition Information per Serving:
Calories: 40
Protein: 0 g
Fat: 0 g
Carbohydrates: 11 g
Fiber: 0 g
Sodium: 0 mg
Cholesterol: 0 mg

Preparation at Home:
1. Combine coffee and cinnamon in a snack-size ziplock bag.
2. Pack honey separately for the trail.

Preparation on the Trail:
1. To prepare a single serving, heat 1 cup water in a cook pot. Pour hot water into a drinking cup.
2. Add coffee-cinnamon mixture and 2 teaspoons honey to hot water; stir well.

Craig "Smitty" Smith
Springfield, Missouri

BEN'S EASY MORNING MOCHA

V-LO

Total Servings: 1
As Packaged for the Trail: 1 serving
Weight per Serving: About 1 ounce
Preparation Time on the Trail: 5 minutes
Challenge Level: Easy

Preparation at Home:
1. Combine instant coffee and cocoa mix in a snack-size ziplock bag.
2. Pack honey separately for the trail.

Preparation on the Trail:
1. To prepare a single serving, heat water in a cook pot. Pour hot water into a drinking cup.
2. Add coffee-cocoa mix and 1 teaspoon honey to hot water; stir well.

Ben York
Alpine, California

1 teaspoon instant coffee

1 single-serving packet hot cocoa mix

1 teaspoon honey

1 cup water, added on the trail

Required Equipment on the Trail:
Cook pot

Nutrition Information per Serving:
Calories: 140
Protein: 1 g
Fat: 3 g
Carbohydrates: 28 g
Fiber: 0 g
Sodium: 180 mg
Cholesterol: 5 mg

PEAKS OF ITALY BITTERSWEET COCOA MIX

Total Servings: 2
As Packaged for the Trail: 2 servings
Weight per Serving: About 1 ounce
Preparation Time on the Trail: 5 minutes
Challenge Level: Easy

V-LO

"This is a morning favorite of mine."

3 tablespoons instant dry whole milk

3 tablespoons VanHouten's Cocoa Powder

3 tablespoons granulated sugar

2 1/4 cups water, added on the trail

Required Equipment on the Trail:
Cook pot

Nutrition Information per Serving:
Calories: 150
Protein: 3 g
Fat: 4 g
Carbohydrates: 33 g
Fiber: 0 g
Sodium: 90 mg
Cholesterol: 8 mg

Preparation at Home:
Combine all dry ingredients in a pint-size ziplock bag.

Preparation on the Trail:
1. To prepare both servings, pour cocoa mix into cook pot along with a very small amount of water. Stir to produce a thick paste mostly free of lumps.
2. Add about 2 1/4 cups water to the cocoa paste in the pot and stir well.
3. Place pot over low heat. Do not boil, but serve cocoa once it's sufficiently hot.

Luca de Alfaro
Palo Alto, California

STORM CHASER'S SPICED MILK

Total Servings: 4
As Packaged for the Trail: 4 servings
Weight per Serving: About 1 ounce
Preparation Time on the Trail: 5 minutes
Challenge Level: Easy

V-LO

Preparation at Home:
Combine all dry ingredients in a pint-size ziplock bag.

Preparation on the Trail:
1. To prepare a single serving, heat 1 cup water in a cook pot. Pour hot water into a drinking cup.
2. Add about ¼ cup spiced milk mix to hot water; stir well.

Vanilla powder can be ordered online. See resources in Appendix B.

Christine and Tim Conners
Statesboro, Georgia

1 cup instant dry whole milk

1 teaspoon vanilla powder

1 teaspoon ground cinnamon

1 teaspoon ground nutmeg

1 tablespoon granulated sugar

1 cup water per serving, added on the trail

Required Equipment on the Trail:
Cook pot

Nutrition Information per Serving:
Calories: 170
Protein: 8 g
Fat: 8 g
Carbohydrates: 16 g
Fiber: 0 g
Sodium: 110 mg
Cholesterol: 30 mg

HIDDEN LAKE HOT MILK

Total Servings: 10
As Packaged for the Trail: 5 servings per ziplock bag
Weight per Serving: About 1 ounce
Preparation Time on the Trail: 5 minutes
Challenge Level: Easy

V-LO

"Hot milk is especially great in the evening. The secret to a smooth, hot, nonfat milk beverage is getting the milk powder dissolved in a little cold water before adding the boiling water."

2 cups instant dry nonfat milk

1 tablespoon ground cinnamon

1/2 teaspoon ground nutmeg

1/4 cup brown sugar

1 cup water per serving, added on the trail

Required Equipment on the Trail:
Cook pot

Nutrition Information per Serving:
Calories: 60
Protein: 5 g
Fat: 0 g
Carbohydrates: 12 g
Fiber: 0 g
Sodium: 80 mg
Cholesterol: 2 mg

Preparation at Home:
1. Combine all dry ingredients in a small bowl. Stir well.
2. Evenly divide ingredients between 2 (1-pint) ziplock bags. Each bag will make 5 servings.

Preparation on the Trail:
1. To prepare a single serving, add about 1/4 cup milk mix to a drinking cup along with a little cold water. Stir to produce a thick paste mostly free of lumps.
2. Boil 1 cup water in a cook pot. Pour boiling water over paste and stir well.

Ann Marshall
Port Orchard, Washington

SACAGAWEA TEA

Total Servings: 1
As Packaged for the Trail: 1 serving
Weight per Serving: About 1 ounce
Preparation Time on the Trail: 15 minutes
Challenge Level: Easy

Preparation at Home:
Combine dried raspberries, optional sugar, and tea bag in a snack-size ziplock bag.

Preparation on the Trail:
1. To prepare a single serving, heat 1 cup water in a cook pot. Pour hot water into a drinking cup.
2. Add raspberries, optional sugar, and tea bag to hot water.
3. Stir and allow tea bag to steep for a few minutes before serving.

Kathleen Kirby
Milltown, New Jersey

1 tablespoon dried raspberries

Optional: sugar to taste

1 single-serving bag raspberry-flavored herbal tea

1 cup water, added on the trail

Required Equipment on the Trail:
Cook pot

Nutrition Information per Serving:
Calories: 50
Protein: 0 g
Fat: 0 g
Carbohydrates: 12 g
Fiber: 2 g
Sodium: 0 mg
Cholesterol: 0 mg

AGUA DULCE HOT CHOCOLATE

Total Servings: 8
As Packaged for the Trail: 4 servings per ziplock bag
Weight per Serving: About 2 ounces
Preparation Time on the Trail: 5 minutes
Challenge Level: Easy

V-LO

¼ cup Nesquik chocolate flavor drink mix

¼ cup powdered nondairy creamer

2 cups instant dry nonfat milk

¼ cup confectioners' sugar

Optional: mini marshmallows

1 cup water per serving, added on the trail

Required Equipment on the Trail:
Cook pot

Nutrition Information per Serving:
Calories: 220
Protein: 8 g
Fat: 2 g
Carbohydrates: 44 g
Fiber: 0 g
Sodium: 140 mg
Cholesterol: 2 mg

Preparation at Home:
1. Combine all dry ingredients, including optional marshmallows, in a small bowl and mix well.
2. Evenly divide mixture between 2 (1-pint) ziplock bags. Each bag will make 4 servings.

Preparation on the Trail:
1. To prepare a single serving, add about ⅓ cup drink mix to a drinking cup along with a small amount of water. Stir to produce a thick paste mostly free of lumps.
2. Bring 1 cup water to a boil in a cook pot.
3. Pour boiling water over hot chocolate paste. Stir well and serve.

Peg Spry
Agua Dulce, California

Meal System Examples

Meal systems, when compared to stand-alone recipe-based menus, offer an interesting, alternate approach to dining on the trail. With meal systems, a predetermined amount of bulk staples are used to mix and match to taste once on the trail. This approach can simplify planning, reduce packaging waste, and, if carefully applied, offer a very wide range of meal variety in the wilderness.

While attractive for these reasons, meal systems should nevertheless be used with caution. For one, it's easy to over- or underpack when using a system filled with food choices with which you don't have previous experience. And, in odd contrast to their promise of providing nearly unlimited variety, meal systems are surprisingly vulnerable to just the opposite if the types of foods selected aren't sufficiently different in flavor, type, and texture. Before using any meal system with which you're unfamiliar, test it out at home for a couple of weeks before taking it on a long trek.

Use the following three examples—one each for breakfast, lunch, and dinner—for ideas on building and customizing your own system.

BREAKFAST 101 HOT CEREAL SYSTEM

Preparation at Home:

Select items from each of the following three categories and pack them separately for the trail. The amount needed for each meal will vary depending on the type of cereal selected and, of course, your individual appetite, but expect to average between 3 to 5 ounces of ingredients per serving per meal.

Preparation on the Trail:

Begin by cooking the cereal using an appropriate amount of water. Continue by adding to taste from the list of spices and condiments. Finally, toss in a handful of chopped, dried fruit.

Option: This system has fruit as the crowning finale, but a whole range of chopped nuts could be used in place or, in addition to, the fruit: almonds, chia, flax, macadamias, peanuts, pecans, pine, pistachios, poppy, pumpkin, sesame, sunflower, and walnuts.

Be careful when using spices, especially with cereal, because odd combinations or excessive quantities can quickly ruin a meal. Add a little at a time, stirring well, then sample before adding more.

Rick Bombaci
Enterprise, Oregon

Category 1: Cereals

Bulgur wheat

Cream of Wheat

Farina

Granola (uncooked)

Grits

Malt-O-Meal

Quick oats

Category 2: Spices and Condiments

Allspice

Brown sugar

Butter Buds

Ground cinnamon

Ground cloves

Ground nutmeg

Instant dry milk

Salt

Category 3: Dried Fruit

Apples

Apricots

Blueberries

Cherries

Coconut (flaked or shredded)

Cranberries

Dates

Peaches

Pineapple

Raisins

Strawberries

Required Equipment on the Trail:

Cook pot

SIMPLE LUNCH SYSTEM

Category 1: Breads
Bagels

English muffins

Pita

Tortillas

Triscuits

Wheat Thins

Category 2: Fillings
Bean mix (rehydrated)

Cheese (block)

Honey

Hummus mix
(rehydrated)

Jam and jelly

Nature's Burger mix
(rehydrated)

Peanut butter

Summer sausage

Tahini

Category 3: Spices and Condiments
Black pepper

Dill weed

Ketchup (in condiment
packets)

Mayonnaise (in
condiment packets)

Mustard (coarse ground,
Dijon, or yellow)

Olive oil

Red pepper flakes

Salt

Required Equipment on the Trail:
None

Preparation at Home:
As with the breakfast system, select items from each of the categories and pack separately for the trail. Expect to carry about 4 to 6 ounces of ingredients per serving per meal.

Preparation on the Trail:
Combine items from each category, first rehydrating any dried ingredients, if required. To round out your lunch, serve with trail mix, jerky, snack bars, or fruit leathers.

Rick Bombaci
Enterprise, Oregon

624 DINNER SYSTEM

Preparation at Home:
A very large variety of dinner meals (at least 624 decent variations) can be produced from the following four-category system of vegetables, meats, carbs, and spices. For each meal select one or more items from each category, packing each separately for the trail. Use about ½ cup ingredients from the list of vegetables, ¼ cup from the meats, ¾ to 1 cup from the carbs, and to taste from the spices. Expect to carry about 5 to 7 ounces of food per serving per meal.

Preparation on the Trail:
To prepare a single serving, bring 3 cups water to a boil then add ½ cup dried vegetables, ¼ cup dried meat, and ¾ to 1 cup carbs to the pot. Stir, then reduce heat to a simmer. Add spices to taste, cover, and continue to cook for about 5 minutes before serving.

Required Equipment on the Trail:
Cook pot

Charlie Thorpe
Huntsville, Alabama

Category 1: Dehydrated Vegetables
Black beans
Broccoli
Butter beans
Corn
Green beans
Kidney beans
Lima beans
Onions
Peas
Pinto beans
Stir-fry vegetable blend

Category 2: Dehydrated or Cured Meats
Canned or pouch chicken
Lean ground beef
Canned or pouch salmon
Summer sausage
Canned or pouch tuna

Category 3: Carbohydrates
Bulgur
Couscous
Grits (regular)
Hash browns (dried)
Noodles
Potato flakes
Rice

Category 4: Spices
Black pepper
Bouillon cubes
Curry powder
Garlic powder
Italian seasoning
Lemon pepper
Onion powder
Red pepper flakes
Sage
Salsa (rehydrated)
Salt

APPENDIX A: COMMON MEASUREMENT CONVERSIONS

United States Volumetric Conversions

1 smidgen.	$\frac{1}{32}$ teaspoon
1 pinch	$\frac{1}{16}$ teaspoon
1 dash.	$\frac{1}{8}$ teaspoon
3 teaspoons	1 tablespoon
48 teaspoons	1 cup
2 tablespoons	$\frac{1}{8}$ cup
4 tablespoons	$\frac{1}{4}$ cup
5 tablespoons + 1 teaspoon . .	$\frac{1}{3}$ cup
8 tablespoons	$\frac{1}{2}$ cup
12 tablespoons	$\frac{3}{4}$ cup
16 tablespoons	1 cup
1 ounce.	2 tablespoons
4 ounces	$\frac{1}{2}$ cup
8 ounces	1 cup
$\frac{5}{8}$ cup.	$\frac{1}{2}$ cup + 2 tablespoons
$\frac{7}{8}$ cup.	$\frac{3}{4}$ cup + 2 tablespoons
2 cups.	1 pint
2 pints	1 quart
1 quart	4 cups
4 quarts.	1 gallon
1 gallon.	128 ounces

Note: Dry and fluid volumes are equivalent for teaspoon, tablespoon, and cup.

International Metric System Conversions

Volume and Weight

United States	*Metric*
¼ teaspoon	1.25 milliliters
½ teaspoon	2.50 milliliters
¾ teaspoon	3.75 milliliters
1 teaspoon	5 milliliters
1 tablespoon	15 milliliters
1 ounce (volume)	30 milliliters
¼ cup	60 milliliters
½ cup	120 milliliters
¾ cup	180 milliliters
1 cup	240 milliliters
1 pint	0.48 liter
1 quart	0.95 liter
1 gallon	3.79 liters
1 ounce (weight)	28 grams
1 pound	0.45 kilogram

Temperature

°F	°C
175	80
200	95
225	105
250	120
275	135
300	150
325	165
350	175
375	190
400	205
425	220
450	230
475	245
500	260

British, Canadian, and Australian Conversions

1 teaspoon . . . . approx. 1 teaspoon
(Britain, Canada, Australia)   (United States)

1 tablespoon . . . . approx. 1 tablespoon
(Britain, Canada)   (United States)

1 tablespoon . . . . 1.35 tablespoons
(Australia)   (United States)

1 ounce . . . . 0.96 ounce
(Britain, Canada, Australia)   (United States)

1 gill . . . . 5 ounces
(Britain)   (Britain, Canada, Australia)

1 cup . . . . 10 ounces
(Britain)   (Britain, Canada, Australia)

1 cup . . . . 9.61 ounces
(Britain)   (United States)

1 cup . . . . 1.20 cups
(Britain)   (United States)

1 cup . . . . 8.45 ounces
(Canada, Australia)   (United States)

1 cup . . . . 1.06 cups
(Canada, Australia)   (United States)

1 pint . . . . 20 ounces
(Britain, Canada, Australia)   (Britain, Canada, Australia)

1 Imperial gallon . . . . 1.20 gallons
(Britain)   (United States)

1 pound . . . . 1 pound
(Britain, Canada, Australia)   (United States)

Equivalent Measures*

16 ounces water. . . . . .1 pound
2 cups vegetable oil . . . . .1 pound
2 cups or 4 sticks butter. . . . . .1 pound
2 cups granulated sugar. . . . . .1 pound
3 ½ to 4 cups unsifted confectioners' sugar . . 1 pound
2 ¼ cups packed brown sugar . . . . .1 pound
4 cups sifted flour. . . . . .1 pound
3 ½ cups unsifted whole wheat flour . . . . .1 pound
8–10 egg whites. . . . . .1 cup
12–14 egg yolks. . . . . .1 cup
1 whole lemon, squeezed . . . . .3 tablespoons juice
1 whole orange, squeezed . . . . .⅓ cup juice
* Approximate

Drying Conversions*

Undried Item	Dried Volume	Dried Weight
1 tablespoon fresh herbs	.1 teaspoon. .	less than 1 ounce
1 tablespoon mustard.	.1 teaspoon. .	less than 1 ounce
1 garlic clove, pressed	.⅛ teaspoon powder . . .	less than 1 ounce
1 pound frozen peas	.1 cup	4 ounces
1 pound cooked and sliced carrots	.½ cup	2 ounces
1 pound boiled and sliced potatoes	.1½ cups . . .	4 ounces
1 pound diced onions.	.1 cup	1 ounce
1 pound frozen French-sliced green beans	.2 cups	1½ ounces
1 pound diced celery	.⅓ cup	½ ounce
1 pound sliced fresh mushrooms	.2½ cups . . .	1 ounce
1 pound fresh green bell pepper.	.¾ cup	1½ ounces
1 pound fresh jalapeño peppers	.1⅓ cups . . .	1 ounce
1 pound frozen mixed vegetables	.¾ cup	3½ ounces
1 15-ounce can mixed vegetables	.½ cup	1½ ounces

1 6-ounce can medium diced olives. . . . . ½ cup . . . . 1 ounce

1 15-ounce can pinto beans. . . . . .1 cup . . . . 2½ ounces

1 15-ounce can black beans. . . . . .1 cup . . . . 2½ ounces

1 15-ounce can kidney beans . . . . .1¼ cups . . . 3½ ounces

1 pound steamed and chopped
    zucchini . . . . ⅓ cup . . . . ½ ounce

1 pound frozen sliced broccoli . . . . . . .1 cup . . . . 1 ounce

1 pound sliced Roma tomatoes . . . . . . .1 cup . . . . 1 ounce

1 6-ounce can tomato paste. . . . . .Leather roll . 1½ ounces

1 pound salsa . . . . ½ cup . . . . ½ ounce

1 pound sliced apples . . . . .1½ cups . . . 3 ounces

1 pound sliced bananas . . . . .1½ cups . . . 4 ounces

1 20-ounce can diced pineapple . . . . . ¾ cup . . . . 2 ounces

1 pound trimmed watermelon . . . . . . .1 cup . . . . 1 ounce

1 pound frozen cherries. . . . . .½ cup . . . . 2 ounces

1 cup whole milk . . . . ½ cup
                                      instant dry. . 2 ounces

* Volumes and weights may vary slightly from those shown here due to a variety of factors, including brand selection, depth of cut, dehydrating method, and equipment.

APPENDIX B: SOURCES OF EQUIPMENT AND SUPPLIES

AlpineAire

www.alpineaire.com

A good source for freeze-dried, ready-to-eat instant meals, AlpineAire's products are available through outfitters as well as at their online store.

Amazon

www.amazon.com

It's well-known that Amazon sells an enormous array of products. But it might come as a surprise nevertheless that it also hosts a very large number of vendors who sell exotic food ingredients difficult to find in your local grocery store. Check out Amazon if you're stumped when trying to find an ingredient.

Asian Food Grocer

www.asianfoodgrocer.com

A wide selection of difficult-to-find Asian ingredients, including dried tofu, fish, and mushrooms, are available at Asian Food Grocer.

Backpacker's Pantry

www.backpackerspantry.com

Backpacker's Pantry is a well-known brand name at outdoor retailers, but their online store is also a very good source of freeze-dried meals as well as single-serving condiments like peanut butter, salsa, and jelly. Backpacker's Pantry also carries a selection of organic products.

Barry Farm Foods

www.barryfarm.com

Barry Farm offers an amazing selection of dry ingredients, including foods you might not believe could even be dried, such as sour cream and yogurt.

Bass Pro Shops

www.basspro.com

Bass Pro is a nationwide retailer that stocks a range of outdoor gear appropriate for the trail. The Bass Pro stores are a good place to go to examine gear firsthand.

Bulk Foods

www.bulkfoods.com

Here you'll find an enormous selection of dried fruits, spices, grains, and nuts sold in a variety of sizes and quantities.

Cabela's

www.cabelas.com

This retailer specializes as a hunting and fishing outfitter but also carries a nice selection of kitchen gear for the trail. Cabela's has dozens of large retail stores located throughout the United States and Southern Canada.

Campmor

www.campmor.com

Campmor's online catalog has one of the most comprehensive selections of gear available anywhere for backpacking and cooking on the trail.

Cascade Designs, Inc.

www.cascadedesigns.com

One of the most respected outdoor equipment manufacturers in the world, Cascade Designs' major brands include MSR stoves and cookware, Therm-a-Rest sleep gear, and Platypus hydration systems.

Eden Foods

www.edenfoods.com

An interesting array of Japanese foods can be found at Eden, including dried tofu, seaweed, spices, and mushrooms, as well as exotic and organic bulk goods.

Emergency Essentials

www.beprepared.com

A good source of dried goods sold in bulk, including whole egg powder and the like.

Fantastic Foods

www.fantasticfoods.com

A culinary voyage across continents and cultures, Fantastic Foods's internet store offers many dried products useful for backpacking, such as refried beans, falafel, hummus, and tabouli mixes.

Harmony House Foods

www.harmonyhousefoods.com

Harmony House carries a large selection of dried vegetables and fruits in bulk.

Harvest Foodworks

www.harvestfoodworks.com

A wide range of freeze-dried and dehydrated meals for the outdoors can be found at Harvest Foodworks.

Just Tomatoes Etc.

www.justtomatoes.com

A wonderful source for bulk individual freeze-dried vegetables and fruits, Just Tomatoes doesn't offer just tomatoes. Their products are so tasty, you can eat them dry, right out of the bag.

King Arthur Flour

www.kingarthurflour.com

Popular at the grocer, King Arthur's online retail store offers not only flour but also a diverse selection of difficult-to-find ingredients, including whole egg powder, dried cheese, whole milk powder, and more.

Mountain Equipment Co-op

www.mec.ca

MEC is a large Canadian cooperative that specializes in outdoor gear via an extensive online catalog and through more than a dozen retail stores located across Canada.

Mountain House

www.mtnhse.com

Mountain House is well-known at outdoor retailers for their freeze-dried meals, but online they also offer a good selection of discounted bulk dried items such as vegetables, eggs, and premade entrees.

My Spicer

www.myspicer.com

An enormous selection of exotic dried vegetables and spices from around the world can be found at My Spicer.

PackitGourmet

www.packitgourmet.com

PackitGourmet stocks a large and unique selection of items with the backpacker in mind, including restaurant condiment packets in smaller lots and powdered citrus drinks.

REI

www.rei.com

REI is a membership cooperative that carries a large array of trail gear and freeze-dried foods online but also retails through dozens of super-stores located throughout the United States, providing the opportunity to see before you buy. Be prepared to be bitten by the backpacking bug once you step foot in an REI.

Sport Chalet

www.sportchalet.com

Sport Chalet is a major outdoor recreation retailer in the southwestern United States. Like REI, this is an excellent place to go to see backpacking gear in general, and trail kitchen equipment and freeze-dried foods in particular, firsthand.

SunOrganic Farm

www.sunorganic.com

This retailer carries a good selection of organic dried fruits and vegetables as well as seasonings, beans, nuts, and sprouting seeds.

Suttons Bay Trading Company

www.suttonsbayspices.com

Suttons Bay Trading offers a large selection of dried fruit and vegetables, including an interesting assortment of flavored powders such as horse-radish, soy sauce, yogurt, and even honey, which is impossible to dry in a home dehydrator.

APPENDIX C: ADDITIONAL READING AND RESOURCES

Books and Periodicals

Cook's Illustrated and *Cook's Country*

www.cooksillustrated.com and www.cookscountry.com

These outstanding periodicals from America's Test Kitchen turn common recipes into wonderful re-creations but with a minimum of effort. Along the way, the reader learns how and why the recipes work. *Cook's Illustrated* explores fewer dishes but in more detail than *Cook's Country*, its sister publication, which comes in a larger format and full color. These are magazines for the home kitchen. But what you'll learn indoors will prove invaluable on the trail.

FalconGuides/Globe Pequot Press

www.falcon.com

FalconGuides is the top outdoor recreation publisher in the country with an extensive catalog of books for every outdoor activity, covering most states and geographical regions in the United States as well as many of the most popular National Parks.

Lipsmackin' Vegetarian Backpackin', Christine and Tim Conners, Globe Pequot Press

A close sibling to the book you hold, *Lipsmackin' Vegetarian* is also filled with recipes well suited for backpacking trips of longer duration. But, as the title suggests, all the recipes are meatless. *Vegetarian* doesn't have to mean "bland," of course, and the more than 150 tasty recipes in this book from over fifty experienced backpackers attest to that. This is a good resource for expanding your list of reliable, durable, and tasty trail recipes.

On Food and Cooking: The Science and Lore of the Kitchen, Harold McGee, Scribner

This is an excellent resource for understanding the science behind cooking. When chefs decipher why recipes work the way they do, they become much more effective at adapting recipes in a pinch or creating new ones on the fly. Be forewarned: This is not a cookbook, much less an outdoor cookbook. But if science interests you, this book will too.

Preserve It Naturally, Excalibur/KBI Inc.
A very good compendium of tips and tricks to make you a wizard with your kitchen dehydrator.

The Scout's Backpacking Cookbook, Tim and Christine Conners, FalconGuides
Written in format and style similar to *Lipsmackin' Backpackin'*, *The Scout's Backpacking Cookbook* contains instructional material and recipes tailored to the needs of the Scouting world. Over one hundred recipes are included, most with durability appropriate for long-duration trips, but with some designed specifically with shorter duration treks in mind, those spanning no more than two or three days on the trail.

Trail Food, Alan Kesselheim, Ragged Mountain Press
This little classic is an excellent reference for those who desire to master the art of drying foods for any outdoor excursion.

Informational Websites

American Hiking Society
www.americanhiking.org
The mission of the American Hiking Society is to be the national voice of those who use and love this country's foot trails. The AHS champions conservation issues, builds partnerships, and provides resources to plan, fund, and develop foot trails. Go to their website to find out more about the work of the AHS and the local organizations whose efforts preserve and protect the trails in your neck of the woods.

Backpack Gear Test
www.backpackgeartest.com
Contemplating the purchase of expensive equipment? This is the place to go to see thorough reviews of the performance of gear in the field.

Backpacking Light
www.backpackinglight.com
A very good reference for those who want to learn more about how to safely reduce that heavy load on their back.

Epicurious
www.epicurious.com
You won't find much on trail cooking at Epicurious. But if you're looking to hone your basic cooking skills and could use thousands of recipes for practice, this is a good resource.

Exploratorium
www.exploratorium.edu/cooking
Exploratorium makes cooking fun by putting emphasis on the science behind it. Even if you're not the scientist type, you'll enjoy this site. Quirky yet practical, recipes flow down the page with relevant science posted in the sidebar.

Gourmet Sleuth
www.gourmetsleuth.com
A good kitchen measurement conversion calculator can be found at this website. Included is the ability to convert between US and British measurement units.

Leave No Trace (LNT) Center for Outdoor Ethics
www.LNT.org
The Center for Outdoor Ethics has been a leader and respected voice in communicating why and how our outdoor places require responsible stewardship. The LNT outdoor ethics code is becoming standard practice in the wilderness. More information about the organization is available at their website, and specific information about outdoor ethics principles, especially as applied to cooking, can be found in Appendix D of this book.

APPENDIX D: LOW-IMPACT COOKING

The Leave No Trace Center for Outdoor Ethics provides a set of principles that are becoming increasingly well-known and applied by those who visit the wild places of the world.

There are seven core principles of Leave No Trace:

- Plan ahead and prepare

- Travel and camp on durable surfaces

- Dispose of waste properly

- Leave what you find

- Minimize campfire impacts

- Respect wildlife

- Be considerate of other visitors

Careful planning, especially with respect to food preparation, is critical to successfully following the principles of Leave No Trace. When preparing for an upcoming outing, consider the following list of application points as you evaluate your food and cooking options.

Decide how you'll prepare your food.

Some methods of cooking, such as the use of pack stoves, create less impact than others, such as open fires. When using open fire to cook, follow local fire restrictions and use an established fire ring instead of creating a new one. Keep fires small. Collect wood from the ground rather than from standing trees. To avoid creating barren earth, find wood farther away from camp. Select smaller pieces of wood and burn them completely to ash. Afterward, be sure the fire is completely out, then scatter the ashes. Learn how to use a mound fire to prevent scorching the ground and blackening rocks.

Carefully select and repackage your food to minimize trash.

Tiny pieces of trash easily become litter. Avoid bringing small, individually packaged candies and other such food items on the trail. Twist ties and bread clips are easily lost when dropped. Remove the wrappers and repackage such foods into ziplock bags before leaving home; or use knots, instead of ties and clips, to seal bags and the like.

Metal containers and their lids, crushed beverage cans, and broken glass can easily cut or puncture trash sacks. Wrap these carefully before placing them in thin-wall trash bags. Minimize the use of glass on the trail. Scan your trail camp carefully when packing up to ensure that no litter is left behind.

Minimize leftovers and dispose of food waste properly.

Leftover food makes for messier trash and cleanup. If poured on open ground, it is unsightly and unsanitary. If buried too close to the surface, animals may dig it up. Leftovers encourage problem animals if not properly managed. Carefully plan your meals to reduce leftovers.

Dispose of used wash and rinse water (also called gray water) in a manner appropriate for your area. Before disposal, remove or strain food chunks from the gray water and place these with the trash. Dispose of gray water in a cat hole covered by several inches of soil in an area free of sensitive vegetation and at least 200 feet from streams and lakes. Avoid excessive suds by using only the amount of detergent necessary for the job. Bring only biodegradable soap on the trail.

Plan to protect your food, trash, and other odorous items from animals.

Consider avoiding the use of very aromatic foods that can attract animals. Store food, trash, and other odorous items where animals won't be able to get to them. Besides being potentially dangerous to the animal, and inconvenient for the backpacker, trash is often spread over a large area once the animal gains access. Follow local regulations regarding proper food storage, such as the use of bear-bagging techniques or bear-proof food canisters.

Decide whether to avoid collecting wild foods.

Don't harvest wild foods, such as berries, if these are not plentiful in the area you're visiting. Such foods are likely to be a more important component of the local ecosystem when scarce.

These are only a few of the practical considerations and potential applications of the principles of Leave No Trace. Visit www.LNT.org for additional information and ideas.

APPENDIX E: THE NATIONAL SCENIC TRAILS SYSTEM

Looking for some of the most challenging, beautiful, and inspiring places to apply your hiking skills? Perhaps you've had a taste of the spectacular majesty of the mountains and are now contemplating where to go next for more? If this is you, then look no further than the National Scenic Trails System.

Created by an Act of Congress to protect corridors of high scenic value, the National Scenic Trails System comprises a masterwork of eleven long footpaths distributed across the United States. Each of these trails is an unparalleled scenic gem. Now spanning more than 18,000 trail miles, they were created to provide ultimate access to the country's most awesome wild places. Each trail presents a challenge like no other.

The following list contains basic information about each of the trails, including length and location. You will probably recognize some of the names. In fact, you may have walked at least a portion of one of these trails in the past. But were you aware of the others? Did you realize just how truly massive this network of long trails is? The opportunities for exploring are nearly endless.

The National Park Service maintains ultimate oversight of the National Scenic Trails System. But day-to-day trail stewardship is accomplished through volunteer organizations that work closely with federal and state government bureaus. These volunteer organizations are often the best source for up-to-date information, and so web links to these have been provided where applicable in the list below. The Partnership for the National Trails System at www.pnts.org is also a good launching point to those organizations directly associated with each of the National Scenic Trails.

And while the National Scenic Trails may be the most famous of the long trails, they are by no means the only ones. Information regarding other backpacking options can be found through the National Park Service at www.nps.gov/nts, the US Forest Service at www.fs.fed.us/recreation/programs/trails, and the Bureau of Land Management at www.blm.gov.

So keep on challenging yourself. Browse the list below, follow the associated web links to learn more about our incredible long trails, and be inspired.

Appalachian
2,174 miles, Georgia to Maine
Appalachian Trail Conservancy
www.appalachiantrail.org

Arizona
807 miles, Mexico–Arizona border to Utah–Arizona border
Arizona Trail Association
www.aztrail.org

Continental Divide
3,100 miles, Mexico–New Mexico border to Canada–Montana border
Continental Divide Trail Society
www.cdtsociety.org

Florida
1,400 miles, entirely within the state of Florida
Florida Trail Association
www.floridatrail.org

Ice Age
1,200 miles, entirely within the state of Wisconsin
Ice Age Trail Alliance
www.iceagetrail.org

Natchez Trace
65 miles, four segments in Mississippi and Tennessee
National Park Service
www.nps.gov/natt/index.htm

New England
220 miles, Connecticut to Massachusetts
Connecticut Forest and Park Association and Appalachian Mountain Club
www.newenglandnst.org

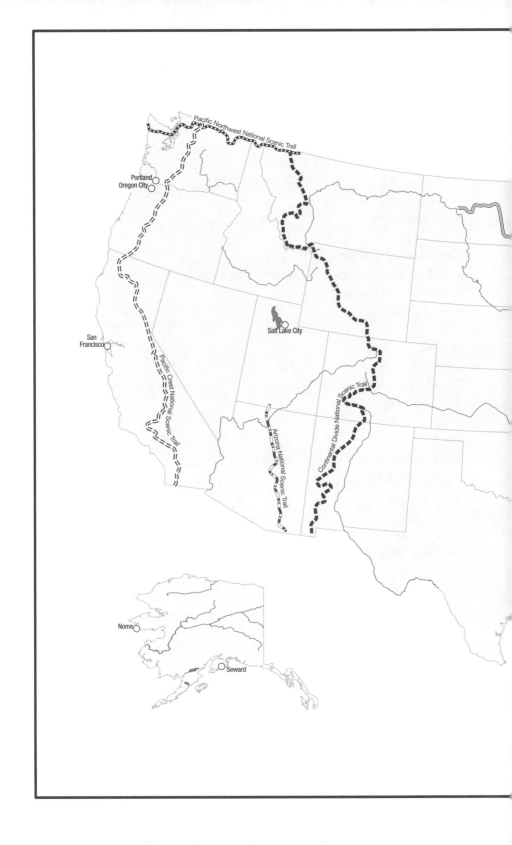

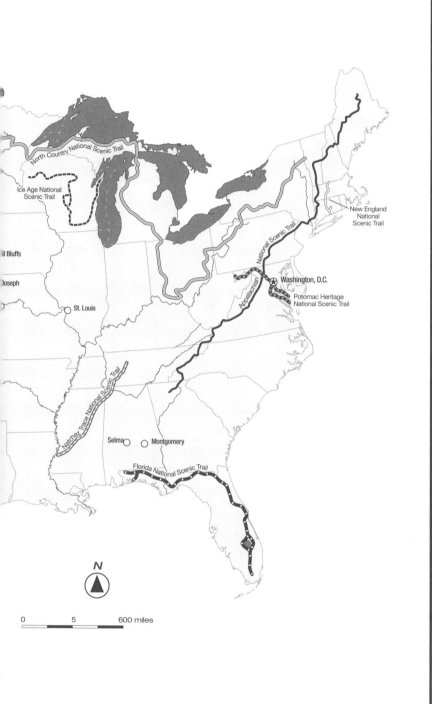

North Country National Scenic Trail

Ice Age National
Scenic Trail

il Bluffs

Joseph

St. Louis

Appalachian National Scenic Trail

New England
National
Scenic Trail

Washington, D.C.

Potomac Heritage
National Scenic Trail

Natchez Trace National Scenic Trail

Selma⃝   ⃝ Montgomery

Florida National Scenic Trail

N

0   5   600 miles

North Country
4,600 miles, New York to North Dakota
North Country Trail Association
www.northcountrytrail.org

Pacific Crest
2,638 miles, Mexico–California border to Canada–Washington border
Pacific Crest Trail Association
www.pcta.org

Pacific Northwest
1,200 miles, Montana to Washington
Pacific Northwest Trail Association
www.pnt.org

Potomac Heritage
830 miles, Virginia to Pennsylvania
Potomac Heritage Trail Association
www.potomactrail.org

INDEX

ABOUT THE AUTHORS

Experienced backpackers, campers, and outdoor chefs, Christine and Tim Conners are the authors of the nationally popular *Lipsmackin'* outdoor cookbook series, including the titles *Lipsmackin' Backpackin'*, *Lipsmackin' Vegetarian Backpackin'*, and, the latest entry to the series, *Lipsmackin' Car Campin'*.

Specifically for the Scouting world, Tim and Christine have produced *The Scout's Cookbook* series: *The Scout's Outdoor Cookbook*, *The Scout's Dutch Oven Cookbook*, *The Scout's Large Groups Cookbook*, and *The Scout's Backpacking Cookbook*. Each title in *The Scout's Cookbook* lineup is a collection of unique and outstanding recipes from Scout leaders across the United States.

Christine and Tim have been testing outdoor recipes for nearly twenty years. At the invitation of Boy Scouts of America, the Connerses have twice served as judges for *Scouting* magazine's prestigious national camp food cooking contest.

The Connerses have four children—James, Michael, Maria, and David—all of whom stay busy in the outdoors by backpacking on the Appalachian Trail, camping and day hiking in the local state parks, and kayaking on the region's lakes and rivers . . . when they aren't writing cookbooks!

Please visit us at www.lipsmackincampin.com, friend us on Facebook at www.facebook.com/lipsmackincampin, or follow us on Twitter at www.twitter.com/lipsmackincampn.